The Privatizati

The Privatization Putsch

by

Herschel Hardin

The Institute for Research on Public Policy/
L'Institut de recherches politiques

Printed in Canada

Legal Deposit First Quarter
Bibliothèque nationale du Québec

Canadian Cataloguing in Publication Data

Hardin, Herschel, 1936-

The privatization putsch

Prefatory material in English and French.
ISBN 0-88645-084-5

1. Privatization. 2. Privatization —
Canada. 3. Government business enterprises
— Canada — Case studies. I. Institute for
Research on Public Policy. II. Title.

HD3850.H37 1989 338.6'2 C89-098525-1

Camera-ready copy and publication management by
PDS Research Publishing Services Limited
P.O. Box 3296
Halifax, Nova Scotia B3J 3H7

Published by
The Institute for Research on Public Policy/
L'Institut de recherches politiques
P.O. Box 3670 South
Halifax, Nova Scotia B3J 3K6

Contents

Note: All money values are in Canadian dollars, unless otherwise noted. Figures originally in foreign currency, such as U.S. dollars, have been converted to Canadian dollars at the going rate of exchange at the time, with annual figures converted at the annual average rate.

Foreword

In a variety of recent publications, this Institute has documented the arguments for privatization of state enterprises and government activities – for "strengthening the market at the expense of the state," in the words of Tom Kierans (*Choices*, April 1985). But at the same time, the preconditions essential for privatization to be effective have also been emphasized. Indeed Kierans himself sets out clearly some of the dangers of privatization in circumstances which amount simply to passing a public monopoly into private hands, without assurance of adequate competitive forces or contestability of markets, without appropriate valuation of the assets or without clear understandings of social responsibilities, performance criteria or accountability, whether or not these may adversely affect the proceeds realized by the government in the sale of assets. (See, for example, Kierans and Stanbury, *Papers on Privatization*, published by this Institute in 1985.)

Such issues are also discussed in several Institute publications dealing with crown corporations or mixed enterprises, such as *Who's in Charge? The Mixed Enterprise Corporation in Canada*, by Stephen Brooks; *Privatization, Public Policy and Public Corporations in Canada*, by G. Bruce Doern and Allan Tupper; *Mergers, Corporate Concentration and Power in Canada*, by R.S. Khemani, D.M. Shapiro and W.T. Stanbury.

THE PRIVATIZATION PUTSCH

In the present volume, Herschel Hardin goes further to redress what he sees as an imbalance in a literature strongly oriented toward the rhetoric of privatization, uncritically embraced in a veritable ideological crusade. He suggests that definitions of "business" have too often been confused with concepts of "enterprise" — that motivations for public enterprise may well go far beyond the profit motive, and may not be well captured by the ability to make lots of money. The motivation for public enterprise, he writes, may be "to provide the best possible service at cost . . . to be competitive, to excel as an enterprise, to innovate, to grow, to thrive and contend, to help Canada (or Saskatchewan or Quebec or Manitoba . . .) in the economic stakes, to build up the community and make it economically strong . . .".

Being forced to examine the process of privatization more closely, he suggests, will force people to look again at the entrepreneurial roles played by public enterprise in the past, and possible added potential in the future. "Finally, people will rediscover the inherent advantages of public enterprise in their own communities: its democratic ownership; its decentralization of economic power; its enhancement of competition in market situations; its regional or national spirit and the entrepreneurial impulse which comes with it; its indigenous control of re-investment capital; its role in helping to gather maximum resource "rents"; its structural efficiencies; its freedom from the debilitating paper entrepreneurship of the private corporate sector; its putting long-term development, productivity, technology, and reinvestment ahead of short-term profit."

As with all Institute publications, this book presents the views of the author, not necessarily those of the Institute's Board, Council or staff. It was initiated as part of the research program on Institutions of Governance under the direction (at that time) of Prof. John W. Langford. The Institute acknowledges with thanks the contribution of Professor Langford to the completion of this project, and is pleased to introduce this provocative monograph as a further contribution to an important on-going debate. While the views so colourfully expressed by the author are uncommon, and may well be controversial — even unpopular — in the present climate, they are seriously considered and clearly articulated, and warrant serious attention.

A.R. Dobell, President
December 1988

Avant-propos

Dans diverses publications récentes, l'Institut a présenté et fourni des justifications en faveur de la privatisation des entreprises d'État et des activités gouvernementales, afin de "renforcer le marché aux dépens de l'État", selon Tom Kierans (*Choix*, avril 1985). Ces publications n'ont cependant pas manqué d'insister sur les conditions prérequises pour que cette privatisation puisse réussir. M. Kierans lui-même expose d'une manière précise certains des dangers de la privatisation, dans des circonstances qui équivalent simplement à transférer un monopole public à des particuliers, sans une assurance des forces concurrentielles adéquates ou d'une contestation efficace des marchés, sans une évaluation appropriée des actifs, ou sans que soit clairement comprises les responsabilités envers la société, les critères de fonctionnement ou la responsabilité que cela entraîne, que cette prise de conscience puisse affecter ou non le montant d'argent réalisé par le gouvernement dans la vente des actifs. (Voir, par exemple, Kierans et Stanbury, *Papers on Privatization*, publié par l'Institut en 1985).

Ces questions sont également traitées dans plusieurs publications de l'Institut consacrées aux sociétés de la Couronne ou aux entreprises mixtes, comme par exemple: *Who's in Charge? The Mixed Enterprise Corporation in Canada*, par Stephen Brooks; *Privatization, Public Policy and Public Corporations in Canada*, par G.

THE PRIVATIZATION PUTSCH

Bruce Doern et Allan Tupper; *Mergers, Corporate Concentration and Power in Canada*, par R.S. Khemani, D.M. Shapiro et W.T. Stanbury.

Dans le présent volume, Herschel Hardin fait un pas de plus pour corriger ce qu'il considère être un déséquilibre dans les études consacrées à la privatisation, qu'il voit fortement orientées en faveur de celle-ci et même engagées d'une manière non critique dans une véritable croisade idéologique. Il lui semble que les définitions des "affaires" ont trop souvent été confondues avec les concepts de "l'entreprise", que la motivation derrière l'entreprise publique va peut-être au-delà de l'idée de profit et qu'elle peut très bien ne pas se résumer à l'aptitude à gagner beaucoup d'argent. La motivation derrière l'entreprise publique, écrit-il, doit être "de fournir le meilleur service possible au prix coûtant . . . d'être concurrentiel, d'exceller en tant qu'entreprise, d'innover, de se développer, de réussir et de se battre, d'aider le Canada (ou la Saskatchewan, ou le Québec, ou le Manitoba . . .) dans ses enjeux économiques, de construire la communauté et de la rendre économiquement forte . . ."

Le fait d'avoir à examiner le processus de la privatisation d'une manière plus approfondie, nous dit-il, obligera le public à revoir les rôles joués par l'entreprise publique dans le passé et à envisager peut-être d'augmenter son efficacité pour l'avenir. "Finalement, les gens redécouvriront les vertus inhérentes de l'entreprise publique dans leurs propres communautés: sa propriété conforme à la démocratie, sa décentralisation du pouvoir économique, son renforcement de la concurrence dans les situations de marché, sa vocation régionale ou nationale et l'esprit d'entreprise qui l'accompagne, son contrôle territorial du capital à réinvestir, son rôle dans l'obtention des "rentes" de ressources les plus élevées, son efficacité structurelle, sa libération des débilitantes manœuvres boursières qui caractérisent l'esprit d'entreprise du secteur privé des corporations, son aptitude à mettre la priorité sur le développement, la productivité, la technologie et le réinvestissement à long terme, plutôt que sur le profit immédiat."

Comme il en est pour toutes les autres publications de l'Institut, ce livre représente les opinions de l'auteur et non pas forcément celles du Conseil, de la Commission ou du personnel de l'Institut. Sa rédaction a été entreprise dans le cadre du programme de recherche sur les institutions gouvernementales, sous la direction (à cette époque) du professeur John W. Langford. L'Institut remercie le

AVANT-PROPOS

professeur Langford du rôle qu'il a exercé pour mener à bien ce projet et il est heureux de présenter cette monographie stimulante comme contribution supplémentaire à un débat qui se poursuit. Alors que les opinions présentées d'une manière si vive par l'auteur peuvent sembler inhabituelles et pourraient bien prêter à controverse, voire même être impopulaires dans le climat actuel, elles ont néanmoins été sérieusement pensées et sont clairement articulées. De ce fait, elles méritent d'être considérées avec attention.

Rod Dobell
Président

Décembre 1988

Preface

My thanks to several people in particular for making this book possible. John Langford was the IRPP research director for governability studies when this project was launched, and shepherded it through to completion. His enthusiasm and editorial contribution were invaluable. My research assistant Jane Oglesby helped build up the files and, most importantly, tracked down the myriad of details involved in such a wide-ranging analysis. Sandford Borins and Allan Tupper offered many useful critical comments. Not least, editor Denise Bukowski, of Pacific Publishing Support Services, did her usual fine job in helping to get the manuscript in order and down to length.

Herschel Hardin
West Vancouver, B.C.

December 1988

1.
The Rigged Debate

In the spring of 1987 in Vancouver, the Honourable Stephen Rogers, British Columbia's minister responsible for privatization, was talking, in a state verging on euphoria, of the Jaguar car company in Great Britain. The privatized Jaguar company was making a handsome profit. Jaguar, as Rogers described it, was an outstanding example of the failure of state ownership and the virtues of privatization. "It's marvellous," he said of Margaret Thatcher's privatization program. The assembled heads listening to the speech nodded assent.

Rogers' protestations failed to note that Jaguar, the maker of luxury automobiles, ended up publicly owned in the first place because its inept and incompetent parent company had gone bankrupt, an outstanding example of private enterprise failure. Jaguar's subsequent recovery took place under public ownership. It had turned the corner and was making a good profit before it was privatized. Margaret Thatcher's government would otherwise probably not have have sold off the company.

There was even a technical term for the process: "hospital-ization." Sick privately owned companies were hospitalized under public ownership until they were well again. Countries like Belgium and Austria, in the early 1980s, went so far as to establish special state holding companies to look after the "lame ducks," or the "canards boiteux" – wrecks of European private enterprise scattered across the economic countryside. Italy had established such a corporation in 1971.

In the most dramatic case, France, nationalization in 1982 had resuscitated whole sections of the industrial economy, from chemicals to electronics. Even the aggressively anti-Mitterand *L'Express* described the nationalizations as a long overdue "kicking open of a gummed-up anthill."[1] It wasn't the first time public enterprise had picked up the pieces of private enterprise failure. In Italy, the Istituto per la Ricostruzione Industriale, the famous publicly owned holding company IRI, was formed in 1933 in the wake of private banking disasters (the banks controlled a large part of industry). In Canada, hospitalization began with the Welland Canal in 1840.

Maybe the greatest failure of private enterprise, in terms of western countries and Japan, was in Great Britain itself. The "British disease" was not quite what the advocates of privatization were making it out to be. Private-sector economic weakness in Great Britain went back 100 years, for which, in the 1980s, public enterprise was serving as scapegoat.

Public enterprise's hospitalization work in Europe was just one part of its role, and not the major part. Publicly owned enterprise was at the forefront of much of western Europe's heady post-war economic development. It was particularly prominent and impressive in France, Italy, Finland and Austria, but there was also a substantial publicly owned sector in countries like West Germany and Sweden where private corporate ownership was less challenged. Public enterprise was as European as *tarte aux pommes* and pasta. The public enterprise success of the lesser known and smaller countries, like Finland and Austria, had its own special interest for Canada, another country having to contend with a neighbouring, dominant economic power.

None of these facts intruded on Rogers's rhetoric and the enthusiastic reception he received. He was appearing at one of many recent "privatization" conferences used as a stage on which to pump up true believers. He didn't dwell, either, on the sad story of the B.C. Resources Investment Corporation, the homemade privatization case. One of his tutors was the ardent privatization advocate Madsen Pirie, head of the Adam Smith Institute. Pirie, as a guest of the National

Citizens' Coalition, had made a rousing privatization speech in Toronto. Tapes of the speech were being circulated in Social Credit circles in B.C.

The conference, of course, was rigged. The virtues of privatization were assumed. The subject matter was set out accordingly. The lead speakers, like Rogers and the federal minister of privatization, Barbara MacDougall, were privatization advocates. The convention kit bulged with a dossier prepared by a preacher of the doctrine, UBC economist William Stanbury, who also chaired the conference. (Stanbury, almost effulgent in his role, was a one-man whirling dervish of privatization paper production).

The keynote speaker, typical of those at such affairs, was a privatization backer from Britain, playing the role of the evangelist reporting from the scene of the greatest conversion. This one was an elderly gentleman from the international accounting firm of Ernst & Whinney, who had been personally involved in the privatization process. He had also been consulted by the French government about its privatization plans, mention of which added significance to his presentation.

Barbara MacDougall, for her part, had shed some of her earlier caution about the virtues of wholesale privatization. She was gung-ho now, too, had her arguments in order, and was warmly received. Among those attending were stock brokers who, as a clan, stood to add a nice chunk of business come the privatization of any more Crown corporations. Also attracted to the get-together was a smattering of business people with an eye open to corporate properties which might become available.

The conference wasn't the only place where privatization doctrine was served up and swallowed whole. The *Vancouver Sun*'s commentator on provincial politics, Vaughn Palmer, wrote two gushing columns about Margaret Thatcher's doings and about the doctrine – as inspirational as any conference speech. One was a summary of Pirie's views. The *Sun*'s Friday columnist, Trevor Lautens, became positively Wagnerian about the Thatcher "revolution." Public ownership in Britain had been responsible for the country's economic stagnation and demoralization, he wrote. Only the shepherdess, Margaret Thatcher, "turning the sheep out to graze on the free range," has saved the day.[2]

The ideology of privatization floated like a low-lying fog into all the crevices of the conference and into newspaper coverage. As one disgruntled University of Victoria professor put it, "There is no debate." It would be ideologically in bad odour, not to mention out of fashion, to protest too loudly the privatization putsch and above all to argue back too broadly. The event in Vancouver, in the spring of 1987, illustrated what was happening and had been happening in the whole country.

The pretentious rigged debate begs to be derigged. This book starts in on it. It looks closely at what the British experience actually has been, and at the real roots of the British malaise. Next, to get some distance on the British case, it moves to the continent — countries like France and Italy where public enterprise has played such a large and dynamic role. Privatization advocates don't like to talk about that very much. Different aspects of privatization in Britain and France are then examined: the hollowness, indeed speciousness, of privatization claims for shareholders' democracy; the manipulative use of mass media propaganda, straight out of *1984*; the rise of a new financial and stock-exchange bureaucracy, self-serving, self-indulgent, pushing for privatization and cashing in on it.

Then the discussion moves to Canada. In pride of place is the mightiest privatization experiment undertaken anywhere, not mightiest in dollar value but in concept: the British Columbia Resources Investment Corporation. Privatization advocates don't like to dwell on that one, either.

This sets the stage for the other side of the story: the great public enterprise tradition in Canada and how destructive and predatory privatization is. Public enterprises are not just publicly owned companies. They are also economic expressions of community, and as such bring with them a whole set of entrepreneurial advantages. Not least is the community impulse itself, adding energy and commitment to the enterprise (a glimpse at the same impulse in Japan and in Europe helps shed new light on the Canadian experience).

Publicly owned enterprise, similarly, avoids the wasteful and debilitating games of paper entrepreneurship. It applies itself to the real tasks of entrepreneurship: long-term development, productivity, technology and re-investment.

Public enterprise also acts as a vehicle for decentralizing entrepreneurship and investment decisions — decentralizing economic power, in effect — as against a growing concentration of ownership and control in private corporate forms. It draws on and develops the indigenous spirit of enterprise. This is important for the whole country but it is especially important for the West.

In competitive market situations, public enterprises enhance the workings of the market, something else which this book looks into. Rather than privatizing companies like Air Canada and Petro-Canada, as privatizers dogmatically insist, we should, it turns out, be creating more public enterprises for market competition.

Privatization acolytes loudly raise their voices in attack and denigration. But public enterprise, a natural entrepreneurial form, remains as appropriate as ever.

2.
Britain: Ideological Tag Teams and Roman Circuses

Trying to come to grips with the privatization arguments as they surface in Great Britain and are repeated by acolytes in Canada is like wrestling against a particularly slippery tag team. Once one argument is defeated, it isn't important any longer; the reason being touted for privatization is an altogether different one. Pin that other argument down and yet another one is cited instead. Since the Thatcher government began its privatization drive in the early 1980s, the tagging of reasons has gone around full circle, and ones that bobbed up at the beginning and were discredited are now bobbing up again.

One of the early reasons given for selling off the nationalized industries was to put a dent in the annual government deficit (the Public Sector Borrowing Requirement, or PSBR, in British lingo), by applying the proceeds of the sale. The same reason was bandied about in Canada, too. Margaret Thatcher was going through a tight-money monetarist phase where the deficit was considered to be evil incarnate and had to be reduced. What better way than to sell off publicly owned companies and use the cash?

The late Harold Macmillan, a true-blue Conservative, disdainful of Mrs. Thatcher's rationalization, said that selling off the state assets would no more provide a lasting economic solution than selling off the family silver. This wasn't all that was wrong with the policy. The one-time effect on the deficit from the sale of assets was undermined by the loss forever of annual income from those assets. Even academic theorists of privatization dismissed the reduction-of-the-deficit ploy as illusory. There is no "free lunch" when it comes to reducing the deficit, said one.[1] It comes in handy for "cosmetic . . . purposes," said another, but that's all.[2] Selling off assets to cut back the deficit, as a reason or excuse for denationalization, couldn't be propped up for long.

More basic, and gradually more prominent, was the argument that the nationalized industries were inefficient just because they were publicly owned. The 1970s were dog days for the British economy, with economic circumstances deteriorating at large. In a growing number of Conservative minds, however, troubles with the basic nationalized industries — steel, coal and rail — came to symbolize everything that was wrong with the country. Adjustment in these declining smokestack industries wasn't easy. The coal industry was burdened with uneconomic pits and a decline in productivity from its high point in 1969; there were frequent losses. British Steel struggled with over-capacity and over-manning, and hence low productivity, compounded by the oil shock and downturn in demand; it began running large losses. British Rail's deficit increased as trucking and the overall state of the economy ate into demand; its productivity lagged as well. All of the problems of declining industry, such as job loss and dislocation, had combined with all of the problems of a sluggish economy and of inflation, at once.

This had other effects. Concern with employment (by the Labour government and its trade union supporters) or the use of the nationalized industries to implement price restraint (by the previous, Conservative government) complicated the objectives of these industries. This made accountability of management more complicated in turn. Price restraint also meant that more money from the treasury was needed for capital investment and any losses. The more disappointing the financial performance, the more frequent and frustrating the contact between sponsoring department and management; this didn't help either. The post office and bus group suffered from lackluster productivity, although other nationalized sectors, like telephones, British Airways and British Gas, far outpaced the private sector (the manufacturing average) in productivity growth. Comparisons with most-efficient operators elsewhere, however, in airlines and telephones, still showed Britain trailing. Service problems in the utilities, when they occurred, added to the distemper of the times. This was particularly so among Conservative voters, ready to think ill of the nationalized industries and their trade unions. Catch-up price increases in electricity, gas, telephones and rail, after price restraint, exacerbated those industries' growing unpopularity.

Privatization advocates pointed the finger at public ownership itself.

According to one version of events, Mrs. Thatcher had actually stumbled on privatization, almost by accident. Privatization wasn't on the top of her agenda. She had simply despaired of the government's ever getting the nationalized industries to do what they were supposed to do, despite valiant efforts on her part. Privatization was the only way around it. The chill winds of the market would brace up the recalcitrant industries.

People in the privatization movement had in fact been working on the doctrine for years, elaborating all the reasons why public ownership was undesirable. One of their arguments was that the nationalized industries were out of control, and that the government was too preoccupied with other things to control them anyway. Another was that there was too much government control and intervention, which only confused and demoralized management and prevented them from getting on with the real job of improving productivity. Too much control and mixed signals were stultifying entrepreneurial creativity. These two arguments were a little contradictory, but the point was that public enterprise was hopeless one way or the other.

Privatization, as if by a theoretical stroke of lightning, was supposed to get rid of the problem of control altogether. The market, the venerable and tireless Invisible Hand, would look after everything. In practice, the Invisible Hand had helpers — the denizens of the stock market and investors who assessed companies in and through their investment choices and thereby rated them on the great scale of stock market prices. The measure of performance to which investors paid the most attention was profitability.

Here was the core of the doctrine. Privatized companies would have to sink or swim. No longer could they depend on government subsidies if they lost money. Management would have maximum incentive to make their companies efficient. They could own shares in their companies and be rewarded in increased share value and dividends if their companies did well. This would spur them on. Workers could also own shares. No longer would over-manning, featherbedding, excess capacity, restrictive work rules and trade union blackmail – backed up by the realization that a nationalized company could not go bankrupt – hold back the economy.

Privatization, in short, would remove enterprise from bureaucratic inertia and the tangle of politics and bring it into the vital, effervescent, creative, stimulating, and above all free world of the market. It would bring on a cultural revolution – would change attitudes, would dissolve diffidence and negativism, would make Great Britain proud of itself again. Poor performance would be exorcized.

That was the hope and the glory, and the theory and the prejudice, behind it all – "the irrefutable conviction that public enterprises are inevitably economically inferior to private ones," as one observer put it.[3] The trouble was that all but one of the first raft of companies which were privatized or broken up were profitable under public ownership, and several were great successes. They didn't need the benefit of a magic wand or cultural revolution. The one exception, a shipyard, was virtually given away. The government was selling off winners, not losers.

If the government were true to the doctrine, it would have first privatized British Leyland (now the Rover Group), the automobile manufacturer, which was going through a long and tortuous rehabilitation and incurring deficits along the way (accumulated net outlay, including capital investment and redundancy payments, would come to almost £3.5 billion). The superior management of private ownership, theoretically, would wipe out future losses, notwithstanding the fact that the company had been mismanaged and gone bankrupt under private ownership not too many years earlier. Nor should the time and capital for its rehabilitation have been a problem, according to the doctrine. Farsighted and vital private investors would look after that. If, on the other hand, the company had no prospects of profitability, then the doctrine called for the company to be abandoned. Everybody knew the government wasn't taking that step because it would mean that the last British-owned general automobile manufacturer would vanish. What then of Britain's hope and glory?

The privatization of British Airways was also held off until later, for the same reason. It was a glamour company which the government intended to privatize early because sale of the airline would generate investor interest. The airline, however, ran into a bad economic patch and was taken off the privatization list until it gained profitability again. According to the doctrine, it should have been privatized anyway. Investors would have known how great the potential of the company was if only it were privatized, and would have paid a high price for its shares accordingly. In reality, faith did not go that far.

There was another problem with the workings of the doctrine. The tenet that privatization would bring increased efficiency was joined by another tenet just as important: that it would increase competition. In fact, increased competition was the nuclear centre of the whole privatization argument. If it was the answer in reality, though, why bother with privatization at all? Why not just open the doors to competition and let nationalized companies contend? The competition, by virtue of the doctrine, would gradually whip them into shape if they needed such flagellation. Managers and employees might not be able to hold shares, but they could be given bonuses for high-grade performance instead. Bonuses were already used in some state-owned companies elsewhere in the world, and were the standard method of rewarding performance in that most competitive of all sectors, Japanese manufacturing.

If that weren't bad enough for the privatization case, the Thatcher government in 1984 began privatizing the large public monopolies while protecting their monopoly status. This meant their profitability would be assured, which meant greater investor interest and willingness, and a better price for the government. British Telecom went first. Then, in 1986, British Gas. Then British Airways. A small company was allowed to compete with British Telecom in a limited way in international long distance and specialized business communications. British Airways wasn't an absolute monopoly, but it was protected on a series of routes from entry by its main competitor, British Caledonian. (Later, British Caledonian, touted as the shining example of private enterprise efficiency and the virtues of competition, began losing a sizeable amount of money and was taken over by, yes, British Airways). You couldn't go wrong buying into a monopoly, free from the mythic bracing winds of free enterprise. Asked if people would buy shares in his company, one Water Authority chairman replied frankly, "Of course, because a monopoly always makes money."[4]

It wasn't that monopolies otherwise didn't make sense in these cases, only that they undermined the excuse for privatization in the first place. A foremost cabinet spokesman for privatization had himself said that the privatization program would "stand and fall by the extent to which it maximises competition."[5] A pair of distinguished economists wrote an essay entitled "Privatization: A Policy in Search of a Rationale," in which they pointed out that, if there is little competition, "regulated private firms do not perform better than public firms and may do worse." The privatization of these protected monopolies as such was "at best pointless and...likely to be positively harmful," they said.[6] The chairman of British Gas maintained that he was presiding over a privatized company which had not changed one jot from its public-sector self. *The Economist*, a heady advocate of privatization, commented acidly that the financial secretary, the leading apologist in the government for privatization, "has given up pretending that privatisation is much more than an accounting device."[7]

The government set up regulatory agencies to protect the public from these private monopolies, but the agencies were seen to be feeble. "A regulatory dwarf," the National Consumer Council complained of the agency in the British Gas case. People knew, too, from experience in the U.S. — the private-enterprise heartland — how regulatory agencies became captive over time to the industries they were supposed to keep in line. "Unfortunately, privatization so far is designed to help the treasury more than consumers," complained *The Economist* as it surveyed the government's privatization plans.[8]

Something else happened during these years. A few sceptics began to look around them to see what did indeed happen when public enterprises were involved in competitive situations. A whole subterranean debate sprang up as to their relative efficiency. Here and there for a particular industry, for example, somebody did a study of "total factor productivity," academic jargon for "taking everything into account." If labour costs or fuel costs were higher for one company than another, and its profits were correspondingly lower, this did not mean it was less efficient or its employees less productive, only that it paid more for certain things.

One of the studies that kept being mentioned, even in Britain, was on Canadian railways. It showed that publicly owned CN in competition with privately owned CP was every bit as productive — indeed, from a considerable handicap, it had slightly passed CP in productivity by the final years of the study ending in 1975.[9] Mentions of Air Canada as an example of publicly owned efficiency also cropped up in the British literature. As for regulated situations, one study showed that publicly owned American electric utilities performed markedly better than private firms.[10] Another found that publicly owned German insurance companies had lower costs than privately owned ones.[11]

Plain British reality was more complicated than doctrine, too. There were all these companies being privatized that had regularly made profits. Several of them, too, operated in competitive market situations or in foreign markets and were entrepreneurial darlings: the British National Oil Company (a North Sea Cinderella); Amersham International (radioactive and other medical products); Cable & Wireless (a high-grade money-maker); the rehabilitated Jaguar; the rehabilitated Rolls Royce; the technologically chic British Aerospace. British Gas was an impressive money-maker (profits in the financial year 1985-86 were $1.3 billion) and was known for its energetic entrepreneurship and its technological forwardness. British Airways had become profitable again. Even British Telecom, which was technologically behind and required a substantial investment program, had managed major productivity gains within those limitations ("an almost breathtaking increase in labour productivity," allowed one critic, of BT's performance in the 1970s) and was reasonably profitable.[12]

Some people even remembered how inadequate private enterprise had been historically in Britain. One of the most demanding critics of the nationalized industries' performance in the 1970s had to admit that "almost any collection of British industries would have shown up badly."[13] The "ailing British private economy," was how another economic historian described the British private sector's post-war history.[14] Profitability of the private sector suffered a considerable decline in the 1970s — the years under contention.[15]

THE PRIVATIZATION PUTSCH

The privatization doctrine also ignored the fact that the much-berated loss-making public industries, such as coal and rail, were in structurally weak sectors where losses were recorded in all western countries. Also forgotten in the general misery of the 1970s was just how much the nationalized industries had already done for the economy – the restructuring of coal, electricity and gas, for example, or impressive productivity increases in the 1960s, increases significantly ahead of the private sector.

Also unmentioned was the American economy, the model on which privatization ideology rested. In the very years that Mrs. Thatcher came to power and began her campaign against the nationalized industries, the U.S. economy was in disarray. These were the days when Chrysler went to the wall and had to be rescued by government. Ford, despite its mercantile power, ran up huge losses (close to $3.5 billion pretax for its North American operations in 1980). Farm machinery and heavy equipment manufacturers were going downhill fast, some recording mammoth losses. The phrase "Rust Belt" was coined to describe the decay and ineptitude. Unexpectedly high capital costs for nuclear power plants became endemic. Losses by the major steel companies began cropping up, with Bethlehem Steel, USX (formerly U.S. Steel) and LTV making their marks as classic corporate disasters. In the two years 1982 and 1983, the U.S. steel industry lost more than $7 billion. Wheeling-Pittsburgh, eighth in the industry, and then LTV, the second-largest, were later to declare bankruptcy. The large annual U.S. trade deficit began in those years, starting from 1976 and getting altogether out of hand in the early 1980s.

According to privatization dogma, in Britain and elsewhere, the threat of bankruptcy disciplined private-enterprise companies, making them superior to public enterprise. The American model mocked that tenet, too. Indeed, the now-familiar "Chapter 11" bankruptcy proceedings in the U.S. provided a luxurious fall-back position where the bankrupt company could free itself of money-losing contracts and interest charges, and then take on non-bankrupt competitors at an advantage. The process of going bankrupt allowed the people who actually operated the business – management and workers – to continue on the payroll until the fatal day . . . and then after the fatal day under new owners who bought in at garage-sale prices. The powerless shareholders got stuck with the loss. These losses thereby "subsidized" industrial adjustment in parts of the American economy, but under another name.

The American model, underlying British privatization doctrine, had other ways as well of "subsidizing" companies that were failing or going through tough times and of picking up the pieces when they went under. Import restrictions (in steel and automobiles, for example), public loan insurance for the many failed banks, a public pension guaranty corporation for defaulted pension obligations, investment subsidies, the notorious defence procurement system with its massive leakages and its "contract nourishment" — these and other devices poured untold billions upon billions of dollars into company balance sheets and helped cover for failures. The emergency restraints on automobile imports put $15 billion into the accounts of U.S. automobile companies for the four years 1981-84 alone.[16] (In Britain, the privatized Rolls Royce will continue to benefit from the 40 per cent of revenues, mostly on a cost-plus basis, that it procures from military business; Rolls Royce also looks to "launch aid" for new engine development. The privatized British Aerospace also rides on the back of military contracts.)

On the other hand, in Britain, no fault or weakness of a nationalized company was overlooked. Similarly, according to the advocates of privatization, the renaissance of British Airways was completely attributable to the drive for profitability leading up to, and for the purpose of, privatization. Without privatization in the offing, it couldn't have happened. The internal logic of the assertion was fine, given the dogma. Somehow, though, no one mentioned Air France just across the channel. Air France had a heavily international route pattern similar to that of British Airways. The French airline was state-owned and was always intended to be state-owned. It, too, had made heavy weather during the recession but had regained profitability and had become highly productive — a level of productivity British Airways was still trying to reach — drawing kudos from *Air Transport World* magazine, one of the industry's favourite journals. Air Canada, of course, wouldn't be mentioned either.

Neither, in the argument, would anybody mention Freddie Laker, the shining free enterprise knight and one of Margaret Thatcher's entrepreneurial heroes, whose discount Laker Airways had ignominiously bitten the dust. British Airways got the blame, for predatory pricing — Laker took British Airways to court and made a fortune for several lawyers. But aren't predatory pricing, squeeze plays and sheer corporate muscle what free enterprise is all about? Ironically, one of the problems that had staggered British Airways was its expansionary discount strategy — following the heralded free-enterprise Laker example.

The privatization claims over the improved performance of British Airways were nothing next to the cries of celebration over the increased profits of several companies after privatization, the living proof of the correctness of privatization ideas. Privatization backers talked of a new spirit of enterprise in the air.

People who were not in a mythology-building mood, however, kept pointing to uncomfortable facts and to extenuating circumstances. Not only had Jaguar, for example, been put on its feet by public ownership, but also its jump from good profitability to outstanding profitability had been forecast (on the basis, presumably, of orders and interim results) before privatization occurred. The biggest factor, though, was the rise in value of the American dollar and the relative decline in value of the British pound; the U.S. was Jaguar's biggest market. (Later, when the dollar began falling, the privatized Jaguar did not look so glamorous.)

Cable & Wireless, another company whose profit leapt up, had established a beachhead in the U.S. telecommunications industry. Privatization backers talked about how the company had been released from a cage. The expansion strategy had been devised, and the initial American acquisitions made, however, while the company was publicly owned. Some of the rise in profitability came simply from increased traffic on its telecommunications network (Cable & Wireless, technologically advanced, was one of the world's largest users of satellites; this, too, was inherited from its public ownership). Movements in exchange rates also contributed to the increased profits, as they had done with Jaguar.

The National Freight Corporation (NFC) was another company invariably cited by privatization proponents. The company was sold to a management-employee consortium (the only case of an employees' buy-out in the privatization list). Profitability shot up from low levels, and there was a great deal of excitement and pride on the part of the new employee-shareholders who had helped to make it happen. That, however, wasn't the whole story. The principal changes at NFC had been completed before privatization, going back as far as 1976, with the introduction of new senior management and a major restructuring of the company. These changes produced much improved results — results which had made the company an early candidate for privatization when Mrs. Thatcher came to power. Other things also had a bearing, as we shall see. Similarly, Amersham International had undertaken a heavy capital expenditure program between 1979 and 1981, before it was privatized, the benefits of which were reaped as privatization occurred.

One study showed that the biggest jump in profit-to-sales ratio for several privatized companies, including Amersham International, had actually occurred in the years prior to privatization.[17] Also in these years (to the mid-1980s), Britain as a whole was emerging from the recession of 1981. The United States, a key foreign market, was also emerging from recession. Sure enough, a second part of the study showed that quite substantial improvements in performance had occurred in companies like British Steel, Rolls Royce, National Bus and, of course, British Airways, which had not been privatized in the immediate post-recession period.

Among the "most informative figures," according to the study, were the ones on privatized British Aerospace. The company, because of its military production and long-term projects, was in less of a position to benefit in the short term by upward market swings. Privatized British Aerospace showed no appreciable improvement in financial performance, improvement which would have been generated by an increase in internal efficiency.[18]

Another factor skewed comparisons: pre-privatization "laundering" of figures and "capital reconstructions" for a number of companies — the writing off of fixed-interest capital debt, for example (debts partly incurred with nationalization), or the making up by the government of pension fund deficiencies. The effect of these "reconstructions" was to show the subsequent financial performance of privatized companies in a better light. The National Freight Corporation, British Telecom and Associated British Ports were among the companies whose books benefited by these pre-privatization changes.

Other factors could also complicate comparisons. In the case of the National Freight Corporation, redundancy payments prior to privatization, for employees cut from the operation, were more than three times what they were afterwards. The publicly owned company paid the costs, the privately owned company reaped the benefit, in terms of financial comparison. Acquisitions and property sales also helped post-privatization turnover and profit-growth figures for NFC, independently of any improvements in productivity.

So amidst the privatization blitzkrieg, questions were being asked, memories were being jogged, and the monopolies were as monopolistic as ever. Competition and efficiency lost their lustre as reasons for privatization. At this juncture, with the privatizing of British Telecom, another reason was taken out of the the ideological grab bag: "shareholders' democracy." It was a great slogan.

Unfortunately, the idea of "shareholders' democracy" was full of holes, too. While the much-ballyhooed British Telecom share distribution was taking place, it was already known that there had been a drastic reduction in the number of shareholders in the earlier privatization cases where the companies were sold to the public. It had happened, too, in just a few short years. Many of the individual share buyers had been doing what the British call "stagging" — selling off for a nice take as soon as the shares began trading in the stock market. It wasn't surprising that, with all the excitement and the potential loot, the idea of "wider share ownership" was politically useful and the government turned to exploiting it — a bit of a Roman circus.

Even without the drastic reduction in their numbers, the shareholders would have represented only a small minority of British households and by and large a better-off minority.

One self-serving irony followed another. Mrs. Thatcher boasted about how privatization had regenerated the economy, as Britain's growth improved. It was her own severe monetarist policy that peaked with the recession in 1981, however, helped along by the U.S. recession of her ideological soulmate Ronald Reagan, that had inhibited growth and exports and created many company problems in the first place.

Gradually the subterranean doubts and criticisms rose to the surface. In early 1987, the business magazine *Management Today*, reviewing Mrs. Thatcher's "private prospects," carefully dissected all the utopian claims that had been made for privatization and the privatized companies, shooting down one overweening generalization after another.[19]   There and elsewhere, the idea of privatizing monopolies in particular was viewed with growing cynicism. A survey of the top 200 companies in Britain found that 63 per cent believed that British Telecom (BT) services "have either deteriorated or failed to improve since privatization." Another found that 52 per cent of all customers rated BT's charges "unreasonable" compared to only 39 per cent prior to privatization. Complaints abounded over long delays in installing new phones and repairing old ones. One in four call boxes wasn't operating (BT, reeling from criticism, managed to get this down to one in 12 later). Several newspapers and magazines had well-publicized disputes with BT over their own telephone systems. Hundreds of companies discovered they were being consistently over-billed. Jokes began to go the rounds, like "How do you get 12 people in a phone booth? You tell them it's working." Even *The Economist* referred to a "storm of criticism and abuse" that privatized BT had created, and conceded that "many people have concluded that privatizing a monopoly intact [without competition] may be worse than leaving it in the public sector."[20] And what if competition results in unnecessary duplication and the loss of the benefits of integration? And who in his right mind would suggest competing, and duplicated, local distribution systems?

Meanwhile, industrial customers of privatized British Gas were up in arms at having to pay the highest rates in the Western world, despite British Gas's North Sea supplies. Gas tariffs in Britain hadn't significantly followed oil prices downwards as they had in some other countries. "Since privatisation, the gap between what British Gas charges and prices in other leading Western countries has, if anything, widened," complained a chemical industry spokesperson.[21]

In electricity, the government announced that prices would be increased 15 per cent to boost the return on assets, in order to make shares more attractive come privatization ("fattening the calf for sale" was how the critics put it). A first-instalment price rise of 9 per cent was forthwith implemented. According to privatization doctrine, privatization should have been attractive with rates as they were; a higher return would automatically be produced by productivity increases brought about by the "miracle" workings of private owner-ship. Nor, for a utility, is a high return appropriate. A survey found that 63 per cent of individuals polled were against electricity privatization.

The London-based *Amex Bank Review*, although pro-privatization, allowed that "while there is a widespread feeling that privately owned companies are more efficient than government enterprises, it is harder to prove than might be expected."[22] Even the London correspondent of the faithfully doctrinaire, stiff-backed *Financial Post* noted how most companies sold off in Britain were already on the road to recovery or were already successful prior to privatization, an irony which also began to be noted in the British press.[23] A report the same year in the Toronto *Globe and Mail* pointed out that "there is no body of hard evidence that shows an enterprise is necessarily better off in private hands or that the public is better served, particularly in cases of near or complete monopolies."[24]

The Conservatives under Mrs. Thatcher were intent on reducing public spending and taxation as proportions of gross domestic product, but into their second term in office the ratios were higher than when they began. On the other hand, they found it technically easier to privatize nationalized industries than they had imagined. So now they were going on a sell-off binge by which they could better reduce taxes or, in the lingo, offer "stimulative tax reductions." Those tax cuts win votes: not bribing the people with their own money but bribing them with the proceeds from the sale of their own assets.

One economist suggests that privatization has also served as an ideological surrogate for the public-spending cuts the government failed to achieve.[25] Another economist acidly calls the sell-off campaign "taxation through privatization," whereby the public is indirectly taxed (by the loss of its assets) to the benefit of the largely well-off middle-class minority which cashes in on the underpriced stock flotations.[26] Similarly, the margin of tax reduction which the application of the proceeds made possible heavily favoured high-income families in the government's new taxation scheme.

Billions in assets – $40 billions indeed – had already been thrown into the ring by the summer of 1987 and the big events were still to come: an estimated $16 billion for the second tranche of British Telecom shares; $16 billion for the remaining 32 per cent of British Petroleum; and the grand *pinnada*, the electricity industry – a tempting target for selling off – with a possible net take of $33 to $40 billion for England and Wales alone, with Scotland and Northern Ireland yet to come. Privatizers boast that this distribution of assets is the greatest transferral of property ownership since Henry VIII expropriated the church's land. They may well be correct. But it's the use of the transferral to help finance current tax reductions – once handed out, all gone – which sticks in the mind.

The year 1987 brought other revelations. The British Post Office announced record profits of $340 million. British Rail was in the process of cutting its deficit in half, from $2 billion in 1982 to $1 billion in 1990, and had achieved the second best staff productivity in Europe, next to the Netherlands (British Rail, like other European railroads, runs passenger trains, which requires subsidies). Given subsidies for unprofitable services, British Rail was expected soon to show an operating surplus. "I see no requirement to privatize bits of the network," the chairman commented. Public financial control over subsidized and monopoly activities had been improved by a new monitoring arrangement stressing profit and performance targets. This latter was the work not of Mrs. Thatcher and the privatization forces but of the previous Labour government.

In fact, the improvements in the basic nationalized industries in the 1980s were foreshadowed by this and other key Labour government measures: ensuring respect for management autonomy, elimination of arbitrary price restraints, and more long-range and flexible investment rules. A "well-constructed boat" was how *The Economist* described the initiatives.[27] The turn-around in the industries' financial performance, from the low point of the mid-1970s, began while the Labour Party was still in power.

Also in 1987, a study showed that, for the period 1978-1985, the improvement in efficiency of nine basic companies still nationalized was quite good, judged in relation either to historical performance or British industry as a whole. More striking, as the study pointed out, was that the most marked productivity gains were made in the traditional nationalized industries – posts, rail, steel – where no privatization was in prospect.[28] Similarly, a government treasury chart, using 1975 as the base year, showed productivity growth of the nationalized industries outpacing both the economy as a whole (since 1983) and private-sector manufacturing (since 1985).[29]

THE PRIVATIZATION PUTSCH

The Rover Group, the automobile manufacturer – one of the most difficult challenges of public enterprise in Britain – was getting back on its feet. The company's main problem was its loss of market share. Nevertheless, it announced a small operating profit (before taxes and interest) for 1987. More important, it had become an extremely efficient, highly automated producer. It had some of the most technologically advanced design and manufacturing systems in Europe. It had a growing reputation for good cost control. It had also developed, through Warwick University, a source of skilled production engineers, otherwise in short supply in Britain. It was a far cry from the hopeless automobile works and corporate culture which public ownership had inherited from private enterprise a decade earlier. One in three Rover cars, moreover, was being exported, whereas the privately owned manufacturers in Britain (Ford and GM) were major net importers. Manufacturing as a whole in Britain (the works of the private sector) had a large and growing trade deficit, hitting $22 billion in 1987.

When the government announced that the Rover Group would then be handed over to privatized British Aerospace, even privatization advocates realized that, in the key areas of manufacturing technology and design capability, it was the publicly owned Rover Group which would be bringing benefits to the privatized British Aerospace, benefits paid for dearly by the public. The controversial sweetheart deal with British Aerospace was effectively a giveaway (and not only did British Aerospace get the plants, it also got the land underneath the plants, valued as high as $4 billion; every time it closes or relocates a plant, it will cash in handsomely). Such was the hollow boast of private-enterprise heroism in Britain that no privately owned British company was willing to buy Rover, and get into the highly competitive automobile business, while paying a fair price for the company.

Most dramatic of all, the nationalized British Steel – the company whose history embodies the nationalization debate more intensely than any other – announced profits of $372 million for the financial year 1986-87. British Steel had become the most productive steelmaker in Europe and was challenging Japanese levels. Also, its staggering adjustment losses, most particularly from redundancy payments and writing off excess capacity, were behind it. (The

American steel industry that year was suffering more losses than ever, with bankrupt LTV alone chalking up a $4.5 billion deficit; only in 1987 did its leading companies manage to get back on even keel. In Japan, Nippon Steel lost money making steel in the financial year 1986-87.) British Steel profits for the following year, 1987-88, were $900 million, making the company perhaps the most profitable integrated steel producer in the world. It was also, by mid-1988, the lowest-cost steel industry by country. It was even ahead of low-wage producers like South Korea and Taiwan, because of lower financial costs.

Naturally, the better British Steel did under public ownership, the higher it rose in the government's privatization priority list. What is even more ironic is that the scapegoating of such British nationalized industries by private enterprise disciples hides the real villain of the piece, the historic failure of British private enterprise itself.

3.
The Historic Failure of British Private Enterprise

At the height of public ownership in Britain before the privatization splurge, publicly owned companies were only 11 per cent of the British economy in terms of gross domestic product. What about the other 89 per cent?

As the British business magazine *Management Today* put it, "The ideology of privatization tends to assume that... the private sector is a burgeoning paradise, replete with fountains of technological creativity, wells of customer services, and streams of production innovation – in which case one might be forgiven for wondering why Britain's postwar industrial performance, nine-tenths of which has been the responsibility of those green-fingered private hands, has been so poor."[1]

The reference by the magazine to "nine-tenths" of the gross domestic product belonging to the private sector is not altogether accurate. The fraction taken up by government services needs to be deducted first. This would leave the private sector in that period with something like 70 per cent of the gross domestic product. The magazine's point, nevertheless, hits home. Britain has been, above all, a private-enterprise failure, comparatively speaking.

The decline, according to American economic historian Michael Edelstein, actually began around 1880, long before there were public enterprises and a Labour party for right-wing ideologues to use as a scapegoat.[2] One of the main reasons: a lack of business enterprise and innovation vigorous enough to attract available capital. This happened, too, when London was the world's leading financial centre and when there were numerous provincial stock exchanges. The great British economic historian Eric Hobsbawm actually said it first, in his provocative *Industry and Empire*, covering the years 1750 to 1968.[3] One chapter in the book is entitled "The Beginnings of Decline." The chronological point of departure for the decline was 1860, when free enterprise ruled both in practice and in doctrine.

Hobsbawm identified the crucial factors involved. The first and most profound change was in the role of science and technology. The second was the development of mass production and the mechanization of machine-making for both factory and consumer use. A mass market of working people with rising incomes was the third. Concentration of production and ownership, to achieve economies of scale, was the fourth.

Hobsbawm continued:

> In every one of the four aspects of the economy we have just sketched, Britain fell behind her rivals; and this was all the more striking, not to say painful, when these occupied fields which Britain had herself been the first to plough before abandoning them. This sudden transformation of the leading and most dynamic industrial economy into the most sluggish and conservative, in the short space of thirty or forty years (1860-90/1900), is the crucial question of British economic history. After the 1890s we may ask why so little was done to restore the dynamism of the economy, and we may blame the generations after 1890 for not doing more, for doing the wrong things, or even for making the situation worse. But essentially these are discussions about bringing the horse back into the stable after it has gone. It went between the middle of the century and the 1890s.[4]

The contrast between Britain and more modern industrial states was particularly striking in the new "growth industries" like electrical equipment, chemicals and steel, Hobsbawm elaborated. "Very feeble," was how he described British performance in these areas. Nationalization, right through to the saving of Jaguar and Rolls-Royce, was in many respects a response to that private enterprise anemia. The unhappy coal industry was no different. Under private ownership, the works were fragmented and inefficient, employers were backward, antiquated equipment and under-investment were endemic, labour relations were bitter – that, too, before coal went into decline as a fuel.

Similarly, the privately owned railways as far back as the 1880s dragged their feet when it came to modernization and reducing transport costs. One of the many archaisms that seemed to last forever was the small size of freight cars transporting coal, half the size of what they should have been. Their inefficiency was apparent well before World War I, but the coal companies and railways couldn't agree on who should put out the capital. It wasn't until both were nationalized in 1947 that anything was done about it.

In chemicals, dyes, electrical technology, machines and machine tools, the British could be full of invention (one scientist began to think about a carbon-filament incandescent lamp two years before Edison was born), but it was the Americans and Germans who forged ahead with the actual manufacturing. The saddest case, Hobsbawm found, was iron and steel where the British led the way in innovation but the Germans, French and Americans profited most. As time went on not only British dominance faded but also British productivity trailed.

The coalmine and railway owners did not protest nationalization too much. They had run down their operations to a point where they couldn't salvage them, and the spectre of facing up to actual competition by oil and trucking respectively did not appeal to them. Let nationalization pick up the pieces. Steel, when it was re-nationalized, was also in a deteriorating position.

Another telltale clue about who was enterprising and who wasn't, as the post-war period proceeded: with the exception of steel, Conservative governments were well able to live with the nationalizations and hospitalizations that occurred. They themselves even indulged: the public takeover of Rolls Royce occurred during the term of office of the Heath Conservative government. These same Conservatives, though, were supposed to be the very guardians and exponents of private enterprise. They in effect recognized in practice what they could not admit in rhetoric.

The privately owned British aircraft industry was sagging by the 1970s, despite millions of pounds of public money for research and development. On the military side – fed by publicly financed contracts – the order books were full. On the civil side, the industry was going downhill. Its major passenger jets (the BAC 111 and the Trident) were coming to the end of the line. Inefficient and costly to operate, the planes had not been a great success to begin with. U.S. aircraft were more economical on fuel, more productive, and their reliability was better. The fragmented British industry meant different companies made similar aircraft, none of which sold well enough to recoup the research and development outlay. Nationalization under British Aerospace amalgamated four different companies, dragging them belatedly into the 1970s, and gave the industry the muscle which it has today.

Or take the automobile industry, the post-war manufacturing sector *par excellence*. In the late 1960s and early 1970s, the French economic "miracle" replaced the German economic "miracle" in the European spotlight. The French economy had grown rapidly. The only thing that seemed to be growing in Britain was its reputation as the sick man of Europe. One of the signs of the sickness was all the imported cars in Britain, including a lot of French ones, and hardly any British ones on the continent. One enterprising English commentator claimed in the late 1970s that if one took away the difference between the automobile industries in Britain and France, including the industrial and economic spin-offs, the two economies would be in virtually a dead heat.

To a large extent, this was the difference between the publicly owned Renault automobile company – the glory of post-war French entrepreneurship – and the privately owned British manufacturers.

Two of the British manufacturers were privately owned American companies with no particular loyalty to Great Britain (General Motors by 1984 was filling 59 per cent of its British market share with imports and the overall foreign content of cars it sold in the U.K. was 78 per cent; Ford and GM between them were net importers of 350,000 cars that year). The other, the only British-owned company, was British Leyland, a classic case of inept and shortsighted management, poor labour relations and under-investment. In 1974, the year before privately owned BL bit the dust, it had £920 of fixed assets per man. Publicly owned Renault had £2,396 per man. Renault's value added per man and gross output per man were double the BL figures. Renault's unit sales per employee were three times the BL figure and the highest in Europe.[5] Its exports were double BL's and also led

Europe. (Volkswagen was the leading European producer in number of vehicles in those years; it had been a publicly owned company and effective control — a 20 per cent shareholding by the federal government and another 20 per cent by Lower Saxony — was still under public ownership.)

That wasn't all. What applied to the automobile industry also applied to manufacturing generally. Post-war British decline began in the late 1960s with the loss by British producers of their share of the domestic market across a broad range of industries. The decline accelerated in the 1970s. This key economic failure was a private-enterprise one; prior to the hospitalization of Rolls Royce in 1971 and of British Leyland in 1975, virtually all of finished manufacturing was in the private sector.

As the chairman of Jaguar and former BL executive Sir John Egan remarked recently about the company in the mid-1970s (it had just been hospitalized at the time): "People thought BL was a uniquely bad British company. In fact it was a typical British company. Looking around at some of our suppliers, I could see that BL was no worse than many."[6]

We know what happens next. The nationalized industries and the idea of public ownership get pummelled. Failed British private enterprise is extolled. British private enterprise gets the money-making public companies as a prize for its historic failure. Once the enormously difficult adjustment has been made by the nationalized industries, after more than 100 years of Britain's falling behind, privatization battens onto public ownership's back and grabs all the credit. A minority of well-off people get a nice piece of loot.

What of the two favourite villains in British privatization mythology: over-manning in the nationalized industries and the wicked power of the trade unions? The two were legendary, in the mythology, and the legend helped conveniently to scapegoat public enterprise while the historic failure of private enterprise was being overlooked.

In this mythology, there were vast legions of unnecessary employees who, by moving slowly, frittering away their time, and constructing inflexible work rules, kept all their jobs intact, with the public paying. The workers could simply manipulate the nationalized companies. They knew that the government would be forced to subsidize the losses or, alternately, that through their unions they could get a Labour government to accommodate them. Worst of all, in Britain, the subsidies were creating enormous and intolerable public debt, wreaking havoc with public finances. Over-manning and sloth in the nationalized industries were making Britain "the sick man of Europe." Only privatization could contend with these debilitating devils. Privatization was first discussed in the Conservative party just in those terms: as a means to reduce the power of public sector trade unions. If, at the same time, it meant a blow to the party's political enemies, all the better.

These mythic villains were summoned up by privatizers in Canada, too – the local doctrine being fed by the British privatization ideologues. It was no coincidence that Stephen Rogers, B.C.'s minister responsible for privatization, searching for a graphic example of over-manning, would pick on a British case: British Airways. Rogers excitedly portrayed the resurrection of the airline as it ascended to privatization. British Airways, went the epistle, having to reach profitability so that it could be privatized, had declared war on its slothful and negligent publicly owned ways and had cut its bloated staffing down from approximately 57,000 to 35,000. Only with privatization in the offing, it was understood, would such cuts have been made. Rogers, a former Air Canada pilot, declined to mention the particular circumstances of British Airways' overcapacity and over-manning, or contrary examples of publicly owned airlines like Air France or Air Canada. Qualifications would, of course, have spoiled what he was trying to do.

It was great mythology, begging to be dissected.

One started with the cases of nationalized industries not up for privatization where the reduction of manning had in fact been much more dramatic than in British Airways. The workforce of British Leyland (now the Rover Group) declined from 150,000 to 50,000 from 1975 to 1987 (including the sale of two subsidiaries).[7] At one point, 1,000 men per month were being dismissed. More relevant, productivity levels rose from 6.5 cars per worker per year in 1977 to a projected 16 cars per worker by the beginning of 1988, to rival the best in Europe although still trailing the leader, Japan.[8] British Steel's workforce, similarly, shrank from 208,000 to 52,000 in the ten years to

1987.[9] Its slimming was the most dramatic among all European steel companies. The cuts were part of a concerted plan by European Economic Community members to reduce excess capacity on a shared basis. The major cuts in the manning of the National Freight Corporation—from 69,000 in 1969 to 25,000 in 1981—were made under public ownership, with little conflict.[10] British Gas reduced its work force by 22,000 in the decade 1968-1978, under public ownership, while almost doubling output and increasing the volume of gas sold by close to four times.[11] The electricity boards in the same period cut manpower back by 60,000, or 25 per cent, while increasing output by about the same amount.[12]

The severe British Airways manning cuts were made under public ownership. Nor was the imminence of privatization (and a board of directors put in place for that purpose) somehow, theologically, necessary to push the cuts through. The downsizing was engineered by attractive severance payments and would have happened in any case.

One of the most striking reductions in manning in British economic history occurred in the original nationalized industries prior to the 1970s, and most of all in coal and rail taken over from private enterprise. In the decade 1958 to 1968, employment in coal mining was cut virtually in half, from 760,000 to less than 390,000 (and was to be cut in half again, to 180,000, by the time of the bitter miners' strike in 1984). The rail labour force was slashed from 590,000 to 330,000, or almost in half; it had been falling steadily, in fact, ever since the war. Overall, from 1958 to 1968, including electricity, gas, buses and airlines, the public enterprise labour force declined from 1,920,000 to 1,310,000. That's 600,000 people, or a third, in one decade while production, at the same time, increased by about a fifth.[13]

These massive cuts in workforce numbers and the broad stride forward in productivity might be compared to the privately owned automobile industry and its notoriously bad labour relations and lagging productivity. By contrast, for that industry, publicly owned Renault in France led the way in good labour relations and productivity. Good management and sufficient investment, as well as the company's enlightened attitude towards labour, helped. The same spirit infused the nationalized industries in Britain in the post-war years. When the railways were taken over after the war, the union members, in their vesting day speeches, spoke of bringing efficiency and honour to the new British Railways, with a service cheaper and better for the public. The coal miners similarly, when the mines were nationalized, pledged themselves to making nationalization a success. They had finally cast off a backward, selfish and class-bound ownership, and now had a situation with decent working hours and holidays with pay where their own contribution would not simply be exploited.

Or compare the reduction of the British Steel labour force with what happened in the free-enterprise United States. There, over-manning and inefficiency, brought about by excess capacity, short-sightedness, and managerial incompetence continued until the industry was on its knees, running up those huge losses and bank-rupting LTV and Wheeling-Pittsburgh.

Probably nothing quite outdid the over-manning and resistance to technical innovation of the production staffs of British newspapers on Fleet Street, privately owned. But that example, taken by itself, is misleading in turn, for the private sector. A recent study found that the overwhelming response by private-sector unions and workers to technical change was positive, often enthusiastically so. Those arch-demons in the anti-union demonology, the shop stewards, liked it even more. Indeed, trade unions often acted as a spur to change, pressing for more investment and the introduction of new tools.[14] Another study found that workers had been unfairly blamed for productivity problems in cases where the real culprit was inadequate capital investment or poor line management. Also overlooked, by the conventional wisdom, was the possibility that strained labour relations might be the result of worker contempt for managerial incompetence.[15] As even the right-wing *Economist* acknowledged, it was "easy to blame the yob on the picket line, harder to blame the invisible board of directors that, five years before, failed to boost the R&D budget."[16] The problem was inadequate British private enterprise and its management again.

If, further, one traced back to its historical roots the class divisions which underlay the lack of industrial accord in Britain — one manifestation of the famous "British disease" — one came inevitably to the arrogance and short-sightedness of British private enterprise. One also came to an unvarnished market doctrine which, among other things, treated labour like just another commodity – the same general doctrine, incidentally, from which privatization springs.

The figures of severe manning cuts in the British nationalized industries tell only part of the story of what was a difficult and complex economic adjustment. It would have been remarkable if, in the declining industries like coal, rail and steel, which had been nationalized, and given bitter historical memories of the dole, there had not been some resistance to job loss and some political concern about it, and productivity problems along the way, especially when private-enterprise sectors of the economy, supposed to pick up the slack, were failing to generate sufficient alternative employment.

Nor did the British have an active labour adjustment policy to ease the transition, a policy similar to the one developed in Sweden, for example. There, retraining programs at close to full pay and job-creation schemes act as a bridge for people who lose their jobs. Such "active labour markets" produce an easy mobility of workers from declining industries into new, technologically different ones – that is, where the rest of the economy, largely left to private enterprise in Britain, is actually producing technologically new work.

The principles of active labour adjustment are: first, individuals should not be made to suffer for technological change of benefit to all of society, least of all where parts of society abound in wealth and luxury and have a habit of exploiting others; and, second, the economy as a whole will suffer and the potential of people will be lost unless there is an active labour adjustment program. By contrast, the ideology of privatization is also the ideology which rejects the very notion that an economy and its parts belong to the community as a whole. In Sweden it was the trade union movement which developed the active labour market policy.

There remained the more basic question: were these subsidies to the supposedly horrible nationalized industries in fact sapping the vitality of the British economy and dragging it down into the mire of uncompetitiveness while others prospered, such as the mythology had it?

First of all, one needed to change the question. All those profitable publicly owned companies, including the lucrative holdings in British Petroleum – the very companies which the Thatcher government privatized – weren't part of the problem. Nor did British Telecom and British Gas – self-sustaining utilities, making large profits, and also privatized – fall into the subsidized category. Also to be excluded were the successful hospitalizations of Rolls Royce and Jaguar; both were a great help to the economy. Another hospitalization case, British Leyland (the Rover Group), had been a costly and difficult uphill battle, but even Mrs. Thatcher had stood behind it. Moreover, despite the outlay on British Leyland, it earned substantial foreign revenue (£800 million in 1979, including Jaguar) whereas Ford and GM in Britain had a combined trade deficit (£40 million in 1979, and £1.1 billion in 1984). What one was really looking at, in this case, were coal, rail, steel and the post office. Were they such a burden, crushing the nation?

At the end of 1978, *The Economist* published a special feature on public sector enterprise which had some interesting details. In 1978 itself, the year before Margaret Thatcher came to power, and several years before another 100,000 coal miners were given the gate, production of British coal was receiving aid of £0.44 per tonne, not much above £60 million in all (whether this included an indirect subsidy from sales to the Central Electricity Generating Board wasn't mentioned). West German coal, on the other hand, privately owned for the most part, was receiving a subsidy of £11.93 per tonne, or slightly over £1 billion in all. Additional aid not related to current production amounted to about £50 million in Britain and £1.7 billion in West Germany.[17] The heavy adjustment costs, for the British coal industry, were yet to come.

In 1975 (the year for which railway figures were given), the subsidy handed out to West Germany's railway was slightly over 100 per cent of its traffic revenues. The similar subsidy for British Rail was less than 60 per cent.[18] In 1977, the cost in purchasing power of a first-class letter in West Germany was just a shade higher than in Great Britain (with the British post office breaking even) but the median cost of business telephone bills was 34 per cent higher and of residential telephone bills 85 per cent higher.[19]

West Germany was the economic miracle *par excellence* up to and including those years, against which Britain was always being compared with sympathy and disdain. One obviously hadn't touched the core of the problem of the British economy here. Nor could one blame steel. All countries in the European Community provided their steel industries with aids and subsidies as steel plunged into crisis in the 1970s, and each country sooner or later had to go through the costly restructuring process of redundancy payments, modernizing and writing off excess capacity. As it happened, by the time those major adjustment costs were incurred in Britain's case, beginning in the late 1970s, the country had long since fallen behind economically.

One had to look elsewhere to get at the heart of the problem. One black hole down which large amounts of money disappeared was agriculture. In later years, these dispensations became enormous. Britain is now spending close to $4 billion annually on agricultural subsidies. For the financial year 1979-80, it was $1.8 billion. The businesses receiving these subsidies are, of course, private-enterprise ones. The subsidized farmers are probably also mostly Tory and fully support Mrs. Thatcher's cries of Armageddon against the nationalized industries and all they stand for. (According to a report on agricultural subsidies done by the Australian government, a coalminer's or bus driver's family in Britain has to fork over something like $1,250 every year in subsidies to these Tory folk in the southern English countryside.)

But the British farms weren't the critical problem either. Great and vigorous economic powers were, and are, also subsidizing their farmers. West Germany forks over almost twice as much as Britain. Japan puts out $15 billion, about four times as much as Britain.

Anybody looking for the main problem sector of the British economy ends up with its historically sluggish private enterprise. Weak and short-sighted private enterprise was the problem all along. Mrs. Thatcher, a private-enterprise grocer's daughter and head of a private-enterprise party, privatized the publicly owned industries instead.

4.
The European Dossier

Privatization apologists in Britain might have inveighed against their nationalized industries, but they weren't so keen to bring up the western European experience just next door. All countries in western Europe had substantial public-enterprise sectors. In terms of percentage of the labour force, public enterprise played almost as large a role in West Germany as in Britain (7.2 per cent and 8.1 per cent respectively, in 1978). The figure for Sweden, always thought to have a relatively small part of its businesses under public ownership, was 8.2 per cent in 1978; the hospitalization of steel and shipbuilding (the latter industry to be subsequently phased out) was a factor.[1]

While Britain was languishing in the 1970s, one of the secret economic successes in the world which nobody much talked about was Austria. Austria was a small country that had managed to diversify and contend next door to a large economic power (West Germany). It did well in the export market and had little unemployment. Its social consensus was impressive. What made Austria particularly notable was how far it had come. Germany and Japan were wiped out during the war; Germany in particular suffered immense physical destruction. Both countries, however, had long and dynamic business histories. The culture of enterprise was instilled in them. They also had national cohesion. Austria, on the other hand, was the left-over remnant of the comic Austro-Hungarian Empire which collapsed during the First World War. Its economic performance in the interwar period was pitiable.

The new Austria had a greater percentage of workers employed in public enterprises and government service than some of its communist neighbours. In a special feature on public sector enterprise late in 1978, *The Economist* ran a chart showing the extent of public ownership in 18 non-communist industrialized countries. Circles were blacked in, in whole or in part, for the various key sectors, to indicate public ownership: posts, telecommunications, electricity, gas, oil production, coal, railways, airlines, motor industry and steel. All the Austrian circles were fully blacked in.[2] Banking, chemicals, mining and metals, electrical equipment, machinery, textiles, paper, glass and building materials could have been added, in various proportions. The largest industrial conglomerate, with companies in six major sectors, was state-owned. The two largest banks were indirectly state-controlled companies. In *The Economist*'s rundown, the percentage of the labour force employed in public enterprise was almost twice as large in Austria as in Britain (13.7 per cent compared to 8.1 per cent) — this, too, before any privatization in Britain occurred.

Finland is another useful illustration. With publicly owned enterprises in electrical power, the forest industry, chemicals, fertilizers, mining and metallurgy, iron and steel, machinery, oil refining and marketing, natural gas and coal distribution, transportation equipment and, later, truck and bus manufacturing, Finland turned itself from a poor and largely agrarian society into a highly industrialized and sophisticated industrial country exporting around the world. Also on the public-enterprise list are automation systems, packaging, plastics, housing and real estate, prefabricated housing, air transport, travel agencies, textiles and textile fibres, explosives, batteries, defence equipment, tractors, special vehicles, paints, shipping, engineering, data processing, biotechnology, alcoholic beverages, hotels, restaurants and catering, and broadcasting. Finland's gross domestic product per capita is far and away higher than Great Britain's and is even higher than Canada's (based on OECD provisional figures for 1987). In late 1986, the publicly owned Valmet Corporation from Finland acquired Sentrol Systems of Toronto from the privatized Canada Development Corporation (CDC), as the

CDC gave up on its high-technology ambitions. Sentrol is involved in industrial automation.

Italy is another instructive case. In Italy, as in Britain, we discover public enterprises rising out of the ashes of private-enterprise failures. It was bad enough for Britain to fall behind France where public enterprise played a central role in the post-war economy. There were, though, in the Common Market, always the hopeless Italians. Recently, ultimate mortification happened. Italy announced gaily — over British charges and counterclaims — that its standard of living had passed Britain's. One of the key elements in the Italian economy is the publicly owned Istituto per la Ricostruzione Industriale — the often controversial and multi-coloured IRI.

Save for the two huge oil companies Shell and BP, IRI in 1986 was the largest industrial company outside the United States, measured by sales. Overall it was the largest employer in Europe.

IRI began with a colossal private enterprise failure: the collapse, in the 1930s, of Italy's major banks. IRI, acting as a lame-duck hospital, took over the companies which the banks owned or controlled. After 1945, it played a major role in Italy's post-war industrial restructuring. It established the modern Italian steel industry. Later it was handed most of Italy's shipyards in a wretched state, and modernized and turned them around. As the conservative *Economist* noted, in its special feature on public enterprise in the late 1970s, the IRI and its venerable chairman at the time, Giuseppe Petrilli, had a "good deal to be proud of."[3]

The holding company controls (although not necessarily wholly owns) the national airlines, public broadcasting service, telecommunications and telecommunications equipment, most turnpikes, three major banks plus other financial institutions (at one time 60 banks in all), Italy's output of pig-iron and a big chunk of its crude steel and special steels, almost all of nuclear engineering, half of all diesel motor output, innumerable engineering firms, most of shipbuilding and a large part of shipping, several electronics companies, plus interests in building construction, public works, plant design and construction, hotels, Rome airport, food, retailing, and much else, including, as a fillip, the Italian end of the tunnel under Mont Blanc. A late 1987 estimate put the number of subsidiary companies under IRI's roof at well over 500 firms.

THE PRIVATIZATION PUTSCH

The IRI isn't alone in public enterprise in Italy. There is the giant ENI group (energy, chemicals, textiles, plant design and construction), now the 10th largest industrial corporation outside the United States, measured by sales. ENI was the baby of the legendary Enrico Mattei. Mattei took on the powerful and arrogant "Seven Sisters" of the oil industry — the old multinationals who ruled the industry worldwide — in the days when it just wasn't done. And he succeeded.

There is also, in Italy, the state-owned EFIM group (aluminum, aeronautics, railway equipment and other industrial companies) and GEPI, created as a lame-duck hospital in 1971. At one time, public enterprise accounted for a quarter of industrial employment and near to half of fixed investment. Currently, the turnover of IRI, ENI and EFIM account for almost 10 per cent of Italy's gross domestic product.

The IRI is of particular interest because of the anarchistic, messy and immensely political environment in which it grew up, namely Italy. Surviving in Italy, it showed how extraordinarily adaptable and constructive public enterprise can be. It should be of special interest to Canadians because it undertook, at government instruction, massive investments in the underdeveloped Mezzogiorno, the south of Italy, to diversify that region's economy. The more physically imposing of this industrial plant became known, both affectionately and sarcastically, as "cathedrals in the desert." The IRI accepted its role in the south — it considered that it had an entrepreneurial "duty to the south" — and, in the 1970s, produced about seven times its fair share of the new manufacturing jobs in the region.

The location of several of these plants did not make sense financially in terms of the IRI itself. However, necessary compensation from the government wasn't always forthcoming, a cause of bitter and loud complaint from IRI's chief executives. In the 1970s, IRI carried other burdens. The labour force in the south was less reliable and skilled than in the north, and the IRI was obliged to take whomever the local labour exchange sent them. In one case, the record of absenteeism was appalling. The trade unions called for anti-cyclical investment. When other companies were holding back, the IRI was supposed to fill in the gap, as it actually had done for a brief period early in the decade. During the economic slump in the 1970s, it was forced by politicians to preserve jobs, and did do so when companies elsewhere were slashing them. It was called in to rescue sick companies — becoming a "garbage pail" for unprofitable companies, as one executive put it — which meant the accrual of huge losses. Its cutbacks in steel production and manpower, when the steel crisis hit Europe, were minor compared to the severe cutbacks at British Steel — a delay in restructuring that would prove costly.

What had been an agency for industrial development became, also, an agency of economic and labour adjustment, to the point where the IRI overall went into the red. The company, once held up as an example to the world for its entrepreneurial achievements, began to get harsh criticism from its ideological opponents. For the economy overall the IRI's actions may have been quite beneficial in the short run. In the long run, without compensating capital from the government, the IRI's entrepreneurial and investment capability risked serious damage.

Free enterprise ideologues might take pokes at the IRI and its losses, and shout that it was a clear demonstration of the inherent inefficiency of public enterprise and how public enterprise would always be messed up by politicians, all the more reason to sell it off. The Italians for the most part, however, did not bite. Even *The Economist*, prior to its apostolic privatization crusade of the 1980s, dismissed the harsh judgement of IRI. The company, it found, had been an "unpaid servant of the state."[4] The executives of the company, while remaining loyal to the broader Italian economic objectives, also helped by refusing to let IRI and public enterprise be blamed for what ultimately wasn't their responsibility. The IRI itself, for example, might point to one of its enterprises that was losing money and explain how many fewer employees it should really have. Its executives similarly argued that even a state business has to be run like a business.

Gradually the government and trade unions made the adjustment. The IRI was allowed to begin rationalizing its operations and, a year ahead of schedule, moved back to profitability, recovering something of its 1960s persona. It became as celebrated for its recovery as it had been for its original economic pioneering, with only the large losses from its steel subsidiary still a major problem. It sold several companies in the rationalization — Alfa Romeo went to Fiat — and floated minority shares in others. The divestitures were pragmatic: the hiving off of companies which didn't fit into the group's basic long-term objectives. With the minority share issues, the IRI took care to retain control.

Both these kinds of privatization — divestiture and minority issues — were much talked about. Powerful forces pushed for privatization. The doctrine also had fashionability about it in certain circles. The head of the IRI saw giving private shareholders a voice as a safeguard against those companies' falling back "into the old, bad habits," as he put it; minority private ownership has in fact been quite common with IRI companies. The new share issues also brought in money and helped the IRI's balance sheet. But there was no sanctimonious scapegoating of the company for the economic problems of the 1970s — no scapegoating, that is, that had sufficient political power. Italy's public enterprises were as proud as ever, and were aggressively implementing the lessons they had learned from tough times and adapting to new technological and economic circumstances.

First, the Italians knew from the great development era of the 1950s and 1960s how capable an entrepreneurial vehicle public enterprise was. The mid-1960s were the country's *miracolo economico*. Italy, with the IRI and ENI in the middle of things, had grown faster than every other European country, including West Germany. The Italians saw, too, that public enterprise's participation in banking, manufacturing, engineering and other areas — by inheritance and diversification — was fruitful and natural. In giving IRI the rundown shipbuilding industry and the mandate for industrial development of the south, they also took it for granted that public enterprise had a special capability. They were right in thinking as much. Public enterprise was not pushed into looking at possibilities narrowly on the basis of a speedy and maximum return on capital. It could take a long-term view. Enterprise was more than just doing something as efficiently as somebody else. Because a publicly owned company had that extra margin of freedom, moreover, it could also be more sensitive to legitimate trade union concerns. Italians could see also that in cases where other countries had a lead or a stranglehold, public enterprise might simply be necessary.

Because public enterprise had such a broad back, however, it could also be abused. This was the lesson of the 1970s. Magnificent and husky as IRI appeared—the great builder of "cathedrals" in the Mezzogiorno, no less—it could not be asked to do everything by itself.

Austrian public enterprise has also gone through an adjustment, one much more dramatic in fact—a wholesale reorganization of the OIAG, the principal state holding company. The restructuring was impelled in particular by the stagnation of the steel market and by the entry into the market of low-wage countries; steel was one of the OIAG's major industries. The adjustment was belated; Austria had become a prisoner of its own success. The corporate shake-up that followed involved not just an organizational overhaul but also an aggressive response to new technological and economic circumstances —a greater decentralization of operations, more managerial autonomy, a distancing of political involvement (which in the past had served so well in maintaining economic consensus), and a high priority on developing international subsidiaries.

France, though, is the most revealing of the European cases and also, by far, the most ironic. At the very time that Margaret Thatcher in England was thundering imprecations at the pernicious evil of nationalized industry, and extolling the redemptive wonders of private enterprise (though why those wonders hadn't yet lit up the British economy wasn't asked), the Mitterand nationalizations of 1982 in France were rescuing whole sectors of the French industrial economy from a decrepit and ossified private enterprise going downhill fast. It may have been one of the most dramatic ambulance rides in economic history. Then, when the government changed: *le déluge* of sell-offs of the companies under public ownership, more ideologically vindictive and absolutist in its motivation than even the most strident absolutism of the Iron Lady.

Public enterprise in the 1970s was already a major factor in France: in communications, rail, coal, electricity, oil, banking, insurance, aviation, automobiles, trucks and chemicals. France's three largest banks were publicly owned. It was a France noted for its prosperity, every bit as impressive, it seemed, as the German economic miracle, except delayed slightly in time. The public enterprises were at the centre of reconstruction. They accounted, however, for only 15 per cent of industrial production and, in 1978, only 7.3 per cent of the total labour force (virtually identical to the West German figure of 7.2 per cent). There was plenty of room for French private enterprise to show its stuff: it had 85 per cent of industrial production and 72 per cent of the total labour force (all sectors) to itself.

One of the things the privately owned steel industry showed was how poorly managed it was. It went bankrupt and was effectively nationalized. This was embarrassing for the Giscard d'Estaing government which took over the industry. The Giscard government was pledged to private enterprise, or at least to the idea of private enterprise, and had just introduced an industrial policy to let lame ducks perish. Given the performance of French private enterprise in the steel industry, though, and also the steel overcapacity and competition in Europe, perhaps Giscard feared that France would end up with no steel industry if it were left to private ownership.

By the end of the decade, a decade in which the new theorists of the Conservative party in Britain were ready to blame the national-ized industries for everything from warts to hailstorms, private investment in France was flagging badly as it was everywhere in Europe. As *The Economist* reported bluntly, "without the nationalised sector, investment in French industry would be at a standstill."[5] This was embarrassing for the Giscard government, too, because it had staked its faith on investment-led growth.

By 1981, several major French industrial groups were in disarray, particularly in new technology areas: falling behind other countries to the point where they risked not being able to catch up. An important part of modern French industrial production and technological advance – the industrial future – risked slowly going down with them. Industrial investment in the private sector had been declining for almost a decade. One executive quietly expressed what a lot of people were thinking: under private ownership these key groups would inevitably be sold off in pieces to foreign-owned companies. *The Economist* was later to call them, with one or two exceptions, "a collection of debt-ridden, wheezing remnants."[6] The Mitterand government acted quickly, nationalizing the six industrial groups covering, among them, aluminum, chemicals, electronics, public equipment, armaments, glass, dredging, construction, telephone equipment, electro-nuclear equipment and computers.

The Mitterand government also nationalized most of the remaining privately owned banks (their record wasn't altogether brilliant either; the Credit Commercial de France, for example, had run up a large total of bad debts and needed a rescue operation). As a result, most banking and 30 per cent of industrial production (including energy) was under public ownership, a far greater role for public ownership than had ever existed in Britain.

Later, Creusot-Loire, the privately owned engineering group, bit the dust, after long agony. No private-sector buyer emerged to buy up the more attractive parts of the company, so the government took it under wing, saving what operations made sense. Creusot-Loire was France's second biggest private company, after Peugeot.

In 1981, four of the six industrial groups that were subsequently nationalized lost money. In 1982, the first year of public ownership and before turnaround measures could have an impact, these losses grew substantially and a fifth group in the collection began to run considerable losses. Upon nationalization, there wasn't a single case of shareholders contesting their compensation; they were glad to get out before the private-ownership roof fell in. "Nationalization without tears," it was called. One official commented sardonically that, in the case of one of the acquisitions, the government could have picked up the company for a symbolic franc if it had just waited a little bit for the firm to sink to the bottom. Another, still more caustic, observer called the takeovers "nationalizing the mistakes of their predecessors."

Under public ownership, badly needed investment capital was pumped into the enterprises. In their private-enterprise incarnation, five of the six groups had distributed too much of their profits in dividends while the rot set in from under-capitalization, virtually forfeiting the future. An official estimated that, in the previous five years, four times as much was taken out in dividends as was injected in new capital. The long term of entrepreneurship and technological development was being sacrificed to the short term. Particularly in the electronics industry, a determination and stick-to-itiveness was required, but had apparently become foreign to the former private ownership and its investors.

Public ownership also brought a long-overdue shaking up of management. Bull (computers), Pechiney (aluminum) and Thomson (electronics) all reduced headquarters staff. Thomson's staff numbers were slashed from 2,000 people in 30 offices around Paris to just 300 people in one building, as part of a plan to cut head office costs by over 60 per cent in two years. The corporate culture of the company, under private ownership, had become inflated and bureaucratic. Top management at Thomson was almost completely replaced. In the past, there and elsewhere in the private sector, chairmen and chief executives were generally chosen by their predecessors as is the private corporate habit, making it difficult to improve the quality of top management. Even the aggressively anti-Mitterand *L'Express* allowed approvingly, through clenched teeth, that the nationalizations of 1982 were like "coups de pieds dans cette inextricable fourmilière" — literally translated, "kicks in this inextricable ants' nest."[7] The Conseil National du Patronat Française, the French equivalent of the Canadian Chamber of Commerce and the Business Council on National Issues combined, and a fierce opponent of nationalization, was prepared to admit that the public-enterprise sector was well-managed by true managers.[8] Part of the old "ants' nest" was the cozy relationship between the large private corporations and the conservative government (and its tax incentives, grants, defence procurement and other public purchases) — a relationship of a special French statist variety but, generically speaking, not exactly unknown in other countries.

The Mitterand government, with the nationalizations, also undertook some important restructuring so that the operations of each respective group had some unity of purpose and so there was no duplication defeating economies of scale. Operations which didn't link up were hived off to other public corporations with a better fit even if, on occasion, the move temporarily lowered the latter's profitability taken alone. The newly nationalized groups in effect were prevented from straying all over the corporate map as several of them had been doing, building up their corporate empires by wandering instead of by enterprise, and losing a grip on their original businesses. Europe's ITT telephone-equipment subsidiary was taken over and merged with the appropriate nationalized group (Compagnie Générale d'Electricité), making the latter the second largest in telephone equipment and the first largest in cable manufacturing in the world. The general objective of these changes: to restructure and modernize.

Performance began to improve. Losses were turned around. The recovery in a couple of cases was spectacular, in others not quite so quick but positive. Three of the five loss-makers when nationalized in 1982 were making healthy profits by 1984, a fourth had virtually eliminated its deficit and the fifth was on the way up. Chief executives of the public enterprises were told that their jobs were on the line if they didn't eliminate losses. Excess staff was cut. New equipment was installed. Production was increased. The *Wall Street Journal* carried an admiring story about "Socialism Inc.," noting that the government was letting firms do what was needed to be efficient.[9] *L'Express*, still fuming about the nationalizations, described them with a mixture of malice and envy as being "seized by capitalism," and observed also that the executive cadres had "recovered their appetite for competing."[10]

The magazine cited every extenuating circumstance it could. You may not know Adam Smith's Second Law: If public enterprise has difficulty, it's because of its public ownership, whereas if public enterprise succeeds, it's because of extenuating circumstances. Notwithstanding the infallibility of this law, the magazine despite itself allowed that the nationalizations had accomplished something notable.

When the new government embarked on denationalization in 1986, the enterprises were worth three times what the Mitterand government had paid for them in 1982.

A mocker of privatization mythology could not have done better in a laboratory. The whole drama was kaleidoscoped in four years. Public enterprise succeeded where mythological private enterprise had failed. It succeeded, also, in all those different ways by which mythological private enterprise was supposed to do the trick. Private enterprise, in turn, had failed while suffering the very symptoms — from weak blood to hardening of the arteries, and contagion picked up from intimacy with government — which the mythology imputed to public enterprise.

As a postscript to these events: Renault, the entrepreneurial star and model of the post-war period, but which had incurred giant losses in 1984 and 1985, went through a severe restructuring and was on the road to recovery. So was Usinor-Sacilor, the steel industry which had gone bankrupt under private ownership.

Margaret Thatcher in Britain, although selling off publicly owned money-makers, was still able to get away with rhetoric about private-enterprise efficiency and vigour and public-enterprise perniciousness, and also with rhetoric about how privatization was

necessary to save the nation. In France, with the 1981 nationalizations, this was impossible. The nationalizations and their prior
circumstances had demonstrated the opposite.

Did this stop, or even inhibit, the French advocates of privatization? Of course not. They simply argued that, while the nationalizations had had a virtuous effect, and might even have been necessary
to introduce the French to real "capitalism" — namely, the hard world
of competition and profits — the companies had better be privatized
right away before their public ownership spoiled everything.
L'Express virtually cackled with delight that these crucial public
enterprise successes could be privatized. It chortled that this was the
"trap the socialists fell into" — that by "getting the balance sheet back
in order, at least for the five large industrial groups, they opened the
way to their denationalization. For it is infinitely easier to privatize
companies in good health than companies losing money."[11] (L'Express
was owned at the time by fiercely right-wing corporate buccaneer
Jimmy Goldsmith who, on purchasing the magazine, made it over in
the image of his own doctrine.)

Other than the fact that nobody said Frenchmen have to be nice
to each other, why this manic crowing over the possibility of privatization? Usually when one takes somebody's success away from them,
one does so more in sorrow than in pleasure, or at least one pretends to
do it in sorrow and reluctance. What privatization does in this case for
L'Express and other defenders of private-enterprise doctrine, however,
is to allow them to suppress the example of public enterprise success
and to keep their doctrine intact regardless of events.

5.
Shareholders' Democracy:
The Counterfeit and
the Real Article

When Margaret Thatcher and her entourage began expostulating euphorically about "popular capitalism" and a "shareholding democracy," privatization advocates must have thought they had died and gone to heaven. The notion of a "shareholding democracy" was a revolutionary idea, it was reported, which Thatcher had virtually conceived herself – a radical breakthrough of historic moment. Power to the people was the message.

The slogan "popular capitalism" had actually been coined by the president of the New York Stock Exchange in the 1950s, and had long been forgotten. Institutional investors had taken over in any case. Even as slogan, it was out of date by the time the Conservatives in Britain got around to it.

It did not take long to demonstrate that instead of a shareholders' democracy – with the intonations in the phrase of puritan, town-hall rationality and serious purpose – what was being created was a casino, fed by a substantial give-away of asset-value belonging to the public. An overly large number of the democratic masses – that is, the alert and well-off minority which took a piece of the action – were buying their allotment at the discounted price and then cashing in for a killing as soon as trading pushed the price up. The British called it "stagging."

THE PRIVATIZATION PUTSCH

The number of shareholders for Cable & Wireless (first tranche) sank from 150,000 to 26,000 within a year, or 83 per cent. For British Aerospace, the total number sank in a year from 158,000 to 27,000, also by 83 per cent; the number of small shareholders (with fewer than 100 shares) sank by 93 per cent, from 44,000 to 3,300. For Amersham International, the number of shareholders fell from 62,000 to 10,000 *within a month*! Similarly, the number of shareholders in Associated British Ports fell by 66 per cent within a year, in British Airways 62 per cent, and in Jaguar 57 per cent. Jonathan Swift could not have done better in satirizing the privatization pretensions. "Millions of punters have learned how to stag a rigged market," commented one economist, as if writing about the track.[1]

When British Telecom was put out for sale, the government attempted to stem this undermining of "shareholders' democracy" with special provisions. To encourage the retention of personal holdings, it issued vouchers that shareholders could use in part-payment of their telephone bills and also promised bonus share issues in the longer term. Who said there isn't a free lunch? Even so, because shares were oversubscribed and underpriced, and hence shot up immediately when trading began — which was becoming typical of the privatizations — one third of the shares changed hands *on the first day of trading.*[2] The "secondary market maker" turned over more than six million shares on that first day.[3] Despite the incentives to hang on, over 450,000 people, or one-fifth the number of shareholders, sold out within six months and within two years their numbers were down a third.[4] They continued to decline.

If there wasn't heavy demand for a stock, as happened with the privatization of some oil and gas fields at the time of declining energy markets, wider share ownership did not occur at all. Enterprise Oil (former British Gas oil properties) is an example. The British-based multinational Rio Tinto Zinc immediately subscribed 49 per cent. The government then tried to limit RTZ's share to 10 per cent. Shortly after, however, the company ended up with 30 per cent anyway. "Going through the City because it was discouraged from making a direct bid, RTZ quietly made a fool of government," reported *The Economist.*[5] But trying to limit the grab by a multinational and to ensure wide share ownership was interference with the market in the first place. Fanciful doctrine will make fools of us all.

50

The idea of employee share ownership did not fare better, either. Despite a variety of concessions, including a gift of shares, free shares for other shares bought (the crudest kind of giveaway) and a discount on additional purchases, the percentage of shares taken up by employees was small. Some of the initial percentages were: Amersham International 3.7, Associated British Ports 4.3, Cable and Wireless 1.4, Jaguar 1.3, Britoil 0.1, Enterprise Oil 0.03, British Aerospace 3.6, and British Telecom (including former employees) 4.6.[6] The only contrary example was the National Freight Corporation, which was sold to a consortium of managers, employees and a bank syndicate and was never put on the market.

The shares in British Telecom were more than four-times over-subscribed as people rushed to take advantage of a sure thing. The premium of the opening day trading price over the offer price was $2.3 billion, a giveaway at the expense of the public. Institutional investors were the beneficiary of almost half that giveaway. The capital gain of foreign investors who were given a piece of the company was over $300 million, quite simply an economic loss to the U.K. A *Guardian* head-line blazoned: "How Maggie sold us £2 billion short."[7] The shares of Associated Ports were over-subscribed 35 times, Amersham Inter-national 22 times, and Jaguar eight times, indicating how much higher their prices could have been. The Public Accounts Committee of the British House of Commons criticized the "windfall gains for the investor at public expense."[8] *The Economist*, a supporter of privat-ization, sneered at the policy of "cheap sales" rigged to make privatiza-tion a success, that is, a success in terms of floating off all the shares.[9] One economist called it "taxation by privatization": tax-payers as a whole paid for the underpricing whereby a group of middle-class people (who succeeded in purchasing shares) got the benefits.

(Imagine if nationalization proceeded on the same basis. The shares of the company being nationalized would be deliberately under-valued by the government. The saving to the treasury would be distributed to households as a "nationalization capital gain." A minority — the shareholders — would lose. Everybody else would win. Nationalizations would take place in an atmosphere of considerable excitement.)

Those who did indulge enjoyed the flutter of it all. "Trading shares is like gambling," burbled a typical new player. "It's exciting,

and once you get started, you're addicted."[10] "It's a bit of excitement . . . the same as doing the football pools," said another.[11] *The
Times* compared a new retail brokerage outlet in a department store to
a betting shop, except the "share shop" atmosphere was benevolent
and relaxed, less threatening.[12] A stock exchange representative in
Manchester reported that the foyer in her building, when dealing
started in the British Gas issue, was "just like a bookie's office."[13]
That the odds were stacked heavily in the punter's favour made it all
the better. But gambling — the appetite for getting something without
effort — is the antithesis of economic application.

The French government of Jacques Chirac also underpriced
shares to float privatization and to make the government and the
privatization program look good. "Clearance sale," "good buy,"
"sweepstakes" and "choice menu" were phrases that came up as the
French sell-off got underway. As a result, the Compagnie Générale
d'Electricité was oversubscribed 6 times, Crédit Commercial de France
11 times, Saint-Gobain 14 times, and so on upwards to Paribas (40
times), Banque Sogénal (46 times) and Banque du Bâtiment et des
Travaux Publics (65 times)!

In October 1987, just before the stock exchange crisis but when
the Bourse in Paris was already beginning to languish, the differential
for some of the companies declined (although not for Saint-Gobain,
which continued to trade at a hefty premium over its privatization
price). Privatization backers used this to argue that the share issues
hadn't been underpriced after all. Given the enormous rates of
oversubscription at the time of issue, however, there was no doubt the
public treasury was shortchanged, and not least in the privatization
doctrine's own terms: issuing shares at the maximum price traffic
would bear.

The French privatizers were both more realistic and more
hypocritical than the British. For some key privatization cases they
created "noyaux durs," literally, hard cores. These were tight groups
of corporate shareholders, represented by major corporate officers,
established to provide stability to the newly privatized companies and,
at least temporarily, to ward off outside corporate raiders. In effect,
this meant handing over control of newly privatized companies like
Paribas and Crédit Commercial de France (both banks) to hand-picked
members of the corporate establishment, and "popular capitalism" be

damned. Furthermore, inasmuch as hostile takeovers would actually be forestalled, the "noyaux durs" would also be impeding a key private-enterprise mechanism, or at least a key mechanism as proclaimed by the privatization doctrine. Hostile takeovers, according to the doctrine, are the way that the shareholders' interests are protected against entrenched corporate bureaucracies. Meanwhile, the small investors, according to one description, were being taken as so many peasants ("des ploucs"). Only two of the newly privatized companies had even a representative of the small shareholders on their boards.

The new French privatization law required that 10 per cent of shares be set aside on the first go-round for applications by employees and retired employees. Even if most employees bought shares – at least 50 per cent did in each case to October 31, 1987 and in some instances participation was as high as 90 per cent – and even if they took up the full 10 per cent of shares issued, their position as small shareholders did not give them any leverage in the company's affairs. Nor was there any assurance, either in Britain or France, that down the line, as shares were sold, employee ownership would be maintained at even its low original levels of shares outstanding.

While all this was happening, nobody asked why shareholders' democracy wasn't already in existence if it were such a fundamental part of private enterprise and a mark of its natural superiority. Nothing constrained it. Many people had savings at different times in British history, for example, and the environment was a private-enterprise one. Even at the height of public ownership in Britain, in 1979, private enterprise was still overwhelmingly dominant. It had been ideologically dominant, too. The London Stock Exchange was there, throughout, to facilitate participation.

What was the point of artificially creating shareholders' democracy by government intervention when private enterprise had failed to generate it as part of its own dynamic? Share ownership in Britain, on its private-enterprise own, had in fact been going progressively downwards. In 1979, only one in 15 of the adult population were shareholders and the numbers were falling. Individual share ownership as a percentage of all shares owned had descended from 70 per cent in the 1950s to just 30 percent 30 years later.

But the idea of shareholders' democracy, private corporate style, was an illusion to begin with. There had already been a revolution, the managerial revolution, whereby management of widely held private corporations assumed control and the small shareholder's ownership became a passive thing. This was known all along. Two American scholars, Adolf Berle and Gardiner Means, in their book *The Modern Corporation and Private Property*, had described the whole phenomenon back in 1932.[14] The ordinary shareholder, they wrote, "is left with a mere symbol of ownership" while the substance is in the hands of management and a friendly board of directors. These groups, in relation to the small shareholder, are effectively "economic autocrats." They also "virtually dictate their own successors" through the proxy committee, becoming thereby a "self-perpetuating body."

Wider share ownership simply extends this economic autocracy. Most corporate annual meetings are routinized and perfunctory. A photograph of the annual meeting of recently privatized French bank Compagnie Financière Suez, held in a large theatre to accommodate all the new shareholders, shows row after row of empty seats — a portent of things to come. All that the ordinary shareholder can do is sell his shares — and, if the company is doing poorly, probably take a capital loss — giving up even the symbol of ownership. Only through hostile takeovers is this pattern broken, and then it's a case of other economic autocrats moving in. Indeed, hostile takeovers, by a larger holding company, a syndicate or a well-heeled raider, eliminate even the pretence of shareholders' democracy in the captured company.

The world of stock markets and share transactions, in which shareholders' democracy is supposed to arise, also produces inequality and growing concentration of ownership. After the broad sale of shares to as many as two million shareholders in the cases of some British and French privatizations, individual shareholders still represented a minority fraction of well-off people. The "financially articulate middle class" was how *The Times* in London described them. Despite the attractive pricing and blitz marketing of the sell-offs, the total number of shareholders of all kinds, including those holding literally just a few shares in one company, was estimated at one-fifth of the adult population of Britain and less than a seventh of the adult population of France, as of mid-1987.

Real shareholders' democracy is something quite different. It touches the substance of entrepreneurial activity: the decision-making power of business enterprise. It also spreads the dividends generated by enterprise as broadly as possible.

There are two ways of doing this. One is to decentralize ownership and control in working terms, physically and geographically, so that ordinary individuals can participate actively in ownership and control. Another is to create broadly based representative governing structures, democratically organized.

The wage earner funds in Sweden are one example of genuine shareholders' democracy. These regionally linked funds, five in all, invest in Swedish enterprises. One-third of their capital comes from an excess profits tax from which smaller companies are exempt. The other two-thirds is generated by a 0.2 per cent increase in the payroll tax. How they are governed, though, is what makes them interesting. A government-appointed, nine-person board manages each of the funds. Five of the nine board members are union-employee representatives. This gives employees and the workforce at large, through their representatives on the funds, an active and meaningful role in investment policy.

Aside from their investment role, the funds must also pay into the national pension system a three per cent annual return (after allowing for inflation) on their capital. This spreads dividend benefits across the population as a whole. In addition, investment policy of the funds can reflect an emphasis on job creation and on avoidance of nonproductive speculation, for example, or matters like regional development, environmental protection and other social concerns. Individual ownership was rejected for two reasons. It would confer special benefits on employees of more profitable firms and it would eliminate any kind of democratic control since small individual shareholders are powerless as policy-makers.

The wage-earner funds are "shareholders'" or "property-owners'" democracy of a real kind. They give to the workforce — the bulk of the population — a greater say in the allocation of profits for investment purposes. They distribute some dividends ultimately to the whole population (through the national pension system). Not least, they work against concentration of ownership.

Or take workers' and producers' co-operatives and co-operatives in general: another genuine form of "shareholders'" democracy. In a typical producers' co-operative in Canada — dairy farmers, grain growers or apple growers, for example — each member-shareholder runs his or her own operation, with the co-operative looking after processing, distribution and marketing. In a workers' co-operative, the employees of a manufacturing or processing plant, or of a service business, are themselves the shareholders. The most famous example is Mondragon, Spain, in the Basque country, which is the centre of a multi-function, technologically advanced manufacturing complex with 19,000 people in 100 workers' co-operatives. As well as the industrial concerns, these include agricultural and service co-operatives, and a retail chain. There are also, at Mondragon, housing co-operatives, secondary educational co-operatives, other co-operatives in research and development, training and social security, and a bank with an "entrepreneurial" investment division which plays a major role in the area's economic development.

Consumer co-operatives are another variation of genuine "shareholders' democracy." Dividends can be paid on the basis of shares or according to how much business a member gives to the co-operative. However, like parliamentary democracy, the fundamental principle is one person, one vote, no matter how many shares a person might want to buy or how much the person patronizes the co-operative. Credit unions are the best-known example in Canada.

Consumer co-operatives in Canada include everything from supermarkets, bulk fuel and agricultural supplies — with oil refining and wholesale businesses supporting them — to cable television licensees, housing and insurance. Because individual co-operatives can gather in federations, there is no theoretical limit to what they can manage. The Mouvement Desjardins, the federation of credit unions in Quebec has financial assets of $22 billion, and as well as its credit unions, operates insurance companies, a trust company, a venture capital firm, an industrial finance subsidiary, an international development society and other divisions. In the Netherlands, the bulk of radio and television broadcasting is done by membership associations — listeners' and viewers' co-operatives. Most Finnish telephone systems, including the Helsinki one, are co-operatives, owned and controlled by the telephone subscribers themselves.

SHAREHOLDERS' DEMOCRACY

In Sweden, the co-operative federation is one of the dominant companies in the retail sector, accounting for 16 per cent of all retail sales. The co-operatives hold a 52 per cent market share for department and variety stores, 55 per cent for discount supermarkets, 30 per cent for supermarkets and 35 per cent for convenience stores. The federation runs its own restaurants, catering service, travel agencies, hotels and summer cottage rental service. The federation also includes a major industrial group, making food and household products, bathroom and kitchen fixtures, car tires, packaging machines and packaging materials, fibres and clothing, paper products, fork lift trucks, cranes, and material handling systems, satellite television dishes and other products. About 90 per cent of its production goes to customers outside the co-operative movement; half of it is exported. Other co-operative branches are involved in insurance, oil, burials and housing. The oil consumers co-operative has its own refinery, tanker fleet and service stations, as well as motels, car-rental system, do-it-yourself centres and attached food stores. It sells a fifth of the country's gasoline and has the largest single share of the oil market overall (including home heating).

Public ownership is also a form of genuine shareholders' democracy — a vehicle of democratization parallel to wage-earner funds and co-operatives and, historically in Canada, leading the way. The governing of Crown corporations is democratic in the only way that widely held enterprises can be: representatives of the shareholders as a whole (the public) ultimately decide. This democratic power, in turn, rests on the most decentralized ownership of them all: the electorate of the country, the province or the municipality, as the case may be. Government parties lose lustre and lose votes, on occasion lose office, or a minister will be fired, if their stewardship of the public's companies is found at fault. Opposition parties provide an organized critical presence, acting as another voice and safeguard of the shareholders.

Unlike a widely held private company, with its self-perpetuating executive and directors, the shareholders of a public enterprise, through their representatives, can actually fire an executive who is not performing well, is responsible for a major bungle, or is involved in scandal. The French nationalizations in 1981, for example, allowed for the breaking up of self-serving corporate clubbiness and for the appointment of new people to leading executive positions. The personnel and character of boards of directors can be changed, reflecting different times and new priorities. The self-indulgent bonuses, perks and golden parachutes in parts of the private corporate world, with which management coddles itself — becoming evermore ostentatious, particularly in the U.S. — are checked by the democratic structure of public enterprise. So is political self-indulgence — the underwriting of lobbies and political parties by private corporations to keep in place public goodies (direct and indirect subsidies) and indulgent public legislation (on labour and environmental matters, for example).

Public enterprise deals with the question of how to combine shareholders' control with managerial autonomy (where the question doesn't arise, as in private corporations, any purported "shareholders' democracy" is a phoney one). Finding the right balance, through precedents and experience, is one of public enterprise's most important achievements. The balance varies according to the nature of the enterprise (whether it's in a competitive market or a monopoly), how well it's doing (is it being subsidized?), and public policy for the company. The balance may change for each company, according to circumstances.

There is also a variety of ways of monitoring the performance of a public enterprise and of keeping management accountable: through the responsible government department; through a Crown holding company; through a minister or deputy minister on the board; or with a mix of these devices (the model in Canada for a Crown holding company is the Crown Investments Corporation of Saskatchewan/ Crown Management Board). Standing committees of parliaments, where executives are questioned by the shareholders' representatives, is another monitoring device — limited but useful nevertheless. Every once in a while, somebody, in response to a turn of events, will cry out that there is not enough public control, or that there is too much intervention and not enough managerial autonomy. This is the process at work. Both enterprise and democracy are too dynamic and various to lend themselves to a static formula.

The shareholders' democracy of public enterprise also works through the expectations the public has of its enterprises simply because it does own them. Public enterprises are expected to be better corporate citizens and to avoid sharp practices. When they don't shape up, elements of the public, including legislators, get after them. One of the most striking examples of such ownership-linked expectations is the CBC. Endless, often conflicting and, in aggregate, unreasonable demands are made of the CBC as to the kinds of programming it should be doing. Public hearings involving the CBC generate considerable, sometimes passionate submissions. On the other hand, the marginal contribution of private television is ignored, despite its outsized profits from distributing American programming and despite, also, being publicly licensed and with a supposed public mandate. But "the CBC belongs to us," people say.

Privatization proponents try to make light of the democratic ownership of public enterprise. At the same time, they betray an awareness of how important it is by borrowing its language, although not its substance, in an attempt to displace it. French privatizers talked about redefining "public ownership" to mean the ownership of shares by the "public." Canadian privatizers talk about how privatization will "transfer shares to the public." They simultaneously complain about what an unfortunate word "privatization" is. "Private" becomes "public" in their mental effort to re-orient perception.

One of the curious events of the privatization campaign in Britain was the happenstance sale of the National Freight Corporation (NFC) to a management-employee consortium. The only such sale of its kind, it allowed privatization advocates to talk about employee ownership with glowing radiance, as if it were one of the major motifs of privatization. What happened was quite a bit different. The Conservative party manifesto stated that the shares would be offered "to the general public." The Thatcher government set about preparing the company for a share flotation. However, the deepening recession in 1980, aggravated by government monetarist policy, undermined NFC's profitability. This allowed a group of interested management people to move into the vacuum and organize a consortium.

Another factor was involved. Privatization threatened a break-up of the company because the company's biggest asset was its properties — obsolete transport and distribution terminals. Somebody with an eye for realizable assets would simply spin off the pieces. The organization of the consortium by management was in good part a response to that privatization possibility. "A desperate defensive ploy" was how business magazine *Management Today* described the creation of the consortium.[15] This "novel version of syndicalism is the outcome of an opportunist . . . initiative following on from an application of Tory ideology," the magazine elaborated. "It was a wry train of events."

Only three-fifths of NFC employees own shares, almost all in small holdings worth less than £ 10,000. Four members of management, on the other hand, have holdings worth over £ 1 million. It's almost as far from a one-person one-vote workers' co-operative as any other company. Nevertheless, a majority of employees are shareholders and their involvement has increased. The lesson to draw from that, of course, is what a good idea workers' ownership and workers' control is. Alas, workers' ownership — a suspiciously socialist idea, a veritable "anarcho-syndicalist" idea — is not a favourite of privatizers, particularly when it comes to companies already in the private sector. Some lessons are less equal than others.

The most interesting British case, however, is the Trustee Savings Bank (TSB), where privatization expressly excluded a shareholders' democracy.

TSBs, begun in 1810, had their roots in nineteenth century paternalism. They were started "as a way of keeping the poor out of the ale house and off the rates by encouraging them to help themselves through thrift and saving," as the *New Statesman* put it.[16] Most of the depositors were working class. Often the TSB was the only bank in their area; the mainstream banks weren't interested in them. They became one of the most popular forms of savings for working-class people and by the 1980s had six million customers. Both by assets and size of the branch network, they were one of Britain's biggest banks.

TSBs had also become a thorn in the side of the banking establishment. Because of their unique "customer-first" philosophy, they had strong depositor loyalty in working-class areas where the traditional banks now wanted to expand. TSBs also did not require large profits, so they were considered unfair competition. The TSBs' decision in the post-war years to issue cheques, and a subsequent decision to lend money, were resisted by both the Treasury and the main clearing banks. Because the TSBs were exercising their muscle, pressure grew to define their status. They had begun under government sponsorship and simply grown. A controversy now arose as to who actually owned the TSBs and their assets. Equally crucial was the question of how the TSBs' ownership would be organized.

Many people long-involved in the TSBs argued they should become a "People's Mutual Bank," operating under laws of association like co-operatives. We would call them credit unions. A commission which looked into the matter in the early 1970s had come out in favour of this concept of depositor ownership. Also, the various legislative acts covering the TSBs instructed them to return to depositors everything generated by their deposits after expenses. The backers of the credit union concept said that this, as well as common sense, demonstrated that the depositors did indeed already own the bank's assets and hence the bank itself.

The government said otherwise. It could not claim ownership itself: that would be tantamount to appropriating somebody else's assets. So it said nobody owned the TSB. The court cases which arose over this issue were academic. The government was ideologically unsympathetic to the idea of depositor ownership. It wanted to privatize the TSB, which it did by launching a share issue. Although depositors received preference in the allocation of shares, not all would take them up, and it would be only a matter of time until the share ownership pattern changed. The management group had control from the beginning in any case. The chance of any democratic control, based on the credit-union concept of one shareholder, one vote, and no proxies to be captured by management, was simply killed off.

One of the problems of the credit union idea for the TSB was that there would be no shares to be traded by stock brokers. Stock brokers (and their investment dealer and merchant bank variations) are one of the most ardent proponents of privatization and play confidant to the government's privatization officials. The theoretical elaboration of the privatization doctrine, with "stock market discipline" as its mantra, is worked out in such a way that the stock market and the brokers' trade are considered *de rigueur*, to keep enterprises up to the mark. Without them, it is suggested, a widely owned business would be a bastard child with poor genes, bound to come to no good in the end. Contemplating the imminent privatization of the TSB, the *New Statesman* remarked acidly that "the City of London will have completed one of the most

6.
Propaganda Inc.
(in Britain, Propaganda PLC;
in France, Propagande SA)

In one of his regular pieces, in the summer of 1986, *London Sunday Times* columnist Philip Norman raged against what he called "Telecom Britain," the brave new world of privatization where all public services were turned over to "state-licensed spivs." The piece was touched off by a small report that plans were on course for privatizing the London Underground ("Oh God, not the London Underground *too*!"). It pointed as an example to the pushing of British Telecom shares in 1984 and the follow-up propaganda — the campaign that set the pattern for major privatizations yet to come.

> Isn't it bad enough to have to live in Telecom Britain? Haven't we learned our lesson from that realm of darkening technical chaos, maniac advertising, and avarice so pettifogging as to have sub-franchised even the Speaking Clock?

> ... Taking British Telecom as our guide, the stages of privatisation can be easily imagined.

> A "watchdog" body will be set up, sworn to maintain the spirit and values of the London Underground. Then the fares will triple. Men wearing Next blousons will be brought in to give the design a "facelift." Six billion pounds will be committed to advertisements telling us there are underground trains, via the medium of talking animals.

> The logo, the map and the clear English will go. Signs will be put up everywhere saying "Thank you," that well-known American preamble to getting kicked in the teeth.
>
> Later on, some whizzkid may get the idea of putting individual lines up for private sponsorship. We shall change (if we can find them) from the John Player Northern to the Durex Piccadilly. Escalators and lifts will be franchised to private operators. Station announcements will include advertising. "The next train is brought to you by NatWest. . . ." And *won't* it be good for all of us.[1]

An estimated $67 million was spent flogging British Telecom (BT) for its privatization in 1984 and 1985. Of that, approximately $43 million was spent by British Telecom itself on its pre-flotation advertising campaign, softening up the public for the share-distribution campaign to follow. The country was blanketed with newspaper, television, billboard and radio advertising. "Massive hard-sell" and "deluge" were some of the ways the propaganda was described.

Any connection between truth and fantasy in this campaign was purely coincidental. Technologically, British Telecom was badly out-dated and, although it was striving to catch up, would require heavy investment in the future. The propaganda campaign, on the other hand, convinced people that it was about the hottest high-technology property on the market. The *New Statesman* remarked caustically that it was "the equivalent of the British public being persuaded that our weather is, after all, not too bad and that perhaps we should stop complaining about it."[2] The public rehabilitation of BT was "one of the more breathtaking achievements of this government." *Business Week*, in the U.S., remarked that the BT propaganda blitz would have been stopped by regulators in the U.S. as "blatant hype."[3] "The Hard Sell That's Turning British Telecom Into a Hot Stock," the headline blazoned. "The odds are," the article exulted, "that the government's effort to transform a once-uninspiring utility into a high-tech Cinderella will have paid off beyond its wildest dreams." It almost seemed as if *Business Week*, too, was accepting the image for reality, not least because, in terms of the business of the stock market, image is interchangeable with reality.

PROPAGANDA INC.

In 1985, according to the U.S. trade magazine *Advertising Age,* BT was the second largest advertiser in the country, spending over $82 million. By 1987, public resentment at the quality of privatized BT's service was surging. The hoax within the hype was leaking out of the package. An advertising campaign asked fetchingly, "Is British Telecom in danger of becoming popular?" "It is not," tersely commented the *Economist* which had so dogmatically insisted on privatizing BT just a few years earlier.[4]

The BT privatization propaganda was only a prelude to the British Gas campaign – something like a military exercise on a limited scale to test new hardware. In the interval between the BT and British Gas campaigns, the Trustee Savings Bank, properly belonging to its depositors, had been "privatized" with the aid of an enthusiastic advertising blitz. As *The Times* put it, the Trustee Savings Bank razzmatazz would be a hard act for British Gas to follow.[5] The skills of propaganda, though, combined with the lottery atmosphere ("the biggest lottery in the world," one reporter described it), were fully up to it.

Over $80 million was spent on marketing shares in British Gas, almost $60 million of which went to the press, poster and television campaign. Like the BT campaign, it was in two phases: the first part designed to create "corporate awareness," the second focussing on the stock issue. A "masterful" campaign, all the advertising bureaucrats excitedly agreed, even if some commentators were enraged (one called it "the direst insult ever offered to the nation's intelligence").[6]

The campaign centred around a fictional character called Sid. "If you see Sid, tell him!" was the slogan. "In a series of sometimes loony TV sketches involving eccentric ladies bicycling through rural villages and retired majors puffing along country footpaths, Sid was chased from Dumfries to Dover, and never found," Southam News reported. Would Sid ever be found? "It will be like the shooting of JR in Dallas," exuded the advertising agency mastermind behind the campaign. "Will he or won't he be found? And I'm not saying." In another ad, Larry Hagman as J.R. Ewing did actually appear, expressing sly disbelief that a *British* company in the *energy* business could make money.

As well as the telescreen campaign, "Tell Sid about it!" was plastered on 20,000 small and 7,000 large posters around the country.

Some 43 million advertising leaflets were also printed. The bombardment extended to radio and even to trains and buses, inviting people to "tell Sid" about the chance to buy a company which he already owned. Sid was immortalized. A senior Canadian financial man involved in the flotation called the campaign "an outstanding success." "Elaborate and minutely executed," was another description. The cost came to almost $85 per shareholder application.

The British Telecom and British Gas campaigns established the game sequence — softening the public up with "corporate awareness" advertising first and the hard-sell connected to the share issue after. The "corporate awareness" advertising was something like corporate "institutional advertising" in Canada — no limit on distortion and omission — with some well-selected and well-placed figures thrown in. The phase one British Airways (BA) campaign, at $10 million, broke with an 80-second spot by Saatchi & Saatchi advertising agency showing famous buildings around the world, like the Sydney opera house, saluting BA. Big Ben chimed like a cash register as a voice-over explained the airline brought in gross revenue of $625,000 every hour. Just in case viewers were not cognizant of how related this was to British patriotism, the dome of Albert Hall lifted off to the strains of "Land of Hope and Glory."

Phase one of the campaign for the sell-off of the publicly owned share of British Petroleum began with an equally huge "warm-up" promotion costing over $13 million. A spate of BP television commercials showed people in hardhats trudging through deserts and icy wastes as they covered the globe.

The Labour Party didn't know what hit them. They could criticize the price at which BT shares were being offered or protest the act of privatization itself, but they were no match for $67 million of propaganda. Each advertising campaign also acted as propaganda for the decision to privatize the next company down the road. Because the propaganda was tied, first, to corporate advertising and, secondly, to a share issue, the possibility of awarding a matching propaganda budget to opponents of privatization, from the same public coffers, never came up. Any carryover of this one-way, publicly financed propaganda to the electoral arena — and some carryover was inevitable — hurt the Labour Party and opponents of privatization in turn.

PROPAGANDA INC.

The French privatizers learned the propaganda lesson from the British with a vengeance:

> It is a dark and stormy night. A powerful stallion shrugs off heavy steel chains and bounds over a rocky hillside. Music rises. The stallion breaks into an open field, rears and gallops away. The music peaks, and an announcer intones: "When you give the economy air, everybody breathes easier."[7]

That particular commercial ran 130 times on prime-time French television. The horse was supposed to be France, "freed of the inherited chains of centuries of state control," according to the chief adviser to the finance minister, the ad's sponsor. It was all part of creating a capitalist, share-owning society, according to sources. The irony of using state propaganda to try breaking the alleged chains of state control went by the finance minister altogether. Nor would he characterize this state propaganda as brainwashing, although 130 times is a good wash. Yet nobody had any doubt what the propaganda was trying to do. "Changing How People Think," was how a sub-heading in the *Wall Street Journal* put it, approvingly.[8]

In another commercial, painter Eugène Delacroix, whose portrait is on the 100-franc note, talked to Montesquieu on the 200-franc note. The painter tells the philosopher that he is thinking of investing his tax-cut savings in shares of soon-to-be privatized state companies. To such a bright gimmick have Delacroix and Montesquieu been reduced by the new propagandists. You can see why the *Sunday Times* columnist had become so jaundiced.

The French privatizers copied the British example studiously, almost chortling at having learned how it was done. Saint-Gobain, the first major French company to be privatized by the Chirac government, beginning in 1986, budgeted a variously estimated $10-$14 million for its corporate-awareness propaganda. "Our first task has to be selling the image," explained the vice-president of advertising agency Publicis.[9] The ads stressed that Saint-Gobain was "solid" and stands for "innovation." That it was made "solid" by nationalization when it was deteriorating under private ownership presumably wasn't mentioned. French advertising specialists sometimes talk about using "des thèmes soft" to insinuate their way into people's consciousness. However, letting both sides to the debate have their say was softer than they and their clients were prepared to get. Paribas, a merchant bank, budgeted $10 million for its campaign. Assurances Générales de France budgeted $20 million. Crédit Lyonnais, on the privatization list but not yet put out for sale, spent $4.3 million just to boast of its merits in newspaper and magazine ads.

Add to that the government's own spending on the actual privatization, as in the $8 million campaign for pushing Saint-Gobain shares. In one feature television commercial, a doctor, a factory worker and a teenage jogger gushed: "Saint-Gobain – I'm buying." In another, a baker brandishing a baguette declared: "Saint-Gobain is like my good bread." Marketing Saint-Gobain, as *Fortune* magazine observed with admiration, was just like selling soap or toothpaste in the U.S.[10]

"The First Winners of Privatization," *Le Nouvel Observateur* reported in a special feature, were none other than the advertising agencies.[11] If Jacques Chirac followed through on all his privatization plans, they would split among them a nice little "gold mine" ("le pactole") of two billion francs ($400 million) in advertising expenditures. "One can understand their zeal," the magazine remarked jokingly. That wasn't all. The agencies anticipated a continuing market in new product and corporate advertising set off by the privatization campaign. "We are building an enduring communications edifice of which the privatization campaign is just the first piece," explained a French advertising executive involved in one of the campaigns. Nor was that all. With more French people holding shares, the investment dealers and brokers saw an opportunity of getting possible new brokerage business, and they would advertise, too. Almost from the moment privatization began, Chase Manhattan in France began running ads in newspapers inviting capitalists to open investment portfolios.

The impact of what this new generation of propaganda could do – how the propaganda, combined with the circus-like, giveaway atmosphere, could even change how people thought – was not lost on observers, especially those who, like the Chirac government, were looking for something like it. French proponents of privatization mocked the opposition for its "Medusa silence" as the privatization campaign, panzer-like in its organization and armament, progressed.

In fact, the opposition continued to criticize the program, but with the mass media bombardment coming from one side and no interceptor planes of their own, all they could do was run for cover. The military analogies came naturally. In describing the propaganda teams at work, reporters talked about their "being on a war footing," "mobilization," and their taking the privatization market "by assault." An advertising agency executive, outlining his strategy, was a veritable field marshall in Guccis:

> A series of events accompanied by the first phase of the campaign, culminating in a day of open-house on a dozen factories. All the means of persuasion are put to work. It's "global communication." It's necessary to mobilize each link in the whole chain [of the process]. And, of course, the public. The second phase of the campaign will attack the public full frontal to the body.[12]

And an exclamation about the big rush he was in: "We've got just three months to transform the attitudes of [the citizenry of the country]!"

The pro-privatization *L'Express*, meanwhile, outdid even its British counterparts in providing fawning and adulatory coverage of the process and its participants. In a piece on the c.e.o. of Saint-Gobain, it even got down to the whisky he had before lunch and the lunch itself (*saumon mariné, sauté de veau-purée, eau minérale et tarte aux pommes*).[13]

Part of the challenge of these propaganda campaigns was to generate enough excitement and expectation so that people who weren't in the habit of buying stocks, or who had never bought them, would decide to indulge. But there was a deeper psychological obstacle to overcome. Many people in Britain and France, especially working-class people, regarded playing the market with moral distaste, as something dirty. Taking a flutter on the horses or playing the football pool was all right. Those were actual games. Making money on the stock market, on the other hand, was sponging on the economy – on the real work of others. It was parasitical. These people had been acculturated by industrial society to respect real work in the first place – to show up on time, to keep their noses to the grindstone, to earn their pay and not to freeload and featherbed. Men in particular dismissed the market as "legalized con" and a way of "them getting money out of us."

The slogan of a shareholding democracy helped to give this pocketing of a windfall the seal of social and moral approval. It attributed higher meaning to the act. Ordinary greed also helped push compunctions into the background. One of the tasks of the massive advertising campaigns was to cover over any remaining ideas of dirtiness left in people's minds.

One wonders what the reaction would have been had the propaganda been delivered by another hand. Imagine that a British Labour government had spent $250 million on wave after wave of inventive commercials and other advertising extolling the energy and innovation of nationalizations. Or imagine that a French socialist government had launched a publicly financed propaganda campaign, with due artistic cleverness, showing public entrepreneurship breaking free from the incestuousness and decrepitude of French private enterprise and from its self-indulgent friends at the Bourse; or if the government, with a pervasive propaganda campaign planned in the utmost detail and sparing no expense, set out, for whatever reason, to "transform the attitudes of the citizenry."

There would have been a violent outcry from private-enterprise quarters denouncing the brainwashing, invoking *1984* and other references to totalitarian methods. Such propaganda, though, is the nature of the advertising campaigns which are now *de rigueur* in privatization cases aimed at wider share ownership, and which gild the privatization lily in a general way. Call it "privatization modern-style," although its manipulative and anti-democratic mentality is only too familiar.

7.
The New Bureaucracy

The investment dealers, merchant bankers and stock brokers swarm around privatization as if it were a honey pot. They ardently advocate privatization. In Britain and France where, previously, stock exchange trading involved relatively few people compared to the champions of paper enterprise (the Americans), privatization helped enormously to expand the investment dealers' and stock brokers' struggling mini-empires. Because of their particular bureaucratic skills, which are the skills needed for privatization, they also counsel governments on how it should be done and participate closely in the privatization process itself. They are also close to the Conservative and RPR parties in Britain and France respectively, and this connection contributed to privatization thinking in these parties and, down the road, to expansion of their territory. Privatization responds to the two parties' natural private-enterprise constituencies, with the merchant bankers in the thick of things getting a piece of the action.

Also in the swarm are their market analysts and in-house economists (for prestige and decoration), plus stock exchange personnel, financial counsellors, investment fund managers and other related orders. Advertising agency executives dart in and out. Hovering nearby are the corporate empire-builders and greenmailers, plus their associated lawyers and accountants. Privatization adds more corporate paper to the private sector, which is always of interest to them. They buzz.

Executives of companies being privatized plunge into these same bureaucratic processes of share issues, stock exchanges, securities regulations, and manipulating the public, and they have their own lawyers, accountants, communications officers, merchant-bank or investment-dealer advisers, and advertising agency arrangements to back them up.

These people are all members of the New Bureaucracy: its stock exchange and private corporate branches. Privatization captures public enterprise for this bureaucracy, adding to its income, wealth, status and comfort, and adding to enterprise a dense, costly bureaucratic layer that wasn't there before.

In Britain alone, prior to 1986, underwriters earned roughly $200 million in fees from privatization. This would be exclusive of the British Gas, Rolls Royce, British Airways and many other issues yet to come. The underwriting fees and commissions for the British Telecom flotation (including bank and legal fees) came to $185 million. The British stock trading companies call the competitions to get this underwriting work from the government "beauty contests." The general bonanza is known, simply, as the "privatization boom." A report in 1986 estimated that privatizations around the world would generate more than $400 million a year in fees for the specialized underwriters that have come to dominate the business. The British Gas sell-off in late 1986 (*The Economist* showed pots of gold at the end of a rainbow) enriched underwriters by $140 million for what one privatization advocate nevertheless admitted was a service "that really doesn't exist."[1] The risks of making British Gas a going concern had already been taken, by the population as a whole under public ownership. Nor did the underwriters risk being left with shares on their hands, since the share offer had been priced so low by the government. In the British Telecom case, sub-underwriters even got a commission on shares they bought for themselves.

But, as the magazine *Euromoney* explained, privatization is even more of a windfall for the banks that "lead-manage" these issues.[2] Their fees for consultation, advice and work in restructuring the publicly owned company to be sold off, to fit the stock market, was estimated in 1986 at $60 to $85 million a year. Advisor fees for the privatization of British Telecom were $25 million for the government and company combined. Britain, however, wasn't the only place where lead-manage work was available or where privatization could be encouraged. Merchant banks even got Turkish jobs, for example. "Charge-out rates of £200 ($350-$400) an hour are not uncommon [in these cases], and since these projects can take a year or two to plan, the fees are substantial if you talk in terms of man-hours spent," said one merchant banker.[3]

France provided others plums. A British firm, along with Crédit Commercial de France, was retained by the French government as advisers on the privatization of Saint-Gobain. In the New Bureaucracy, one firm alone is never retained as an adviser when two, or four, can be hired. Saint-Gobain, in this case, added two advisers of its own to the government's pair. The fee for both the advice and the underwriting was expected to be in the $70-million range. There were mutterings about conflict of interest — the advisers, in this case, were also doing the underwriting — but these were not heeded. Since one corridor of the bureaucracy was not be outdone by another, two French banks and a Swiss bank got retainers from the government for advice on privatizing Paribas, number two on the list. Paribas, a merchant bank itself, hired an outside adviser anyway.

"Come One, Come All, To The Great French Sell-Off," trumpeted *Business Week*.[4] The trumpets in the article weren't for people who might want to buy shares in the companies scheduled for the guillotine of privatization but for investment dealers who would be the functionaries of the process. There would, for a start, be a "windfall" for the foreign banks chosen to advise on that fraction of placements to be sold overseas. This branch of the New Bureaucracy doesn't scrimp, either. Morgan Stanley & Co. in New York had hired the former U.S. ambassador to France to drum up business. "There's room for lots of people," he said, impressed with what there was to be had in the French privatization program.[5] No civil-service-style cafeterias for Morgan Stanley and their British and French counterparts. The New Bureaucracy has its own expense-account rules. The teams of high-level investment bankers did their jockeying for position over elegant Parisian dinners, *Business Week* reported.

William Schreyer, the c.e.o. of Merrill Lynch, and hence a bit of an icon in the trade, was interviewed in his Wall Street office for a special feature by *L'Express*. Merrill Lynch's French office had acted as privatization adviser to Paribas and was in the bidding for the next 15 state-owned companies in line. "His entourage call him Bill," the magazine disclosed to its yuppie readership. "I believe in the virtues of privatization," Bill Schreyer declared.[6]

Conflicts of interest between a merchant bank as adviser and the same merchant bank as a subscriber weren't new. In the British cases, at least up to 1985, the banks who advised the government were, in each case, the initial subscribers. When the trading price jumped from its original flotation level (set with the bank's advice), the same bank then stood to make a nice capital gain on its subscription. The merchant bank advisers "appear so far to be the chief winners from the privatisation policy," one study of the early privatization years observed.[7]

The "privatization boom," with its rich adviser fees and its bonanza flood of commissions, is just the first step in this expansion of bureaucracy. Every time the shares are traded, another commission is collected. When, share issue after share issue in Britain, masses of shareholders, sometimes close to half a million, flipped their shares, brokers who relished their take from the original flotation got even richer.

For the private-sector bureaucracy of the City centred on the London Stock Exchange — and it was already a large bureaucracy — privatization was something to be adored. As if symbolically, Kleinwort Benson, one of the most active in the privatization process, spent what bankers described as "a small fortune" setting up a massive 20,000-square-foot stock market dealing room. Kleinwort Benson would have the British Gas privatization issue to see it through the "big bang" (deregulation) bloodletting.

If the British branch of the New Bureaucracy was excited about privatization, the French branch, much smaller to begin with, was in ecstasy. Previously, there had been minimal trading in stocks, although the bond market was substantial. In 1985, the value of all shares on the Paris exchange was equal to only about 13 per cent of its country's gross national product compared to market capitalization of 50 per cent in New York. Now *L'Express*, the champion of the new bureaucrats in France, ran excited features about the exchange, complete with stories about high school kids buying financial magazines to consult the market listings and talking animatedly about Paribas shares (the second company privatized by the government).[8]

"The large lines of stock slowly spun out of state-controlled industrial sectors have now revitalized stock exchanges," commented *Euromoney* approvingly.[9] The reality behind the observation: a languishing bureaucracy has been puffed up by privatization. There is something mordantly ironical about public enterprises acting as a transfusion for aenemic stock exchange bureaucracies which, in the mythology of privatization, are supposed to be the repository of genuinely red-blooded enterprise.

The general objective of these bureaucracies is to increase the volume of trading — a kind of institutionalized make-work project in the best (that is, the worst) of bureaucratic traditions. The most experienced of these bureaucrats, the New York brokers, make no bones about the nature of their work — buy or sell, up or down, keep 'em trading. The New York Stock Exchange is the bureaucratic ideal, with the *annual* volume of trading amounting to 85 per cent of the total capitalization of companies on the exchange. That is, the equivalent of almost all those huge and middle-sized companies on the exchange put together moves in and out each year in trading. U.S. mutual fund managers and investment advisers help right out, replacing an estimated 60-65 per cent of their portfolios every year.

The bureaucratic apogee is when, in flurries, the speculation up and down feeds on itself although the companies, which are nominally the objects of the speculation, continue operating the same as ever. Add options and futures, particularly on commodities, and also the churn of takeover raids and of arbitrageurs playing the takeovers, and you have the "paper economy" or the "symbolic economy." The stock exchange bureaucracies work like fury, piling up commissions and margins as the players vie against each other, detached from the real world of producing goods and services.

Privatization adds to the paper and symbols. By significantly augmenting the number of shares and the total capital of companies listed on the stock exchange, the privatization of large and substantial companies expands and fattens the stock market bureaucracy indefinitely. For the frequency of trading to be pumped up, however, a popular culture of speculation and of continuing excitement has to be created out of the huge wave generated by privatization in the first place. Research undertaken by the London Stock Exchange's advertising agency after the British Telecom issue (the first broad privatization share distribution in Britain) showed that more than 60 per cent of the new shareholders were "passive." Something had to be done to "energise these dormant shareholders." "These are people who have shown enough interest to go into the waiting room," said the advertising executive in charge, "now we want to get them on the train."[10]

The bureaucracy goes to work. The London stock exchange underwrote another wave of advertising. The massive propaganda campaigns of individual privatizations helped, in London and elsewhere. "It is a chance to interest tens of millions of Frenchmen in the Bourse," said the honcho from Publicis, the agency that handled the Saint-Gobain privatization.[11] Underpricing the shares in privatization cases also helped; it made stock speculation look good almost automatically.

The obliging media also help, effusively, shamelessly. Here is *L'Express* lauding the case of a middle executive in some anonymous corporation buying shares for the first time and, in the stock market upsurge, almost doubling his money within a year. The man is enchanted, *L'Express* reported. He spends half an hour each day and four hours every weekend studying the charts, we learn. Nor is there any doubt what is being celebrated. "If before they always lined up in the cafes to play the horses and lotteries, the French of every age have ended up surrendering massively to another passion," *L'Express* exulted. "The Stock Exchange, that they long held under suspicion, today amazes them and, at the same time, lures them with its repeated exploits."[12] This was before the October 1987 crash.

The rules of the game and what to watch for were spelled out for novices. A photograph proudly displayed in *Fortune* magazine, in a feature on privatization, showed an intimate little club of Parisian high-school boys sitting around a table discussing stocks. The club's name was "Bigwigs on the Bourse."[13] *The Times*, in a special feature on "share shops," one of the by-products of privatization, gushed over the arrival of somebody actually wearing a cloth cap . . . yes, a worker. True, he was using only a small sum, which he described as "play money." True, also, most of his savings were in a building society (a mortgage trust company). True, as well, he was dabbling in shares in the industry where he worked and which he knew something about, much like having a jockey friend at the track for betting on the horses. But that didn't matter to the image. "On the fourth floor of Bristol's Debenhams, at least, the age of Cloth-Cap Capitalism has arrived," *The Times* report declared.[14]

Other sectors of the New Bureaucracy were also expanded by privatization. Pension-fund and other investment-fund managers had more tokens to play with, adding exponentially to the possible permutations and combinations, hence to their assumed role and status. "The prospect of mature businesses, among the biggest enterprises in the country, being offered for sale, is a pleasing one," said the investment manager of a large British pension fund as he contemplated, with feelings of effulgent expansion, the oncoming privatizations.[15]

Financial counsellors (and their money letters), financial magazines, and financial writers generally also expand and proliferate, by the microbiotic action of bureaucratic growth. Their daily and weekly "analysis" and reporting of the minutest real and imagined factors that might have caused this shift and that in the market — their endless elaboration of the game — help keep the trades churning over. Several new financial papers doing just that showed up in France upon privatization, as publishers joined the new bureaucratic rush. Circulation numbers for investor bulletins in Britain shot up. The print mass media added services and ran how-to features about the game, and sold more advertising aimed at the players.

The growth of pure market analysis expands, too. This is perhaps the most esoteric and layered sub-branch of the stock market bureaucracy, pullulating forth with theories, prognosticatory rites, and examiners of entrails — some pulling in extraordinary incomes — not excluding sub-sub-branches like the "Contrarians" whose mission is to recommend the opposite of what everybody else is recommending. If any branch of the "old bureaucracy" in government departments had ever harboured like esoteric activities of paper and symbols, there would have been enormous scandal and ridicule, and one would have heard the loudest imaginable braying of condemnation of the public sector. The New Bureaucracy's power is such, however, that it is impregnable.

Gradually the culture of this bureaucracy makes itself felt. One of its more pernicious effects is in contributing to harmful short-term attitudes in the management of industrial companies themselves. Wall Street, where the New Bureaucracy is most entrenched, is the model. Market players, by the nature of their game, are oriented to maximizing income from one short-term period to another. Most professional (institutional) investors in the U.S. are paid to beat the market every quarter. They move in and out of stocks, huffing and puffing, trying to gain advantage. Price-earnings ratios – the profits per share of a company compared to share value – receive particular attention; they are an objective measure in a sea of information and speculation. Individual players frantically buy and sell, looking for profit opportunities. This is the supposedly all-knowing "verdict of Wall Street." Corporate management adopts income-maximizing strategies to match, to produce the steady quarter-to-quarter increases in profits that so please the financial players.

The reasons for their doing so are obvious. The verdict of the market establishes the pay-off to top management from stock options (so much touted by privatization advocates as a managerial incentive). It affects, too, other compensation. The executives' professional standing also becomes tied to these results. So does the ability of the company to raise money in the securities market, based on the price-earnings ratio. Also, if the stock goes down at any one point, it leaves the company more vulnerable to corporate raiders, which forces management to focus attention even more assiduously on short-term earnings. However, entrepreneurship and economic development, with their high up-front costs in technological development, worker training, design, and market development, are long-term – quite a different kettle of fish.

Industrial engineering professor Seymour Melman, in his book *Profits Without Production*, documents all the economic horrors that result from this managing for short-term profit, from industrial decline (with graphic U.S. examples) to breaking the law.[16] Not all companies are affected, and the stock market bureaucracy is only one of the factors that contributes to "short-termism." But it can be a potent one. Melman's major interest was the U.S. There is now also a growing debate in Britain about short-termism as the New Bureaucracy there more and more resembles its American counterpart. The churning of shares by British institutional investors, as they search for short-term advantage, doubled or tripled in the six years 1981-87, depending on the category of investor.

The most creative periods of economic development for different countries have been when their stock markets either were marginal and didn't count or when their pressures could be ignored. The post-war development of Japanese enterprise, financed largely by debt and retained earnings, is only the most recent and most impressive of such examples. As a rule, historically, stock markets have battened on to surges in industrial and technological development after they have taken place.

Privatization rhetoric celebrates capture by the stock-market bureaucracy regardless. It indeed insists upon it — has to insist upon it. The "discipline of the stock market" is a central tenet of the doctrine. The phrase is thrown up again and again, unquestioningly, when privatization advocates are put on the defensive. It has virtually a religious value for them. It is bureaucratic cant. The games the stock market bureaucracy plays with itself may have only a tenuous relationship to the real economic world and to the investment requirements of entrepreneurship. The discipline of something that is undisciplined or predatory is the discipline of fools.

The examples, over and above short-termism, are never-ending. To cite only the latest: The frenetic bull market that culminated in October 1987 occurred at the same time that economies were improving at an ordinary incremental rate (in the United States, the bull market coincided with the alarming rise of the American trade deficit and with U.S.products retreating in the face of foreign competition). Then the dramatic break in the bull occurred although the actual operations of companies and of economies continued apace. Nobody talked about discipline there, except in a perfunctory, ritualistic way, and then the talk applied not to producing companies but only to speculators and other paper game-players. What people really were talking about was "jitters" and "nervousness," a reflection of the vast second-guessing, paper-shuffling, make-work, tail-chasing apparatus of stock-market bureaucracies in their symbolic world. Even Michael Wilson, Canadian finance minister and an investment dealer by trade, was driven, in a moment of frankness, to dissociate the goings-on of the stock market from the "real economy."

Privatization also opens the door wide to paper entrepreneurship and the playing of takeover games. Publicly-owned companies make acquisitions, but usually they are closely related to the basic business or have some economic rationale. The rampant empire-building for the sake of empire building, the greenmailing, the costly defensive measures (from pay-offs to "poison pills"), the financial weakening of companies and diversion of energy, the abandonment of difficult entrepreneurial areas in order to increase share value (and the use of the increased value as leverage for more takeovers), the pimping by investment dealers of acquisitions and mergers of every conceivable style and corporate coupling in order to earn a fat rake-off, corporate executives turning to takeovers because financial games are where their skills are (and because financial vice-presidents may not have anything else to do), the enormously lucrative fees of lawyers and tax accountants ... this is the world of paper entrepreneurship and its byzantine, elaborate bureaucratic manoeuvring, that now beckons.

The newly privatized British Aerospace bought Sperry Gyroscope's British operation, Royal Ordnance (armaments and munitions, privatized), a West German optics company, a Dutch-based construction firm, and then the Rover Group (automobiles, another privatization). The newly privatized British Telecom took over Mitel in Canada. Newly privatized British Gas effectively took over Calgary-based Bow Valley Industries, in a manipulative arrangement to circumvent Canadian government regulations. The newly privatized British Airways got involved in a troublesome takeover game with British Caledonian, for which it ended up paying £250 million, more than twice the original offer of £119 and two-and-a-half times BCal's total assets, and, at that, for an airline which was losing money. The newly privatized telecommunications equipment manufacturer CGE in France picked up a majority interest in Générale Occidentale (incidentally, from privatization advocate Jimmy Goldsmith). The acquisition included an oil company in Guatemala, a U.S. forest company, *L'Express* magazine and a large publishing firm.

Privatized companies can also become acquisition fodder for existing paper entrepreneurship, accentuating concentration of ownership and control in the process. Effective control (30 per cent) of newly privatized Enterprise Oil fell to British-based multinational Rio Tinto Zinc at the moment of privatization. Enterprise Oil represents the former North Sea holdings stripped by the government from British Gas before it, too, was privatized. The privatized Britoil, the former oil and gas holdings of the British National Oil Company, fell to British Petroleum, whose government share itself was recently privatized.

The new French privatizations limited any individual or company to five per cent of the shares for an initial period, but that doesn't stop a closely knit circle, like a billionaire's club reported by *Le Nouvel Observateur*, from getting together to take control, once things settle down.[17] The American magazine *Business Week*, before the five-per-cent rule, speculated about cash-rich European financiers being "certain to change the French corporate landscape as profoundly as raiders such as T. Boone Pickens Jr. have altered Wall Street."[18] Nobody will be surprised when such paper games begin. One of the major reasons for the creation of the "noyaux durs" (hard cores of controlling shareholders) by the government, for several large privatizations, was to temporarily protect the companies against hostile takeovers even though it meant sacrificing the notion of shareholders' democracy. That, however, won't indefinitely stop the takeover games, either. After the two-to-five year protection period, it's open season.

Another growing function of the New Bureaucracy is public affairs and lobbying. British Telecom appointed the retiring Conservative Party chairman to its board, in a deft turn of the revolving door. The ex-politico, as a cabinet minister, had supervised BT's privatization in 1984. One of the roles of the new director would be to advise the company on how best to advance its cause within Whitehall (the government) which was taking so much flak from the public over deterioration of service. Where the New Bureaucracy is most entrenched, the United States again, corporate lobbying is a whole service sector by itself — an extraordinarily lucrative one where increased expenditure by one participant leads to increased expenditure by another in exponential elaboration.

Also part of the bureaucratization that comes with privatization, for widely held companies, is removal of shareholders' control over what the top corporate bureaucrats get paid and over how they otherwise look after themselves. The executives of newly privatized companies partake of the indulgent habits and customs of the existing private-sector corporate bureaucracy. At British Telecom, just to get into the spirit of things – as part of restructuring for privatization – the chairman's salary was raised 63 per cent in the two years 1982-84 leading up to privatization. This brought him up to $160,000 a year ($225,000 in today's equivalency). This was only the beginning. The privatization prospectus noted that one of the first things the BT board intended to do after the sale was "to implement substantial increases in the salaries of the executive directors to levels commensurate with those prevailing in other commercial companies." By way of comparison, the chairman of a BT supplier and competitor got $350,000 in 1984 ($482,000 in today's terms). At British Gas, privatization magically changed the chairman's salary from $150,000 to more than $350,000.

At British Telecom, the executive directors all signed contracts taking them to the age of 60 so that they would have to be bought out after privatization if they were to be pushed out the door. This was in keeping with the private corporate spirit where, more and more, "golden parachutes" are contractually acquired on the way into a corporation so that on the way out the floating is easy. In the same spirit, the Thatcher government doubled the salaries of the directors of British Coal while at the same time 21,000 coalminers were losing their jobs (the *Economist* reported that the doubling of the salaries was presumably an incentive to further retrenchment).[19] Not that reductions in the work force were uncalled for, and not that the cuts wouldn't ultimately improve British Coal's financial picture, but *doubling* executive salaries while masses of people in the company were being put out on the street only could happen given the logic of private corporate bureaucracy, American style.

Much more is yet to come, to judge by the corporate and stock-exchange cultures in the United States, which are the privatization model. There, executive remuneration often appears to be not merely out of control but also out of this world (the highest in 1987, including stock options, was $80 million). Outlandish pay-outs to management are commonplace even when companies are losing money, in decline, closing plants, or playing financial games of no productive value and often hiding an underlying economic deterioration. Such inflated management emoluments, plus perks and corporate entertainment to rival the Sun King, have become regularized in the New Bureaucracy.

Other bureaucratic variations abound. Golden parachutes are now studded with diamonds (the record: probably the $48 million to get rid of the chairman of Revlon, in 1985). In a revealing case of what was jokingly described as "hushmail," one corporate bureaucracy (General Motors) effectively paid $10 million to a director they were kicking out, on condition that he not criticize the company (this was just part of a lucrative share-purchase buy-out of an estimated $965 million, at nearly twice the current market price for the shares at the time). In such easy-spending ways do these private corporate bureaucrats try to cover their collective behind and to keep life comfortable. The New Bureaucracy does not stint, either, on gladhanding (recently British-based Allied-Lyons, a player of takeover games, spent $1.2 million on a publicity junket for 90 people; imagine the brouhaha if, let's say, a publicly owned British Gas had done it).

The irony of all this is that public enterprise is stigmatized with the label of bureaucracy while private enterprise is touted as the model of bureaucracy-free entrepreneurship. In reality, the latter generates a vast and open-ended, top-heavy bureaucratic superstructure, with rank upon rank of people playing paper and symbolic games of little or no productive value and being vastly overpaid while they are at it. The body of public enterprise, on the other hand, gets on with entrepreneurial tasks uncluttered and undistracted by that bureaucratic overlay.

Privatization feeds the New Bureaucracy and, not surprisingly, the members of the New Bureaucracy are among the doctrine's most ardent pushers.

8.
Back in Canada:
BCRIC and Other Privatizations

The finest and most illuminating example of privatization occurred right here in Canada before Margaret Thatcher even got started: the British Columbia Resources Investment Corporation (BCRIC). As privatization models went, BCRIC was the fairest of them all. Shares were distributed to everybody. A large amount of new equity capital flowed in whereby the privatized company could show what it could do in its own right. BCRIC quickly became an entrepreneurial disaster. It was an unforgiving, terrible embarrassment to privatization "pietists."

A "revolutionary plan," said the news release from the office of Bill Bennett, the premier of British Columbia, on January 11, 1979, when the BCRIC privatization was launched. "It is a unique, once-in-a-lifetime opportunity for the greatest number of people to become owners and not tenants in our own land . . .," the release went on. "We want people to be able to see and feel their ownership in the form of a tangible share certificate."

The premier was announcing that "every eligible man, woman and child in the province" — or about 2.4 million people — would be receiving five shares in the British Columbia Resources Investment Corporation. Other shares would be available for purchase. Premier Bennett went on to say that no large corporation or individual could ever own more than one per cent of the shares, "thus preventing this company from ever being controlled by a few and ensuring that it will always be held by our own citizens." Thrown into the BCRIC pot by the government were three forest companies, 1.2 million shares in Westcoast Transmission, and oil and natural gas licences covering 2.3 million acres in northeast British Columbia.

The largest of the forest companies involved, Canadian Cellulose (Cancel), 81 per cent Crown-owned, was a public-enterprise Cinderella story. The company, acquired from Celanese Corporation in New York, was an operator of three pulp mills and two sawmills, split between the Northwest and the Interior. Under its previous American owners, it had a woeful record of financial, production and management problems, with continuing losses, a negative net worth, and deteriorating plant. Helped by a rising market, Cancel, under majority public ownership, turned itself around so that just a few years later even the private-sector business press was praising the deal. *Executive* magazine described the "once-sickly discard" as "one of the most dramatic turnabouts in recent corporate history."[1] Cancel was the centrepiece of the BCRIC properties.

In the end, applications representing 2.07 million people were received for the free BCRIC shares, or 86 per cent of the population as compared to less than 4 per cent of the population for the later, conventional, and much ballyhooed issue of British Telecom shares in the U.K. About 7 per cent of British Columbians also bought additional BCRIC shares, almost double the ratio for the British Telecom issue. A total of $487 million of new capital was raised by the additional share issue.

So "shareholders' democracy" wasn't invented by Margaret Thatcher in the 1980s after all. It was invented in 1977 and 1978 by Bill Bennett and the coterie of philosopher-advisers and investment dealers in southwestern British Columbia who put the plan together for him. The first group of advisers, involved in the incorporation of BCRIC, were representatives from A.E. Ames & Co., McLeod Young Weir, Pemberton Securities and Richardson Securities. They even gave it a code name, "Project West."

When the original incorporation bill was being debated, and a straight sale was envisioned, the leader of the opposition attacked the concept. "The people of this province are now being given the opportunity to sell off something to themselves that they already

own . . . sold off to the few rich who can afford to buy that stuff off."[2]
The privatization coterie dismissed this as illogical. If BCRIC and the publicly owned assets which went into it were sold off, the people of the province would receive the share-purchase payments or a block price in return. It would be an ordinary money-for-value transaction.

Still, the opposition attack had a powerful political impact because it was indeed quite logical in its own terms. It was an attack on the proposed concept of ownership. What belonged to all the people of the province — what was democratically owned — would end up in the hands of a few, a small minority of the well-off. The subsequent free share distribution was a political stroke which appeared to cut the opposition's argument off at the feet.

The accent on the idea of a "tangible share certificate" — something you could hold in your hand — added to the counter-attack. It raised ownership to a different aesthetic level, something exquisitely grabbable. Mind you, at the issuing evaluation of $6 per share, you couldn't buy too much with just the five free shares you got. That skirted the point, though. Unlike a person's share of public ownership, one had an individual choice over the disposition of one's shares.

Left unsaid, and a tremendous political bonus for the scheme, was that the price paid by the province's people for the BCRIC properties in the first place wasn't visible unless one bothered to look up the figures in old public accounts or newspaper articles. So the assets represented by the giveaway did appear to be free. Also lost to sight was the incremental value of the properties in the interim, plus oil and gas exploration rights to some 2.3 million acres of Crown land that were also handed to BCRIC. That wealth all in all, recovery of which was forfeited in the free share-certificate distribution, would be paid for invisibly by the public in taxes or in diminished public services. It came to $106 million in 1978 dollars.

The revolutionary part of the "revolutionary plan," however, lay elsewhere. "People's capitalism" was the phrase Bill Bennett used. By becoming shareholders en masse, the people of the province for the first time in large numbers were participating in private-enterprise capitalism — were entering the business world (big business, in fact) and the heretofore mysterious universe, for most, of share certificates and stock exchanges.

BCRIC, in the sale of additional shares, was also proffered as an unprecedented investment vehicle which would gather up the private savings of British Columbians and put them to work making British Columbia... well, making it great again. The theme was another forerunner of the kind of sales pitch that would be used in Britain. Because of the publicity and prestige associated with the share offer – Premier Bennett himself bought a sizeable clump of shares – because, also, it touched a well-spring of provincial patriotism and involved assets which, in another form, had belonged to everybody, the share offer was enormously successful. "Galloping capitalism," Bennett proudly called it. The shares were also priced at a discount to the appraised book value, something the Thatcher government and also the French government would later do as well to make sure privatization sales went off with a loud bang.

Between the free share distribution and the additional share offer, the scheme was also to have an educational effect. The masses of people would become active parts of the private-enterprise corporate culture. Distribution of the free share certificates alone cost $4 per person in processing fees. Other administrative costs included computer-screening the applications, the high-quality engraving of share certificates to prevent counterfeiting, the advertising and other printing, the prospectus, share registration, and commissions for the share-sale part of the operation. All told, the overheads came to a conservatively estimated $40 million. Next to launching a cultural revolution, though – and, above all, getting rid of public ownership of the enterprises – the expenditure hardly counted. A vengeful spirit of suppression of the previous government's successes and orientation pushed the whole exercise.

The mystical "tangible share certificate" was joined in the privatization mantra by another key phrase, "individual ownership." "Our commitment is ownership for all of our people on an individual basis, as opposed to big government ownership which neglects the individual," the premier said. So BCRIC wasn't just a share giveaway. All the evangelical and utopian elements of "shareholders' democracy" exulted over by Mrs. Thatcher and her government – the incantations and "revolutionary" protestations – were there. One privatization advocate was inspired to write about "bricking-up" Crown corporations and government offices in general across the country.[3] The BCRIC share distribution scheme made its way ultimately into utopian privatization literature as far away as France and perhaps beyond.

That was the "revolutionary" setting, but the actual operation of BCRIC turned out to be less impressive. The first major move was to use the large cache of money left from the new share issue, plus debt financing, to buy controlling interest (67 per cent) of Kaiser Resources, whose principal business was coal mining in southeastern B.C. BCRIC paid a prodigious 70 per cent premium for the shares, $55 as compared to the market price of $32.36. To make matters worse, it earlier had an option to buy a sizeable block of Kaiser Resources stock, although not control, for $44, which was passed over for the takeover. To make matters worse yet, Edgar Kaiser Jr., the single largest beneficiary of this caper, retained the right to buy back certain choice Kaiser Resources assets not at a premium price (as BCRIC had paid for the whole of Kaiser Resources), or even at market value, but at what was likely to be the much lower book value.

To make matters even worse, Kaiser was given an exclusive contract to look after the coal marketing at a generous 3.5 per cent commission, which worked out to $1 million a month. To make matters worse than even that, three BCRIC directors, including the president and secretary, plus the president's wife, owned Kaiser Resources shares and profited by the BCRIC takeover. As a fillip, a flurry of options trading had taken place during the takeover negotiations, which led to an investigation by the Ontario Securities Commission to determine if there had been any insider leaks.

Yet the BCRIC president and board could defend, and did defend, what they had done, in private-enterprise terms. They pointed to other takeovers where the premium had been even higher. This was private enterprise in operation, they were in effect saying. As for some directors profiting personally from the takeover through their holdings in Kaiser Resources, they had declared their interest to the board and had not voted on the takeover decision. True, one of the benefiting directors, the president, had recommended the takeover, but there was nothing illegal in that. "The board is entirely satisfied that the actions of these individuals were proper and correct in every respect," a BCRIC statement declared. The president of a leading investment firm commented vigorously, "In my view, it's a bit of a storm in a teapot because none of them has done anything wrong."[4]

BCRIC shares, which had originally shot up from $6 to $9.25, began declining and fell past the issue price. One of the privatization zealots that had been party to the planning of BCRIC, now in his capacity as a director of research for a prominent investment-dealer firm, commented, "We view the shares as a buy at current levels based on their excellent value . . . [and there seems] very little downrisk."[5] This judgement — or was it an expression of faith? — wasn't enough to block a slide to the $3 level.

BCRIC sank under its high debt level incurred by its deals. Losses, sell-offs and write-offs followed. A North Sea oil holding and a costly development agreement attached to it, which BCRIC carried for years, was finally sold, with a considerable write-off involved. The company surrendered altogether in pulp. It acquired a small oil and gas operation in Saskatchewan of not much significance and of no relevance to B.C. Exploration of its B.C. oil and gas properties was limited and produced little in the way of results (later, most of the licences would be sold for a fraction of their original evaluation). Almost from the beginning, people complained that BCRIC was not really doing anything constructive for the province and its people, such as starting new business and creating new jobs. The shares kept falling, ultimately all the way to 75 cents.

The idea of shareholders' democracy didn't fare any better. One of the first things that came up was the mechanics of distributing dividends to 2.07 million people, mostly with a few shares. A Conservative member of the legislature charged that it would cost more than the dividends themselves. And how do you get 2.07 million people, or even a meaningful fraction of them like the 136,143 registered shareholders (100 shares or more), into an annual meeting? The first president of the corporation denied the magnitude of the bureaucratic task. First, you had to subtract 600,000 from the total shareholders, for children. Their shares were the absolute property of their mothers, like family allowance. A lot of people would be trading their shares for cash. By the time dividends were to be paid, many years down the road, the free shares would have aggregated in relatively few hands. Or so the president appeared to hope. The problem was, however, that such a scenario would defeat the original concept of people's capitalism.

In fact, for annual meetings, nobody ever expected large numbers of shareholders to turn up—large, that is, compared to the total number. What was the point? Only those who had bought at least another 95 shares, incidentally, had voting rights. People with just the five free shares didn't qualify. The revolution was over the moment it was supposed to have begun.

The shares were listed on the Vancouver and Toronto stock exchanges. In the first five months, more than a quarter of the shares eligible for trading changed hands. Ownership was already beginning to move out of the province. After three years from the opening of trade, Bennett lifted the restriction which had limited individuals to only one per cent of the shares and institutions to only three per cent. There went the solemn assurance that the company never ever would be "controlled by a few [and] will always be held by our own citizens," the prior condition of any "shareholders' democracy." (Much later, in 1988, the prohibition against foreign shareholders would also be lifted.)

One of the reasons for lifting the restriction was that the value of BCRIC shares was plummeting, an embarrassment for Bill Bennett, the father of BCRIC. Without the restriction, speculative action for more shares would increase share value. It even allowed for a takeover. The "market" would treat BCRIC as it should be treated, namely hoisting its share value back up. This was the theory. It didn't happen that way. Over time the share price kept falling. Unsaid in the theory of the manoeuvre was that if you wanted the "market" to act properly, you had to kiss shareholders' democracy goodbye.

For the first annual meeting in 1980, BCRIC, faced with the unknown, booked the cavernous 17,000-seat Pacific Coliseum. Only about 1,400 people showed up, of which only 678 were registered shareholders with voting power. For the second annual meeting, only registered shareholders with tickets were allowed (others were plumb out of luck). With dissatisfaction over the company's performance on the rise, 1,550 such registered shareholders were present. The dissenters did not get far. The next year, with even those diehards realizing the lie of the land, only 799 showed up. Management, "stodgy and at times arrogant" as described in the *Vancouver Sun* report, used its proxies to push everything through.[6] The show of hands might vote one way; the ballot count, with the proxies voted, would vote another way. One shareholder declared that "there is no point for us to come and vote, it doesn't make any difference and, at least, I suggest you can save the cost of renting the room and decorating it." More than three-quarters of the shareholders went home before all the resolutions were dealt with.

"The famous experiment in people's capitalism pays little regard to the people of B.C.," another shareholder said. One commentator a couple of months later sardonically noted that BCRIC directors "had roughly the same authority as an absolute monarch."[7] For the 1983 annual meeting, only 320 registered shareholders showed up, not many more than the numbers in a good-sized legislature. By the time of the 1984 meeting the newspapers had stopped counting.

BCRIC wasn't long in picking up other self-serving undemocratic habits typical of private corporations. In 1984, it issued a special package of flow-through shares, giving buyers lucrative tax breaks at the expense of the tax-paying public; flow-through shares are a typical private-corporate draw on the public purse. BCRIC didn't even bother offering the shares to the common folk, including long-suffering BCRIC small shareholders, because it would have been administratively awkward. The offer was made in a private placement to outsiders instead, in minimum $102,000 lots, except for BCRIC's own highly paid executives, plus officers and employees, who were allowed to buy $6,000 lots. The price of BCRIC shares at the time was $3.15. For investors in the 50 per cent tax bracket, the effective price of the flow-through shares was $1.95.

The first president of BCRIC moved up to chairman for a while, where he retained his $125,000 salary – not exactly suffering from the company's disastrous performance. The second, who came from the presidency of MacMillan-Bloedel, checked in at $250,000 plus future cash bonuses if any, and, to boot, an assured lifetime pension of half the figure ($125,000 plus half the bonus level) after his seven-year contract expired. He turned out to be uninspired and eventually left under a cloud of criticism and unpopularity, but not hurting in his pocketbook, either. At one point, this second president, to make sure he had control of the annual meeting, paid a hefty fee to get brokerage houses to solicit proxies on management's behalf. Another gambit considered at the time was to issue new treasury shares at low prices to a select group of corporations and businessmen who would back the existing management.

BCRIC management and the board functioned like a private club, supporting themselves, renewing their nominations and bringing in new directors by their own self-perpetuating choice. Naturally they drew from their own corporate, political and social circles, representing existing power. The original BCRIC board consisted of the chief executive officers of the Bank of B.C., Okanagan Helicopters, Daon Development, Woodward Stores, and Finning Tractor, all of considerable business experience ("captains of industry," they were called), but all of the same mentality and hence collectively limited in economic imagination. One of the results of the private-sector cosiness was the costly and excessive deal for Kaiser Resources which helped put BCRIC in the glue. "I'm friendly with the guys sitting on the BCRIC board," explained one company president, "and I'm very friendly with Edgar [Kaiser]. There's just too many friendships around."[8] When a disgruntled shareholder in 1981 told the press that all the company could do was "line the pockets of the corporate elite," he was sounding off angrily out of personal discontent but he was also touching on something close to the bone of what BCRIC had become in the privatization process.

What happened to BCRIC in reality was only extraordinary because of the ideological fantasy which preceded it. BCRIC was a typical privately owned corporation, quite unexceptional in its undemocratic ways. Annual meetings of corporations are typically perfunctory. Individual shareholders are typically powerless. Successors to positions of power in private corporations are chosen internally, unless there are takeover coups, something in administrative method akin to making replacements in the Soviet politburo. The preferential flow-through share deal was par for the course. The BCRIC boards of directors were probably no more stodgy and arrogant than any others.

For the week ending September 30, 1988, BCRIC shares closed on the Vancouver Stock Exchange at 90 cents.

In the rigged privatization debate, hardly anybody cited the BCRIC case, large and instructive though it was. Long and reflective articles by imposing authors appeared in such magazines as *The Report on Business Magazine* and *Policy Options*, pushing privatization and exploring the subject in often exotic detail, but inspirationally avoiding any mention of BCRIC. Subsequent privatization in Canada, in the 1980s, took place in the ideological slipstream of partisan British privatization claims and rhetoric instead.

De Havilland and Canadair, the country's two airframe manufacturers, were sold off, in the first case to foreign owners (Boeing), after a great deal of money had been spent over the years, and misfortune suffered, on development and keeping the industry alive. Fisheries Products International in St. John's, rescued and restructured by public ownership from a gaggle of unprofitable companies, then turned around and making healthy profits, was sold off, as was a smaller company in Quebec, Pêcheries Canada Inc. These had all been hospitalization cases of one kind or another, where public ownership had stepped in to pick up from failed or departed private enterprise. Alberta, similarly, sold off Pacific Western Airlines (PWA). The airline had originally been acquired after the Alberta cabinet had tried unsuccessfully to organize a consortium of Alberta private-sector investors for the task. Now that public ownership had done the job and protected Alberta's interests when it came to the airline, PWA, too, was handed over. The federal government also reduced public ownership in the Canada Development Corporation from 47 per cent to a nominal 13.5 per cent. The CDC was effectively privatized long before. (Its initial asset was publicly owned Polymer, now Polysar, handed over by the government of the day. It was still the company's main asset 15 years later when the hapless private-sector holding company, Polysar and all, fell into the hands of Nova Corporation of Alberta.)

These privatizations, however, were only at the edge of the growing privatization putsch, British-style. More telling, the highly profitable monopoly utility, Teleglobe, was sold — virtually turned over as a prize — to a small Montreal-based company called Memotec Data Inc. Teleglobe was Canada's international telecommunications carrier. Memotec, with shareholders' equity of only $40 million, thereby acquired a company worth $345 million net of outstanding debt, merely for the asking. The acquisition was a "leveraged buy-out," with the acquiring company and its management using the profits of the acquired company to pay for the acquisition, getting it in effect for nothing. Teleglobe's profits in the previous year were $63 million and rising. Debt financing would be required but, because the acquisition was a monopoly utility, Memotec would have an assured cash flow. Arranging the debt financing for the takeover would be as easy as pie.

Two months after the deal, Memotec shares had doubled in value despite the enormous debt the company had assumed (debt represented 93 per cent of all its liabilities). This reflected the value of the Teleglobe prize. Some stock players got into the action early, generating a sharp price run-up a week before the Teleglobe acquisition was announced and, indirectly, taking a piece of the prize with them. The main reason Memotec succeeded in the manoeuvring for Teleglobe was exactly because it was so small. To give Teleglobe to a larger company would, it was said, add to concentration of ownership. Three months later, Memotec sold almost a third of its shares to Bell Canada Enterprises (BCE) and added to concentration of ownership anyway.

The transaction made BCE by far the biggest shareholder. The two firms that previously controlled Memotec would together own 14 per cent, less than half BCE's holdings. Memotec's shares jumped almost 25 per cent with the announcement of the BCE purchase. The government could have collected this margin itself if it had sold the 30 per cent of Teleglobe directly to BCE. Indeed, a few months before Teleglobe was handed over to Memotec for $488 million (including the assumption of Teleglobe's debt), industry analysts estimated Teleglobe could sell for between $700 and $800 million. It was anticipated that BCE would get the biggest piece of Teleglobe in any case. In the sale to Memotec, the government had set guidelines limiting future telephone company ownership in Teleglobe to 40 per cent, and participation of any one telephone company to 33 per cent. This left substantial room for BCE.

Ammunition manufacturer Canadian Arsenals was also sold by the federal government. Privatization advocates began beating the drum yet once more for the privatization of Air Canada, Petro-Canada and now, also, of CN. The companies are known to privatization devotees as the "big three." Air Canada and Petro-Canada had long been a target of privatizers but the government had delayed privatization because of troublesome public opinion. An opinion poll published March 31, 1988 showed that 53 per cent of Canadians opposed the selling of Air Canada (35 per cent in favour), 54 per cent opposed the selling of CN (31 per cent in favour), and 49 per cent opposed the selling of Petro-Canada (37 per cent in favour); this despite the constant drumming of private-enterprise ideology. Then, in a surprise announcement less than two weeks later, the government declared its intention to put 45 per cent of Air Canada on the block, with the remainder of the public's ownership to go later. Until the public's ownership was totally disposed of, moreover, its shares were to be voted automatically in accordance with the private shareholders. The government didn't dare privatize the airline all at once. Enabling legislation was duly presented to the House of Commons.

Ontario sold the Urban Transportation Development Company to a Montreal engineering firm. Quebec privatized the prime gold-mining assets of the Société québecoise d'exploration minière (SOQUEM), also the province's controlling interest in forest products company Donohue Inc., and sold off several other holdings. A privatization-bent committee put together by the government recommended that all "strategic enterprises" — that is, all commercial enterprises — be privatized.

The government of Grant Devine in Saskatchewan, in a kind of ideological orgasm, is attempting a wholesale sell-off of publicly owned companies — enterprises at the heart of Saskatchewan entrepreneurship. It has privatized a controlling share of SaskOil (the majority of whose private shareholders are now outsiders). The Saskatchewan Mining Development Corporation and the federal Crown company Eldorado Nuclear have been merged and a phased-in privatization is about to be launched. Saskatchewan Minerals, a small but profitable producer of sodium sulphate and peat moss, was sold in two parts to an Ontario and a Quebec company. The large gas reserves of Saskatchewan Power were sold to the privatized SaskOil in exchange for SaskOil shares, then SaskPower bonds were issued which private buyers could convert for those SaskOil shares. Earlier a SaskPower coal mine and dragline were sold to an Alberta coal company. Saskatchewan Forest Products, with a treatment plant, sawmill, plywood plant, planer mill and stud mill, is being broken up and sold off. The Saskatchewan Computer Utilities Corporation (SaskComp) and the computer operations of Saskatchewan Telecommunications (SaskTel) have been folded together with two private companies, one a leasing company in Alberta, to form a new entity, Westbridge Corporation; a private share-issue is planned.

The general insurance division of Saskatchewan Government Insurance (SGI), with a notable history of improving insurance service in the province, will be privatized in 1989 through a 60 per cent share offering. (The original plan was also to contract out the management and operational side of SGI's automobile insurance — ersatz privatization where the real thing was too politically risky; this idea was so peculiar, and so transparently involved privatization, that it was ultimately dropped.) The Prince Albert Pulp Company went to giant U.S. forestry company Weyerhaeuser. Some of the private sales, like the one to Weyerhaeuser, have been marked by sweetheart arrangements and, in two cases, loan guarantees (directly or indirectly financing the private purchase of public property with public money). Prince Albert Pulp, sold at a low point in the forest products economic cycle, immediately began to ring up extra-large profits for its U.S. buyer when the cycle inevitably improved. The Potash Corporation of Saskatchewan (PCS) is also being considered for privatization. A couple of British proselytizers were brought to Saskatchewan on visits to expound privatization doctrine. "Devotees with a religious fervor," Dale Eisler, political columnist for the Regina *Leader-Post*, described them, not without a little awe for their messianism.[9]

The Bill Vander Zalm government in British Columbia has sold off the natural gas and rail divisions of B.C. Hydro. The rail division went to a San Francisco subsidiary of a Chicago company. B.C. Hydro's research division and the B.C. Systems Corporation were actively considered for privatization. The original talk of privatizing the Insurance Corporation of British Columbia (ICBC) was hastily abandoned when it quickly became clear that not even absolutist doctrine could cover over the advantages of the public corporation. Still, given the government's ideological disposition, there is always hope for predators. A syndicate headed by an American (a former president of ICBC) and underwritten by the private insurance lobby in Toronto (the Insurance Bureau of Canada) launched a $1 million "public relations" campaign to soften up the public on the idea of breaking up the corporation, but that effort failed abjectly. In one of the most bizarre developments – a testimony to the transcending power of belief in dogma – a proposal was floated to privatize most of the Robson Square complex in Vancouver. That idea went up in smoke and ridicule. Victoria was "propelled by the successes of Britain's Iron Lady," reported the *Vancouver Sun* of the Vander Zalm privatization push.

Not to be outdone, privatization promoters in Alberta began lobbying for the sell-off of Alberta Government Telephones and Edmonton Telephones. CKUA, the radio side of the ACCESS provincial broadcasting authority, was saved from privatization only when its listeners flooded the government with letters and telephone calls.

As in Britain and France, members of the New Bureaucracy – the investment dealers and consultants – moved in on the scene, looking for fees and prizes (the underwriting of privatization issues), giving advice (also for healthy fees), pushing politically for privatization in their own right, and envisaging the day when the additional assets from privatization would be listed on stock markets, beefing up the share-trading pool and their business. As in Britain and France, too, their connection to the political parties behind the privatization is a close one.

In British Columbia, investment dealers were reported as "bullish and pawing the ground, waiting for a shot at some B.C. Crown corporations." The dealers were telling the government how good it was, encouraging it to turn up the burners on privatization.

Salomon Brothers in New York was brought in by the Canadian government to advise it on privatization of Canadian Crown corporations (it wasn't clear what it was supposed to do, and it didn't do much, but presumably it collected a nice fee for its troubles). S.G. Warburg from Britain also acted as an adviser to the Mulroney government on some of its privatizations. Wood Gundy was retained to advise the government concerning the sale of Petro-Canada. Three financial advisors took in $2 million for work on the sale of De Havilland to Boeing and a similar group of three (Burns Fry, Merrill Lynch, S.G. Warburg) received $2.6 million for high-priced advice on the sale of Canadair.

Advisers have been picking up fees in some Canadian provinces, too. British Columbia retained representatives of British firms N.M. Rothschild & Sons and Schroders to advise it. N. M. Rothschild has what it calls an "international privatization unit." Its man, one of the British proselytizers who visited Saskatchewan, is a defeated Tory candidate.

The two federal cabinet ministers most closely associated with the privatization putsch come from investment-dealer firms and carry with them the cultural baggage of that bureaucratic world and, no doubt, some of the old fraternal connections. Barbara McDougall, the federal minister in charge of privatization, was a vice-president of A.E. Ames and, briefly, of Dominion Securities, when the two companies merged. Finance Minister Michael Wilson was an executive vice-president of Dominion Securities.

The leading proponent of privatization in Alberta is Keith Alexander, a former MLA who ceded his Edmonton seat to Premier Don Getty. Alexander is a vice-president of Dominion Securities, too, but it could have been any other firm. Dominion Securities (Alberta) Ltd. has been commissioned by the government to do a study on the economics of privatizing Alberta Government Telephones. Dominion Securities overall has been instrumental in numerous privatization studies for various governments.

Underneath it all is the ideological hype. Grant Devine has already shown himself no slouch in using Orwellian propaganda techniques, by calling his minister of privatization (an unpopular word in Saskatchewan) the Minister of Public Participation. The shameless ruse has become a point of humour in Saskatchewan, but, of course, there is a serious side of it, too, as the *Sunday Times* columnist realized in his broadside against "Telecom Britain." The manipulation of language and ideas, and the brave new world of privatization, go together.

9.
Canadian Public Enterprise in Economic History

The more important, enduring Canadian story is on the other side of the issue — our public enterprise itself. We know, from our own experience, how successful and vital public enterprise has been and, when we think about it, how much a part of us it is. We have, in public ownership, some of the world's best electrical utilities, best telephone companies, best broadcasting networks, the most efficient automobile insurance companies, a leading airline, a first-class railroad, a top-notch national oil company, a grain marketing agency which has liberated prairie farmers from speculative markets, provincial companies instrumental in regional entrepreneurship, and other ongoing enterprises wherever ideological bias has not stood in the way.

They provide, without subsidy, some of the western world's lowest electricity rates, the lowest telephone rates in Canada, the highest pay-out for the automobile insurance dollar, and air fares and freight rates that help keep Canada competitive with the much denser American market. They also provide first-class service in terms both of the service itself and the equipment and technology used. This, and their low rates, are not passing phenomena. They go back to the very early days of these companies, the oldest of which, like Ontario Hydro and the prairie telephone companies, are heading for the century mark and coincide with the history of modern industrial Canada.

Other public enterprises provide efficiencies and economies in ways that most Canadians don't think about. For example, the overhead cost of financing broadcasting publicly — the cost of getting the money together through the tax system — is marginal. The cost of doing it in the private-enterprise way, with the overheads of the commercial bureaucratic apparatus, amounts to about half a billion dollars a year for television alone, or $5 billion every decade uncompounded (almost twice that, compounded annually at 8 per cent), an enormous waste.

Medical insurance is not a business enterprise as such in Canada, but for the most part it is in the United States, where it is handled largely by private corporations. As insurance, it represents a business function. A U.S. study found that a medical insurance system there comparable to ours would save a minimum of $36 billion annually (and possibly as much as $66 billion annually) in administration costs alone, for the year 1983.[1] Based on this figure, our public medical insurance system is saving us, relative to American private insurance, at least $3.8 billion annually or $38 billion every decade (about $82 billion compounded at 8 per cent), and possibly as much as $7 billion annually or $70 billion every decade.

A Toronto investment dealer who was involved in British privatization couldn't help pointing out, in an article on commercial Crown corporations, that Canadian consumers of state-owned rail, broadcasting, electricity, airline and telephone services "have enjoyed standards consistently ranging from fair to superb, on an internationally comparative basis."[2] One unnamed dealer cited by the *Globe and Mail*, too honest for his own good, confessed that "the big problem with privatization is there's no economic rationale, ideological or pragmatic."[3]

Our public enterprises are also technologically forward. This is one of their major defining characteristics and a key element of modern entrepreneurship. Research and development is also an area where, with exceptions, private enterprise in Canada has a dismal record.

Ontario Hydro is one of the world-leaders in nuclear power. Hydro-Québec is a technology innovator and has its own research institute (IREQ), as compared to the previous, privately owned Montreal Light Heat and Power which was technologically backward and parasitical. Petro-Canada does its own research and development. This forwardness isn't necessarily a function of size. Air Canada, although a substantial company, is small compared to major corporations but is one of the world's most technically advanced airlines and has a long list of innovations to its name. The Insurance Corporation of British Columbia had an autobody shop used not only as a measuring stick for autobody repair rates but also as a laboratory for more technologically advanced and efficient methods of car repair; it was discontinued by a government that ideologically wanted to curb public enterprise. Atomic Energy of Canada (AECL) has developed one of the world's most successful nuclear power technologies, all the more remarkable given the theoretical futurism of the endeavour when it was begun and the small technological and engineering base in the country that the company originally had to work with.

This technological forwardness goes back to the early days when Canadians were not supposed to be capable of doing new things on their own. Our public enterprises gave us the chance to show the naysayers differently. Ontario Hydro was a pioneer in large-dam construction and in high-power long-distance transmission at a time when it had barely got on its feet, in the early part of the century. CN in the 1930s, when railroads were still firmly in the age of steam, developed the first experimental diesel locomotive (the railway also pioneered network radio broadcasting in Canada; CN Radio was the precursor of what was to become the CBC). The prairie telephone companies extended service into the countryside when the previous privately owned Bell companies were only interested in wiring up the lucrative cities; one of the major reasons for taking over telephones was to take the lines out to the towns and farm families in these predominantly agricultural provinces.

Our publicly owned enterprises make up a great entrepreneurial tradition in other ways. We all own them. They are a genuine rather than a bogus form of "shareholders' democracy" — indirect it's true, but representative, governed in effect by a delegate system, the only way a widespread shareholding can be effectively democratic. Public ownership also captures in this way some vital qualities of entrepreneurship: indigenous ownership and control, self-reliance and originality. Even the ordinary things about this are of considerable importance. The corporate headquarters physically are in the country or in the region. This means that the decision-making people in operations, corporate strategy and investment are on hand at the centre of the company's activities. They also bring to the community around them entrepreneurial presence, knowledgeability, and skills which are passed on, formally and informally, to others. In a country where there has been extraordinarily high foreign ownership of the economy—where so much enterprise has been colonized and made subsidiary—indigenously owned public enterprise has been a powerful counterforce.

Public enterprise is an economic expression of Canada's own identity—the desire of Canadians, together or in their different provinces, to be a distinctive and independent community on the North American continent. Like the rest of the public-enterprise culture, this element goes back in history, too, indeed to the building of the Rideau Canal for military purposes after the war of 1812 against the United States. The Welland Canal followed, to protect the commercial heart of Canada (the St. Lawrence system) against the building of the Erie Canal in New York state (the construction of the Welland Canal, begun as a private enterprise, was our first significant "hospitalization" case). The building of the CPR, publicly conceived and supported—a public enterprise in all but name—tied the country together as we know it today and kept the great Northwest Territories (western Canada) in Canadian hands. Ontario Hydro was created not just to keep electrical power out of the hands of financial tycoons and provide the cheapest possible rates for the citizenry but also to provide cheap electrical power for southwestern Ontario manufacturers so they could contend against American competition. The publicly owned prairie telephone companies were established in the same period, just after the turn of the century, to bind prairie settlement together. Winnipeg Hydro, Edmonton Power, 'edmonton telephones' and other municipally owned electrical and telephone utilities were also established, and were going concerns, prior to World War I. The local electricity distribution systems in Ontario were municipally owned.

As the interwar period began, the CNR was created and made into a great railway out of a gaggle of bankrupt private companies (another hospitalization case). The CBC, Trans-Canada Air Lines (Air Canada), the Canadian Wheat Board and the Treasury Branches were also created in the interwar period.

CANADIAN PUBLIC ENTERPRISE IN ECONOMIC HISTORY

The World War II Crown companies – aircraft manufacturers, Polymer (synthetic rubber), an advanced technology company called Research Enterprises (radar and optics) and a host of others – helped turn Canada into a modern industrial state. Then, among many others, came the post-war corporations like Atomic Energy of Canada (AECL), Saskatchewan Power and many smaller Saskatchewan Crown companies (including a bus company, forestry company, an airline and a sodium sulphate producer), Manitoba Hydro, the automobile insurance companies, Hydro-Québec, B.C. Hydro and later Petro-Canada. Equally dramatic was the partial breakout of public enterprise provincially into the resource and manufacturing industries – most particularly the Société générale de financement in Quebec (a manufacturing holding company), the Saskatchewan resource companies in oil, potash and mining (SaskOil, Potash Corporation of Saskatchewan and the Saskatchewan Mining Development Corporation respectively), and the mixed-ownership steel company IPSCO and the Alberta Energy Company. Manitoba created small oil and gas and mining companies. The B.C. Petroleum Corporation was established in British Columbia in the early 1970s as a natural gas marketing intermediary. Cancel and other forest products companies and the Dunhill Development Corporation (land development) were also established in that period under public ownership in B.C. Major provincial broadcasting corporations were established in Ontario and Quebec, and broadcasting organizations in Alberta and then B.C. were also set up. The provincial railways, like B.C. Railway (formerly the Pacific Great Eastern) and Ontario Northland, went back in time.

It wasn't just that public ownership could raise the necessary sums of capital whereas private enterprise could not. In most cases it wasn't that at all. In the 1930s, despite the depression, there was sufficient capital in the country as a whole for a national radio network. Organized in private-enterprise terms, however, radio here would have been just an offshoot of the American networks which had already staked out Canadian territory as their own. In the post-war period, there was plenty of capital to underwrite the oil industry but, unlike our publicly owned electricity and telephone companies, the major companies in the field, generating investment capital through operations, were foreign, mostly American-owned. Our money went into their ownership. Our banks then bankrolled the takeover by those foreign companies of other oil companies that had been established by Canadians, companies, also, whose owners did not have the tenacity to fight it out. Canada's automobile industry, earlier, had gone the same way. Imperial Oil was originally founded by Canadians, only to be sold to Standard Oil (now Exxon). Only when public enterprise was finally untied and Petro-Canada was formed did indigenous ownership establish itself among the major national oil and gas companies.

The same applied in other cases. Ontario and Manitoba hydro power were coveted by private enterprise, with plenty of access to necessary capital. Air transport was also coveted by private enterprise. The privately owned CPR, financially, could have easily managed to buy up the bankrupt roads that went to form the CNR. Prairie telephones, automobile insurance, hydro power in B.C. and Quebec and potash in Saskatchewan were taken over in the face of opposition from private enterprise. So were grain elevators (by the wheat pools) and grain marketing. The Treasury Branches were established notwithstanding the existence of well-heeled chartered banks. In all of these instances, Canadians chose public enterprise consciously as the better alternative.

There were setbacks. Some efforts at manufacturing in agrarian Saskatchewan in the 1940s — a woollen mill, tannery and shoe factory — to make use of natural materials from the province, weren't well thought out and were given up. Several post-war hospitalization cases in Manitoba (from small aircraft to bus assembly) couldn't overcome difficulties. Quebec's abortive attempt to re-establish its steel industry on the ashes of privately owned Dosco proved costly and, in retrospect, was ill-timed. There were embarrassments as well, like AECL's hospitalization of a corroded heavy water plant in Glace Bay, which ran into expensive problems (AECL's two heavy water plants in Nova Scotia eventually had to be closed down when expected nuclear expansion didn't take place). Sysco, the steel plant in Glace Bay, has been a story of difficulties unto itself.

Most of these and similar cases were attempts to pick up after private enterprise despite the odds, in order to maintain employment or an industrial sector or, on the Prairies, to promote additional manufacturing activity. They functioned on the economic margins.

106

Aside from that, public enterprise is not immune from mistakes and failures. But economic development never occurs in a straight line.

The accomplishments of public enterprise in Canada are all the more impressive when one considers that the establishment of many Crown corporations faced fierce political battles and often the wholesale hostility of predominant private business, and that public enterprise in most cases could not diversify, especially into manufacturing, without raising howls about intruding on "private enterprise's territory." The detailed story of this entrepreneurial tradition I tell in *A Nation Unaware*.[4] It is one of the notable success stories of economic history – only one of a great number, of course, but no less significant and instructive for all that.

Now, the more sophisticated and intellectual proponents of privatization in Canada realize that it is hard to argue with success. Some of them will even allow that public enterprise was necessary for Canada in putting capital and skills together (ignoring that in most cases this wasn't the reason for its establishment). They will even admit that public enterprise has done a good job. Nevertheless they ardently urge – almost as if they are afraid it isn't true, or won't be true if action is delayed – that whatever the achievements and vigour of public enterprise in the past, its entrepreneurial culture is no longer relevant.

If their ideological wishing would make it so, they would, of course, be right. Nothing, however, could be more doctrinal, and more fanciful. And the aspect of public enterprise which they criticize most strenuously – namely, its community impulse – is exactly the aspect which gives public enterprise its particular entrepreneurial strength.

10.
Community-Centred Enterprise

Adam Beck, the founder of Ontario Hydro, was a crusty and fierce protagonist, whose entrepreneurial intensity was legend. He isn't alone, in the annals of Canadian public enterprise, for having had a special entrepreneurial energy. Henry Thornton, the first president of the CNR, set out to make a proud national railroad from a grab-bag shambles of bankrupted private railway companies. He also set out to build up the economic confidence of the country and increase settlement in order to support the railway. Thornton was more important than the prime minister, some people said, and better known too – an entrepreneurial pop star when Lee Iacocca was still a toddler. The creative vision and determination of Alan Plaunt and Graham Spry, two exceptional figures, led to the creation of the CBC. The formation of the publicly owned radio network in Canada, with the ambitious and powerful American networks about to move in, ranks as perhaps the greatest entrepreneurial innovation in Canadian history.

One could trace the same forces of determination through the development of most public enterprise in the country, federally and provincially, although the main protagonists weren't always as colourful as a Beck or a Thornton. Some, because of their style, were hardly known by the greater public, like Gordon McGregor. McGregor, who was president of Trans-Canada Air Lines (now Air

Canada) from 1948 to 1968, led in the creation of a foremost and innovative airline in a country where much of the rest of business was in awe of the United States. Or some, like Norman Bortnick, are simply forgotten. Bortnick, as the first general manager of the Insurance Corporation of British Columbia, engineered the creation of the largest general insurance company in the country, building the corporation from scratch, overnight as it were, when the private insurance companies withheld claims information and accident records. Canadians, probably even most Quebeckers among them, wouldn't be able to name the executives who led in the building of Hydro-Québec and the James Bay project, but was there ever, in the whole country, an entrepreneurial achievement quite like it?

Where does this special entrepreneurial energy come from? Individuals themselves had a lot to do with it, but there was always something much broader, and deeper, animating the enterprise. The building of the CNR in the 1920s involved a nationalist stirring and self-assertion throughout the country, of which Henry Thornton was only a spokesman, albeit an eloquent one. Ontario Hydro was the product of the same community self-assertion: the determination of southern Ontario and southern-Ontario manufacturing to have the lowest possible electricity rates and not to fall irretrievably behind the industrial power of the United States. Québecois patriotism gave to Hydro-Québec, the symbol of Québecois self-assertion, a special edge of entrepreneurial animation. And so on, in one form or another, through the different parts of the entrepreneurial stream.

This is "community-centred enterprise" — enterprise animated by a sense of community. Different forces can touch such enterprise: the impulse to do things in a better way for the community; to build something in one's own country or region; to show what one's people can do; to develop indigenous entrepreneurship and innovation; to eliminate gouging of the public by exploitive companies; to keep alive or resuscitate a vital industry and give it the technological and capital base to contend; to meet an important strategic need; to create enterprise sensitive to workers, the environment and other elements of one's community; to keep one's own region or country abreast of others, without which it falls behind and, if it grows dependent on others, even loses some of its decision-making powers. Not least is the impulse to do things as part of one's community. Individual pride as a member of the community – sharing its objectives and ideals – comes into it.

These are powerful entrepreneurial impulses, that combine with the ordinary motors of competition and achievement. They are present in some strands of private enterprise. They work in often indirect and intangible ways, day to day, touching the workforce as well as management. They are carried forward in the aspirations of the community and in the corporate culture, although their intensity varies as the enterprise matures or as the community changes, or in response to external challenges.

The impulse to move one's country or region forward is also a powerful force for meeting international competition. The community impulse in an enterprise also enhances competition in market situations. Community-centred enterprise is both of the past and of the future. And of this entrepreneurship, Canadian public enterprise, not surprisingly, is a leading example.

Privatization doctrine is blind to this entrepreneurial force. It excludes community. At the core of the doctrine is an idea of enterprise which quite simply leaves public enterprise out. In the doctrine, the entrepreneur is the profit-maximizer impelled by nothing more than acquisitiveness, whether in selling goods or services or trading in corporate properties. Stripped down to its naked doctrinal purity, the image is one of enterprise as greed, as if greed were a transcending emotion that puts the market to work and sweeps the interference of anything else away. In this notion of enterprise, further, the community impulse is a foreign body, a kind of malignant tumor that only gets in the way and needs to be excised. It not only hinders the untrammelled spirit of enterprise, but it also may alter or deflect, and therefore detract from, the beneficent workings of market forces. Even where this may happen ever so slightly, it is to be deplored, according to the doctrine.

This image of enterprise has become increasingly prevalent in North America in the last decade. It is no accident that this is also the image of enterprise entertained by the stock market bureaucracies and the world of paper entrepreneurship, which have been on the rise and have imposed themselves. It is also the image drawn up by many branches of business schools and the business press, themselves increasingly catering to and reflecting the New Bureaucracy, and by the mass media which, with a delayed reaction, have followed in their train. Nor is it an accident that in the privatization campaign in Great Britain this singular image of enterprise should be celebrated, and that greed and the accumulation of wealth by financial manoeuvres ("sexy-greedy" in fashionable London jargon) should be lauded in its wake.

In real life, however, greed is a limited motor of entrepreneurial creativity and is often destructive of entrepreneurship. The major factors of entrepreneurial creativity are personal and social pride and the sheer zest and satisfaction of practical striving and invention – these in turn coming from achievement, building, creating, excelling, winning in competition, contributing to one's community and even to mankind. This is no less the case for private enterprise. Even in the brash days of early industrial development in the United States – where the imagery of entrepreneur as greedy buccaneer took root – it was the case.

Look at some of the major figures. Henry Ford regularly denounced the profit motive and did not care for money. Excessive profits, in Ford's view, hindered progress and the access of the ordinary person to the new products of industry. William Durant, the driving founder of General Motors, on more than one occasion turned a deal over to his company without a dollar for himself. "Successful leadership . . .," an acquaintance once wrote, "really counts more with him than financial success." Sensitivity and pride were Durant characteristics. John D. Rockefeller, the embodiment of puritan acquisitiveness, did care for money, but as part of an ordered, rational, almost divine mission of economic progress. "I believe the power to make money is a gift of God . . . to be developed and used to the best of our ability for the good of mankind," he once said. His rationalization of the oil industry into a "pool" was a move to bring order out of grasping and greed. The great inventors of that era, from Thomas Edison to Alexander Graham Bell, were interested in ideas, innovation and development. Mere greed would not have got their mental engines even to turn over. "The stereotyped old-style entrepreneur with his preoccupation with profits and profits alone was a myth," wrote two historians of American business. "The owner entrepreneur or the manager with a large personal stake in his company was interested in much more than profit."[1]

Greed, on the other hand, could be predatory and destructive. Its practitioners were recognized even in those days — maybe more so in those days — as an inferior species. The more notorious stock market players of the post civil-war era in the U.S. — equivalent to the paper entrepreneurs and the greenmailers of today — were known as "wreckers" and "hyenas," and wreck they did. People like Andrew Carnegie and Henry Ford, great entrepreneurial prototypes of the steel age and automobile age respectively, scorned the stock exchange crowd and found the culture of it repugnant.

Economic development and entrepreneurship are much more than a few notable individuals in any case. Entrepreneurial currents and the multitude of people who participate in them are products of their societies. The work ethic and scientific education have been basic factors in modern industrial development (the U.S. and Germany overtook Britain economically in no small part because of their educational systems; today, the one factor most singled out by observers of the economic rise of Japan is its educational system). With the advent of the assembly line and the modern corporation, organizational and social skills also came into play. Co-operation became important. Also, starting in the nineteenth century, the thrust of commercial expansion and empire-building, and, in some cases, sheer proximity to the economic leaders (Great Britain and then the United States), brought home to one country after another how far they were behind or how economically vulnerable they were. Another factor, and by no means a new one, began to play a role in modern economic development: economic nationalism stemming from the sense of community in countries. This sensibility was intertwined with enterprise throughout much of western Europe, especially in countries like France, Germany and Italy. Western Europe's varied public enterprises grew out of it. Public enterprise in Canada is by no means alone, as a community-centred entrepreneurial tradition.

Perhaps nowhere did the sense of community play a greater entrepreneurial role and frame the very nature of enterprise, however, than in the country whose success now has private-enterprise America on the run, namely Japan. The Japanese case is worth looking at by itself.

In 1955, long before Japanese entrepreneurship became a fashionable subject, Gustav Ranis, an historian at Yale University, published a short article on what he called the "community-centred entrepreneur" in Japanese development, in a journal called *Explorations in Entrepreneurial History*.[2] It's from Ranis' essay that I have borrowed the term "community-centred entrepreneur."

Ranis discussed how Japanese entrepreneurship developed, starting from the days when Admiral Perry of the U.S. navy dropped anchor off Japan in 1853 and made demands for trading rights and port concessions. Unable to fend against the power of western gunboats, feudal Japan set out to modernize and to strengthen itself.

All kinds of people in all kinds of structures can fulfill the entrepreneurial function – closing the gap between the actual and the potential, Ranis commented of the process. At one extreme, he wrote, is the caricature of the government official, "an individual with very few intense desires of any kind, least of all for change." Even if we soften the caricature, the government official is likely to emerge as "the tradition-oriented type with a formidable stake in the preservation of a routinized approach to doing things."

At the other end of the spectrum is the "auto-centered entrepreneur" who "wants to accumulate wealth or power for himself by his individual action," although, as a byproduct, he may accumulate wealth or power for the community. This is "the time-honored Faustian individual motivated by the inexplicable inner springs of his being to search, to change, to juxtapose" – the ideal free-enterprise prototype. Ranis observed, simply, that "this ideal type will not be found in Japan."

Somewhere between the two lies the "community-centred entrepreneur" who "seeks to accumulate wealth or power for the community by his individual action; as a byproduct he may, and very likely will, accumulate wealth or power for himself." The motivation is "to further the ends of the community; the individual seeks to grow, not so much in the reflection of his wealth, a private good, as in the prestige of the cohesive unit, a social good."

If an obsession of some sort, a prime mover, is required to explain entrepreneurial behaviour, Ranis continued, "we encounter it here in the form of an obsession with national strength and survival, a desire, in the small, to perpetuate the family fief in the service of the country. This is what community-centred entrepreneurship connotes." And this was the heart of the new Japanese entrepreneurship.

Ranis traced the development of this entrepreneurship from its initial post-feudal days to an era of major government enterprise and to government investment in infrastructure and in developing expertise. Having established one successful enterprise after another under government ownership, Japan then began transferring factories to private ownership. Almost all of them went to the zaibatsu, the industrial oligarchy, at ridiculously low prices. It was much like transferring property within a family, however, for the zaibatsu were another branch of the same entrepreneurial tree, grafted on, and could be depended upon to make the right decisions. Indeed, the zaibatsu were often led by the community-centred entrepreneur from government. Other personnel transfer was frequent. It was a case of moving community-centred entrepreneurship about.

Ranis characterized the situation this way: that "throughout the business community there was room for individual action within a conscious social framework built largely on the basis of quasi-hierarchical obligations; the traditional super-family concept continued to permeate the modern Japanese economy to an amazing degree." Decisions were made "in the light of collective goals." The "primary human relationships" of community "never weakened sufficiently here to bring about attempts at compensation solely, or even largely, through the accumulation of money or power for the individual."

The zaibatsu were broken up by the American occupation authorities after World War II, but the distinctive community-centred Japanese economic culture remained, with the sense of community and of national achievement a powerful entrepreneurial factor. Its most vivid and direct expression was in the famous Ministry of International Trade and Industry (MITI) which virtually ran the post-war economy. The former holding-company role of the zaibatsu was recreated in terms of their banks, but the entrepreneurial role of the banks was in turn both financially underwritten (with "overloans") and managed by the state-owned central bank, the Bank of Japan, according to MITI industrial strategy guidelines. Other publicly owned banks, like the Export-Import Bank and the Japan Development Bank, underwrote enterprise with direct loans, again following MITI policy. The practice of *amakudari* ("descending from heaven"), by which leading MITI and other officials in their mid-fifties "descend" to major executive roles in corporations, maintained and enriched the community-centred corporate culture. Even companies like Honda and Sony that eschewed this indirect government sponsorship were part of Japan's community-centred entrepreneurship where country comes first and company comes second. The pride in craftsmanship by workers in the countless supplier companies was also, in part, an expression of this entrepreneurial culture; the connection between this commitment and a sense of common endeavour went back to the earliest days of industrial development. This is the true meaning of "Japan, Inc.," not its governmental industrial planning or its developmental subsidies, incentives and financial guarantees.

Community-centred entrepreneurship takes different forms in different social environments or countries, depending on the traditions and make-up of those countries themselves. In Canada, it has been Crown corporations. Remember where in the entrepreneurial spectrum Gustav Ranis located community-centred enterprise. At one extreme is the auto-centred entrepreneur, wanting to accumulate wealth for himself. At the other extreme is the stereotype of the routinized bureaucrat. In the middle is the community-centred entrepreneur "who seeks to accumulate wealth or power for the community . . . to further the ends of the community." This is where Crown corporations are located in the spectrum.

Culturally speaking, it may be impossible to altogether privatize a major company in Japan. It will always be part of Japan Inc. The interventionist and entrepreneurial Japanese administration has controlled privately owned Japanese companies more closely in many cases than Canadian governments control some of their Crown corporations. But Canada isn't Japan, which is why we have Crown corporations. They capture the community impulse for purposes of entrepreneurship in a way that would not otherwise happen here. Private enterprise in North America is too much private enterprise.

Paul Frankel, the English business journalist, described the same community-centred entrepreneurship in France.

> French public enterprise was initiated by civil servants and
> run by a curious, but in many cases remarkable, brand of
> business administrators dedicated to their task, efficient,

intelligent, single-minded and incorruptible . . . . That French public enterprises attracted a certain *elite* of industrialists might to some extent have been due to the scope for them there to fulfil certain technocratic ambitions for which private investors were not (or not yet) ready. There is, however, another essential element: the opportunity of doing a big job, which the man of action cannot easily resist, was enhanced by the underlying knowledge that the effort was expended not to swell the coffers of some capitalist or other, but directly in the interests of the nation — 'All this and Heaven too. . . .'3

The prototypical example was Pierre Dreyfus of Renault.

In Italy, the ENI and IRI played the same community-centred role. They gave Italy an entrepreneurial zest and pride by harnessing the longing not to be forever trailing in the wake of Germany, France and Britain because, by an accident of geography, Italy had missed out on coal and iron ore.

Frankel refers to the same community-centred impulse in, yes, of all places, Great Britain:

In Britain nationalised coalmining, railways and power generation have drawn into their orbit a galaxy of men such as Beeching, Robens, Hinton and Edwards who, coming from very different ways of life, had in common the idea that they were not there merely to administer what there was, but to set a high standard of industrial performance as a service to the community.4

Frankel's book, in which this appeared, was published in 1966. The decade 1958-68 was an age of impressive productivity growth in the nationalized industries.

Like Japanese and other community-centred enterprise, and unlike many Canadian companies, Crown enterprise in Canada is not interested in selling out to foreign owners for a capital gain. A sell-out would be abdication. It would remove the enterprise from the community of which it is a part, and sacrifice the long run of entrepreneurial development.

A community-centred enterprise may establish or buy subsidiaries abroad, and may contract production abroad, but if, at the same time, it abandons enterprise and work at home, it is betraying its own nature. It has been said that one of the reasons the Japanese hesitated in taking over companies overseas was fear of offending, yet the Americans have never had that fear. Could it be that the Japanese, their own enterprise so "community-centred," were unable to conceive that other countries would not be offended if significant parts of their entrepreneurial base were bought out from under them?

Community-centred enterprise, in particular publicly owned enterprise, relates to the community in other ways. Ready to invest in new ventures or to expand, it acts as protection against investment blackmail – what is known in academic jargon as "capital strikes." It protects, in this way, the political freedom of elected representatives. Governments don't have to abjectly give way on proper resource "rents" (royalties, taxes, stumpage), tax levels in general, labour laws, and environmental and safety regulations every time a corporation or industrial group threatens to take its capital and expertise elsewhere. They don't have to play investment beggar, with cap in hand.

Public enterprise provides the public, through government, with a "window on the industry" – a level of expertise and information about industry which comes only through direct involvement, and without which the public is at the mercy of corporate manipulation. This was one of the reasons for the establishment of Petro-Canada, the Potash Corporation of Saskatchewan and Manitoba Mineral Resources. Information about technology and costs from a publicly owned participant can also be used for gauging efficiency and price when it comes to public contracting – promoting efficiency and preventing the padding of tenders. During World War II, Crown corporations in each of the major wartime industries – small arms, munitions and aircraft – enabled the government to assess the efficiency of privately owned plants in war production. The creation by ICBC of a test body shop allowed the insurance company to introduce new technology and to assess body shop prices.

Another characteristic of the community-centred model is the high priority it places on the long-term development of productivity, technology and a skilled and educated work force. It is not alone in doing this – the best of enterprise everywhere takes a long-term view – but the community-centred model generically is more resistant to the pressures of short-termism and the hoots and hollers of stock-market players. Enterprises still need to make a profit over the long term and seize opportunities. Not the size of profit, though, but the development of the enterprise is what matters.

Crown corporations, by giving economic expression to Canada's sense of community, or to a regional sense of community, also add to and reinforce that sense of community. They amplify our identity. They underscore the point that people are members of a community first and not just participants in an impersonal economic game. Privatization, as a result, does make Canada, or a region within Canada, the less.

At the same time, the public ownership of Crown corporations avoids one of the critical disadvantages of the old zaibatsu in Japan and of corporate private-enterprise generally. It is democratic ownership. It does not create oligarchic or minority ownership power – power as often as not built at the expense of the general public in the first place. The zaibatsu industrial enterprises, for example, did not arise out of some heroic entrepreneurial feat in an unforgiving environment. They were built up through manipulation of the tax rate by the government and through an exemption-riddled definition of the tax base. They were built, in other words, on the backs of the farmer, the labourer and the small businessman. The idea was to tax away the surplus from ordinary people, who might spend their money in any old way, and channel it into areas that were deemed by national policy to be important and where the zaibatsu could be depended upon.

Tax policy in West Germany after World War II, similarly, heavily favoured profits so as to maximize retained earnings for new investment in priority sectors and help rebuild the shattered economy. It did stimulate reconstruction, but it had an intractable negative side-effect. The small minority who got into business on the ground floor after the war grew asset-rich as their retained earnings piled up without their paying a fair share of taxes. The rest of the population, which was putting its shoulder to the wheel, got the short end of the stick. Something much the same happened in post-war Japan. In the same way, corporate and investment tax expenditures and loopholes in Canada, supposedly for community goals (investment and economic development), ended up accentuating the wealth of a minority of people and helped to create some extraordinary family fiefdoms – and did not achieve the increased investment and innovation for which they were intended, thrown into the measure. The asset ownership of Crown corporations, on the other hand, is equally distributed.

The stronger the sense of community, the more powerful is the added impetus that community-centred enterprises enjoy. Similarly, if the idea of community in economic enterprise is always being denigrated — if private ownership and private-sector activities are put on a pedestal while public enterprise is ideologically downgraded — then the community impulse in the enterprise is diminished and the entrepreneurial imagination is weakened, although the enterprise can continue to function quite successfully in private-enterprise terms. Given the ideological environment in Canada and the impact on Canada of private-enterprise ideological doctrine in the U.S., what is most remarkable about our public enterprises is how strong they are. It shows, indirectly, that Canadians' sense of community is a stubborn, underlying force of its own.

The Americans, whose business ideology has denied community-centred enterprise even where it exists, are now groping for some kind of answer as to why their mastery is in decline. Dissident American observers like Robert Reich, who have documented this American syndrome, attempt to develop a philosophy of economic community. Reich bemoans the fact that Americans are "losing the competitive struggle because we cannot work together," and calls for "ideals and institutions that inspire citizens to work together" without fear of being victimized by the opportunism of others.[5] Many in the United States are now belatedly, painfully, discovering what the creators of public enterprise in Canada always knew. Community does count. But where a prominent investment dealer like Ivan Boesky can extol unvarnished greed to the most eminent business school in the country and not be hooted at, and where stock exchanges are treated like economic temples, propagating the idea of a community-centred economy is hard-going.

Community-centred entrepreneurship also applies to the larger picture of economic strategy and planning, and has for centuries. Economic competition between communities goes back all the way to the mercantile days of Queen Elizabeth I in Britain and Charles V of Spain in the sixteenth century. John A. Macdonald's National Policy is another example. A community works together, sometimes limiting competition and assuring markets at home so as to better vie and contend in the world.

Two of the most telling cases of containing local competition recently, as part of a community-centred entrepreneurial strategy, occurred in Japan. In one, all computer companies were brought together into a single research and development organization, called the Co-operative Laboratory. This laboratory, in turn, was given a hefty subsidy in the form of interest-free loans. The aim was to close the gap in computer technology between Japan and the U.S., and then pass the Americans. Once the new-generation technology was developed, the three computer groups (reduced from six companies) could market the results separately.

In the second case, the publicly owned Japan Development Bank organized a leasing company for robots. It guaranteed the makers of robots a market for so many thousands of units per year. It then offered the robots to industries on an annual-lease basis, saving them large up-front costs and allowing them to return the robots if they didn't work. The scheme constituted a considerable risk on the part of the leasing company – a community risk. The robots, however, did work, and because of the scale of production, the makers of the robots got down the learning curve so fast that it was extremely difficult for the Americans and others to catch up.

Similarly, while doctrinaire privatization advocates rail against public monopolies not having to face competition, they may have been facing it all the time: not market competition, or restrained private-enterprise oligopoly competition, but community-centred competition against other regions and other countries. This has always been the case with major Canadian publicly owned monopolies. Ontario Hydro from its inception fought against, and measured its rates against, the privately owned power companies across the border (Ontario Hydro, incidentally, won hands down). Canadians look upon their publicly owned hydro utilities to give them the cheapest possible power so that they have some kind of comparative advantage over the United States. The prairies look to their telephone companies, in telecommunications, to keep them abreast of Ontario and Quebec and their much denser populations. Air Canada, when it had a domestic trunk route monopoly in the 1950s, measured its fares and service against the American airlines. So did its customers, and that competitive pressure was fierce too, sometimes so unreasonable that Air Canada finally welcomed mere market competition domestically, as a relief.

Ironically for privatization doctrine, when a monopoly like British Gas is privatized, the public gets the worst of both worlds. There still isn't any market competition to speak of, and to artificially introduce market competition for its own sake would break up economies of scale and of integrated operation. But, also, the community pressure that was behind the public enterprise – making comparison with other countries and regions – loses its edge. Privatization of monopolies takes the community-based competition out.

Often, too, a domestic monopoly makes eminent sense structurally, and not only in utility cases. The Canadian Wheat Board is a monopoly that eliminated speculative depredation at home and enabled farmers to make the most out of having to compete in world markets. When the CBC radio network monopoly in the 1930s was established (first as the Canadian Radio Broadcasting Commission), people at the time insisted that the Canadian effort not be fragmented because only with its efforts concentrated could Canadian programming contend against what the powerful American networks were offering. The Air Canada (Trans-Canada Air Lines) monopoly in the 1940s and 1950s enabled Canadians to vie with the Americans and their much denser traffic, by allowing for the most efficient matching of capacity and equipment to demand.

These cases are variations of community-centred entrepreneurship at work, where competition against other countries is foremost. Privatization doctrine, which denies any value to community-centred entrepreneurship in general, also flies against this particular form of it. Privatization theology plumps for untrammelled market competition, a tenet almost as fundamental to it as private ownership itself. But what does it profit a country if it denies community, and allows untrammelled competition, speculation and corporate game-playing at home, while entire sectors are being outpaced by community-centred entrepreneurship from abroad?

This has finally hit home in the U.S. semi-conductor industry, where member companies, staggered by Japanese competition in the mid-1980s, have been trying to patch together an industry co-operative for developing new chip-manufacturing technologies. One company president, reflecting on the situation in a television interview, wistfully noted how this was happening to the most private-enterprise of players, the mavericks of the Silicon Valley. One such executive cowboy told the *New York Times*, "I think when we have a national purpose, we can reverse the tide."[6]

Did he indeed say "national purpose?" He was talking almost like a community-centred entrepreneur.

By the same token, selling off public enterprises in Canada is more than just an account-book transaction. It undermines community-centred entrepreneurship — Canadians' sense of being in the economy together — by giving what belongs to all of us to financial gameplayers with loyalty to no one but themselves.

Public enterprise, in short, represents the community incarnate in at least a few economic enterprises and the privatizer doesn't want to be reminded of it, is offended by it, feels uncomfortable with it. But, as examples as diverse as Canada and Japan have shown, in expunging community one is expunging as well one of the deepest of economic wellsprings.

11.
Public Enterprise in the Competitive Marketplace

Like a lazy dog howling in one yard, and another dog picking up the howl, and then another dog responding, and another, until there is a motley and comic barking everywhere in the neighbourhood, privatization advocates have been howling to the sky about "competitive market situations." They try to use mere barking of the phrase to get rid of public ownership.

The clamour goes like this. If it's a monopoly situation, then a public enterprise may be all right; it protects the public against rate-gouging. (A true privatizer isn't even satisfied with that concession.) A public enterprise established for development purposes in a money-losing situation, like the Cape Breton Development Corporation, is also acceptable. Hospitalization of a failed private firm, if hospitalization is agreed on, is similarly fine. By the same token, a publicly owned Air Canada was all right in the past, although not in the present, because, in the past, there was cross-subsidization of routes. Air Canada (Trans-Canada Air Lines) was also appropriate for pioneering air transport when the traffic densities in Canada were not so commercially attractive.

If, however, there aren't any such "social policy" functions to Crown corporations, we must sell them off pronto, the argument continues. "Competitive market situations," where private enterprise is willing and able to take over, are just such cases. Get Air Canada,

CN and Petro-Canada out of the way. Dedicated privatizers will similarly try to insert into any monopoly situation at least a little colour of competition around the fringes — a sliver of business communications here, access to the gas distribution system there, anything at all regardless of whether it makes sense or whether it's meaningful — in order to provide an excuse for privatization. "Look, ma, no monopoly," they can say, "we can privatize now."

The *Globe and Mail* bays the most eloquently on the subject. "Why should Ottawa own Air Canada or Petro-Canada as we contemplate the 1990s?" it asks rhetorically in an editorial. "Surely the onus is on the state to justify such dominant participation in private markets."[1] Why the onus should be on public ownership to justify being part of our economy, and why markets should be described as being "private" as if they were a club from which public enterprises should be blackballed, the *Globe and Mail* doesn't say. It is just assumed, as if public ownership's being in the market were abnormal, a perversion of nature.

Some people even point to the commercial success of public ownership as its own downfall. As long as companies like Air Canada, CN and Petro-Canada had their "social policy" functions, they weren't in danger of being privatized, goes the argument. Once those social policy functions are stripped away, however, they become sitting ducks for privatization. If only they were money-losers, then some vague, residual social policy might be assumed: the maintenance of some worthwhile activities or services despite the loss of money. But, wouldn't you know it, the public enterprises are commercially successful instead. Before, their public ownership was attacked for not being commercial enough. After, their public ownership was attacked and privatization demands rang out because they were commercial.

Petro-Canada is a classic case. Part of its original mandate was to lead the way in long-range frontier exploration and act as a catalyst where privately owned corporations were loath to go. It did this resolutely, with most notable success in the Hibernia field. Critics charged, however, that all this long-range expenditure was a misallocation of resources. Then oil prices fell. Frontier exploration was deemed to be not so much of a priority. It also cost a lot of money without any immediate cash flow in return. Petro-Canada was instructed to act like a commercial company. It did this resolutely as well. It cut back on its frontier exploration and wrote down its frontier assets. It was as impressive a performer under its new orders as under its old ones. Now critics shouted that "it's just another oil company" — that it's behaving commercially — and should be privatized. Public ownership was damned either way.

The Air Canada case is a similar one. Some detractors of the airline suggested that Air Canada executives were hanging on desperately to their airline's social policy mandate because, as long as it existed, the executives could get protection from out-and-out competition due to the company's role as the national airline with its many responsibilities. The hidden inference was that somehow Air Canada, although it appeared to be extraordinarily successful as an airline and competed widely, was actually second-grade and its executives were cowards, just what we should expect to get from public ownership. Then, as circumstances changed, Air Canada responded, almost too eagerly. It had to defend itself from charges of abandoning social responsibility with such decisions as discontinuing jet service to some smaller centres. It was now accused of being too commercial. Its original critics have changed their tune. They now charge that since Air Canada has become "commercial" — is quite willing to operate without social policy obligations and the presumed protection that goes with it — the reason for its public ownership no longer exists and the airline should be privatized forthwith.

But contrary to all this, and aside from the other advantages of public enterprise, there is a compelling reason for public ownership which has to do with commercial operation and "competitive market situations" themselves: *a publicly owned participant in any major sector makes the market work better.*

It was old Adam Smith who wrote that "people of the same trade seldom meet together, even for merriment and diversion, but the conversation ends in a conspiracy against the public or in some contrivance to raise prices." How can one best protect the consumer and the public from oligopolistic price-gouging? A public-enterprise participant — which has no interest in excessive profits, which is owned by the public itself, and which is part of a public-service tradition — provides potent protection against private-enterprise oligopoly. It also can provide market leadership. The different ownership – different from private corporations – is the key.

Ever since 1920, we have had a publicly owned and a privately owned railroad facing off against each other – in the early days not only in freight but also in passenger service and first-class hotels. Canadians instinctively did not trust a private CPR monopoly or a privately owned duopoly. We have had similar competition between Air Canada and, in the past, CP Air (now part of Canadian Airlines International). Critics liked to point to what they saw as the co-operation of the two airlines – their filing identical fare-increase applications, for example. Notwithstanding that, Air Canada kept fares so low that, overall, they matched or bettered American fares. While providing sufficient return, the fares allowed so little surplus margin that they eventually forced the most powerful holding company in the country, CP Investments, to get out of the airline business.

A co-operative participant in any one market similarly enhances competition ("maintains competitive markets") and for the same general reason. Its ownership is different in kind and it is part of a different entrepreneurial tradition (in this case, the co-operative movement, dedicated to its customers as member-owners). Take credit unions. They pioneered innovation after innovation in retail banking – from daily interest and automated teller machines to variable mortgage payments and personal lines of credit – often a decade or more ahead of the chartered banks. It wasn't too long ago that if the earner in a family was a woman of child-bearing age, she couldn't get a mortgage from her chartered bank. The banks were not only arrogant, insensitive and hidebound, they were culturally behind the times. Credit unions, from a different and socially rooted entrepreneurial culture, provided those mortgages. Daily interest is another interesting case. The banks simply refused to provide it, and dragged their feet even after the credit unions went ahead. Vancouver City Savings Credit Union, which first offered daily interest, did so because its general manager, steeped in the co-operative tradition, decided that since the credit union itself was getting daily interest on its loans, it could not very well deny its member-owners daily interest on their deposits.

If there had been a large publicly owned national bank, or even regional banks, the banking system overall would have been even more diverse and responsive. Dave Barrett, as NDP premier, was a supporter of a provincial publicly owned bank. So, to a degree, was W.A.C. Bennett, Barrett's Social Credit predecessor, who fought hard for a provincial bank with 25 per cent government equity. Both realized that the privately owned national chartered banks were not the be all and end all, despite their numbers and the facade of market competition, and that B.C. economic development was being hindered by the lack of an alternative. In 1944, Ernest Manning, the Social Credit premier of Alberta, had applied for a charter to operate a provincial bank in that province, to no avail against a rigid Ottawa and the political influence of the existing banking oligopoly.

There should be a Crown enterprise and a co-operative enterprise in a range of "competitive-market" sectors, including manufacturing, where the possibilities arise; this not just for the buyer's or consumer's sake but also for entrepreneurial liveliness and economic development. In some cases, there might be two Crown corporations, one federal and one provincial, in oil and gas, for example. Add to that the co-operative movement on the prairies, which has had an oil refinery for decades, plus bulk fuel distribution and service stations, and is now a joint partner in a heavy oil project. Recently, the Co-operative Energy Corporation, with 50 per cent co-operative and 50 per cent federal Crown ownership, has been added; its operating company is Co-enerco. The co-operative oil business in Canada had revenues in 1985 of more than $1 billion. The Mouvement Desjardins (Quebec credit unions) has an investment subsidiary which holds equity in various enterprises, taking an active role in economic development.

The creation of Crown-owned mining companies in Saskatchewan (SMDC) and Quebec (SOQUEM) was a step in this direction, leaving aside the controversial question of uranium mining in Saskatchewan. So was the public ownership of Cancel (forest products) in British Columbia and Rexfor (forest products) in Quebec. In broadcasting, there are co-operative radio stations as well as the publicly owned CBC and the existing provincial networks. One of the great missed opportunities in broadcasting for Canada was the failure to create a new national channel financed and governed co-operatively by cable subscribers. The idea of municipal enterprises has yet to be developed in this country: another area for innovation. There aren't enough public and co-operative enterprises in the market economy, and some which have been created have been kept marginal (like SOQUEM) or suppressed (like Cancel).

Variety of ownership brings different entrepreneurial cultures and different crowds to the scene, and new ways of looking at things. It challenges clubbish old ways. Or to put it another way: public and co-operative enterprise adds socially rooted competition (one might even say ideologically rooted competition) to market competition. Socially rooted competition is a powerful force. Market competition by itself can often be weak, as like-minded corporate bureaucrats settle into a working arrangement with each other, something which Adam Smith's comments foreshadowed. Post-war retail banking in Canada is an example. More than just oligopoly was at play in that case. Corporate culture – the headquarters in Montreal and Toronto, the clubbish routines and pretensions, the interlocking bank and corporate boards, the self-image of banking executives as part of a corporate world, the conservative politics, the cultural homogeneity – the restricted outlook.

Compare this with the competition of the CNR and the CPR, particularly in the 1920s when passenger service was important and before the depression hit. Nothing beat it for intensity. What was at stake was not mere market share but the idea of a publicly owned railroad fighting against the long-established position of a privately owned railway which was also the central-Canadian corporate leader and the symbol of private economic power. The creation of the CNR brought into the competitive fray, over passenger train times and over the building of branch lines, an energy that the exclusively private-owned chartered banks, left to themselves, could not imagine.

Australia recognized the same competitive impetus by consciously pitting a publicly owned airline and a privately owned airline against each other within highly structured rules, like putting two boxers of the same weight category inside a ring. Market competition in air transport in a country like Canada with relatively light traffic densities – hence the use of smaller than economic aircraft and insufficient integration of traffic – is a questionable proposition, but if nevertheless you insist on market competition, a publicly owned versus privately owned arrangement is one of the best ways of getting the real thing.

One of the underlying social dynamics in Canada is the tension between the regions of the country and central rule, particularly the struggle of the West and the Atlantic against central-Canadian economic power. Why not have federally and provincially owned Crown companies competing against each other in the oil industry, and put that powerful underlying competitive dynamic to work? Imagine a Crown oil and gas company owned by the three westernmost producing provinces with Alberta in the lead. Imagine, also, that the company took over one of the privately owned integrated majors with service stations across the country, let's say Shell, and faced Petro-Canada head-on. It wouldn't be tepid competition between the likes of privately owned Esso and Shell any more. The competition would always have that little bit extra edge to it as long as Canada remained the country it is. Ironically, at one point the suggestion was made in Ottawa that a Crown competitor to Petro-Canada be set up, but the idea was dropped.

Similarly, one of the best possible innovations for Canadian television would be to establish a federated network of provincial publicly owned broadcasters to compete against the CBC in general programming. It was a profound mistake to establish the private CTV stations, which would inevitably function as offshoots of the American film and television industry, instead of setting up a public broadcasting network competing against the CBC but structured differently. The mistake was doubly compounded with the establishment of Global and similar stations later on. Canadian broadcasting gets all the challenge of American-style television it needs directly from American stations whose signals come across the border.

Many of the great innovations of public enterprise in Canada have been made in monopoly situations. Often the idea of a public monopoly was the greatest innovation of all: the rapid extension of telephone lines to rural areas on the prairies on a cross-subsidized basis, the automobile insurance companies and their savings to the public, the service-at-cost electrical utilities, the balanced marketing of the Canadian Wheat Board.

THE PRIVATIZATION PUTSCH

In competitive market situations, the different entrepreneurial cultures of public enterprise and of co-operative enterprise also come through, although not always in obvious ways. The CNR, when it was established in the 1920s, brought a new and positive attitude to labour relations far ahead of its time. It also brought a positive attitude to the development of new technology when Canadians habitually left such ambitions and possibilities to Americans and others.

One of the railway's greatest pioneering ventures was network radio. The first step was to bring radio programs to CNR parlor cars crossing the country. The railway then went on to organize the first network service in the country, with programming and stations of its own. Because of its public enterprise culture, the railroad realized both the potential of radio for the country and the need to develop a genuinely Canadian, public-service broadcasting. The CPR, in those early days of the medium, was deaf to radio. The CN Radio network precedent eventually led to the Canadian Radio-Broadcasting Commission and the CBC.

Air Canada is known in the air transport industry for its high safety and maintenance standards – a special consciousness and commitment in the airline which comes from its public-service roots. The airline is also known for its considerable effort in providing services for handicapped passengers. Air Canada introduced non-smoking flights, a public-service innovation which its chief privately-owned competitor in Canada (Canadian Airlines International) imitated only when its commercial acceptability had become obvious (major U.S. airlines belatedly followed two years after Air Canada, in the wake of government regulatory interest in the matter).

The environmental practices of Petro-Canada in frontier areas set the standard for the oil industry and helped advance environmental protection practices. The CBC does the same for Canadian content on television. Belatedly, recognition is growing that Crown corporations can lead the way "in fostering competition, encouraging private enterprise to improve the standards of its products and services, and setting the pace for standards of health and safety at work."2 Co-operative enterprise – think only of credit unions – brings other differences in entrepreneurial culture into play.

The different ownerships also bring varying structural elements with them. One of the differences between the Japanese rise in

132

manufacturing and the American competitive decline has been the greater debt financing of Japanese enterprise in the past and its greater freedom from short-term stock-market pressures. The Japanese entrepreneurial culture also looks down on hostile takeovers; they are virtually unknown in Japan. According to American doctrine (and privatization doctrine), hostile takeovers are the ultimate, indispensable way for applying the "discipline of the stock market" to inefficient companies. They usually create havoc with – and add distraction to – the entrepreneurial process instead. Crown enterprise in competitive market situations faces the discipline of the market – the market in goods and services – but avoids destructive stock market pressures and takeover games.

Crown corporations in Canada have been attacked in the past for not acting just like private corporations: not sharing the management mentality, the corporate structures, the financial gamesmanship, and the business administration tenets – written in stone and propagated in business administration schools – of the U.S. corporate model. Everybody is willing to admit now, largely because of the Japanese, how rigid and backward those dogmas were. But why ask Crown corporations to be the same anyway? Is Petro-Canada disliked by the rest of the players in the Calgary oil patch, or at least some of them? Pray God that it is so. It would be disturbing if it were not. Why do we have a publicly owned oil company in the first place, if not to make the other guys uncomfortable? For the sake of enhanced competition and entrepreneurial variety, we should be cultivating and exploring the differences. Let a thousand flowers bloom, let a thousand schools of business thought contend.

The unpredictability of public enterprise, as seen by private enterprise, may be its most competition-enhancing characteristic. Paul Frankel, the biographer of Enrico Mattei, the renowned founder of the Italian publicly owned oil company ENI (Ente Nazionale Idrocarburi), provides a graphic case history. Mattei, when he took on the Seven Sisters, accepted some of their rules and conventions but not all. He was never a member of the club. A couple of meetings between spokesmen of the majors and Mattei ended unhappily; they were too far from being the same kind of people. Mattei did all kinds of unpredictable things. He pioneered concession agreements with oil countries which gave them a participatory role in development rather than leaving them just passively collecting whatever royalties were going; this led ultimately to changing the face of the oil industry. He built refineries for third world countries which allowed them to save foreign exchange (on the refining value-added) and to buy crude from the most advantageous source, eroding the Seven Sisters' control over the "power of disposal." Caught in a supply squeeze-play himself, he imported Russian crude when any such idea was altogether taboo. Frankel cites a conversation with a senior oil executive in which the executive expresses wonder that, given the provocation, nobody had yet murdered Mattei. He was serious.

Troublemaking to the point that one would literally expect murder? That's competition! As it happened, Mattei was to die shortly in a plane crash, an accident many Italians were convinced was caused by sabotage.

Similarly, liberal Italian economists in the past — the believers in market competition — saw public enterprise as a way of checking private oligopolies and providing competition. Adam Smith, were he alive today, would plump for public-enterprise and co-operative participants in the market. If the likes of the C.D. Howe Institute, the Conference Board and the Fraser Institute really believed in the transcending virtues of market competition, they would be fighting for the inclusion of public enterprises, too. They instead want to blot them out completely — to leave no traces. Perhaps, when we look at how those "think tanks" are financed, we should not be surprised.

The privatization of Canadian Cellulose (Cancel) in 1979, as part of BCRIC, provides another case history. Cancel accounted for only 3 per cent of B.C. forest-industry production. It was a great success in commercial terms, turning an absentee-owned money-losing operation into an impressive profit-making concern on the way to long-term rehabilitation. The company was run autonomously on a commercial basis. Its board consisted of conservative businessmen, none of whom likely would have voted NDP. Nevertheless, when the government changed, it was deemed that Cancel had to go. The idea of a publicly owned forest company represented a departure and an alternative — and hence a threat — which could not be tolerated.

Imagine, instead, that private corporations, public enterprises, and co-operatives each had roughly a third of B.C. forest industry operations over the years and were equally well-established (Quebec, incidentally, has both a public-enterprise and co-operative sector in forestry). Foot-dragging over more intense reforestation, with the enormous negative long-term consequences it will have for British Columbia, might have been challenged because of the differing entrepreneurial composition of the industry. New silviculture practices might have been introduced. Badly needed diversification into new value-added production, patriating the added value from the U.S. and elsewhere – creating in effect a whole new sector – might have occurred. So might increased diversification with linkages to machinery and automation equipment. The government would have had comparative operating measures by which to assess more appropriate stumpage rates, gathering for the public treasury (and for silviculture) hundreds of millions of dollars lost in recent years – stumpage rates which were only readjusted because of U.S. countervailing measures. The cozy relationship between the privately owned companies and the government, complete with revolving door, would have been broken up. The industry would have been largely under indigenous ownership instead of out-of-province and foreign control, with all the entrepreneurial, spin-off, and financial benefits which indigenous ownership brings. Labour relations might have improved and lost production been saved instead of what recently happened: the forest companies inexplicably tried to stab the International Woodworkers of America in the back with "contracting out." This was a union which had accepted (indeed pushed for) technological change, suffered major reductions in its numbers, and held back wage demands to see the industry through difficult adjustments.

All those might-have-beens! One thing is certain, though: that the entrepreneurial variety of publicly owned and co-operative participants would have allowed entrepreneurship in the B.C. forest industry to take in breaths of fresh air – to get its lungs full of the oxygen of new ideas and of new ways of looking at the forests at home and at the world outside.

Rexfor, the publicly owned forest company in Quebec, has had its mandate artificially restricted. It is supposed to take the lead in developing new products, but always as a minority partner regardless of its contribution, and then, when the innovation begins to bear fruit, it will be obliged to get out. The same applies to the development of new forest-industry technology. Again, as a custodian and developer of forest lands, it is supposed to share as much work as possible with the private sector. It is now forbidden to expand in sawmills except in specially designated situations. It has surrendered major holdings in two operations, under the new policy developed by the government and its minister of privatization. Rexfor is supposed to do all kinds of other wonderful things as well, from developing new markets to saving operations in difficulty in marginal areas, but if the rescue operation succeeds it is to remove itself forthwith. In no circumstances is it to enter into competition with the private sector. In other words, it is to be a handmaiden to the private sector and to be locked in an entrepreneurial chastity belt if, for one reason or another, it has to leave the scullery. Genuine entrepreneurial competition is lost.

Or take SOQUEM (the Société québecoise d'exploration minière) and the SGF (Société générale de financement) in Quebec. SOQUEM was established in 1965 to step up mining exploration in Quebec when exploration, left to the private sector, was languishing ("erratic risk capital investment" is the euphemism). SOQUEM was also to be a vehicle by which francophones working in French could rise to leading executive positions in the industry. Despite starting from scratch with meager capital and being excluded from the part of the Abitibi area where the private sector was most active, SOQUEM turned out to be highly successful in making discoveries. Then, acting on a privatization scenario, the government decided to strip it down, first by obliging it to get rid of a major gold property. A committee on privatization struck by the government, made up of private sector people, did not even want to let SOQUEM exist as a charity ward exploring in high-risk areas where the private sector was unwilling to go.

Private-sector exploration has been artificially inflated and kept afloat by what are euphemistically called "fiscal incentives." Among them are the notorious "flow-through" shares, by which high-income earners are given lucrative tax breaks for putting money into mining exploration — privileged public subsidies to private mining companies, paid for by the rest of us (about $1 billion extra in our tax bill for the years 1983-87). An industry executive, when the flow-through giveaway was threatened by tax reform, cried that exploration would collapse. Add to that the Quebec Stock Savings Plan with similar tax-reduction breaks favouring the wealthy. This giveaway has cost the Quebec government $600 million in non-compounded lost revenue in its first seven years (1979-1986) alone, of which an indeterminate amount went to mining exploration. SOQUEM may be the only mining company in Quebec which isn't effectively subsidized by government to the everlasting benefit of the well-off. Aside from that, though, why this passion to get rid of little, energetic SOQUEM? Why bother? Who is it harming (in fact, ironically, its discoveries and joint ventures feed the private sector), while it provides at least something of an entrepreneurial alternative?

The same goes for the holding company SGF. The SGF was originally formed as a mixed private-public corporation but was taken over by the Crown because of mediocre results. It was a rare kind of Crown corporation in Canada inasmuch as it was involved in a substantial range of manufacturing and forest industry activities. Its task in the early years was particularly demanding in having to resuscitate firms facing difficulties or critical situations. Even the 1986 Quebec privatization committee were obliged to allow that the creation of the SGF constituted a significant addition to French-Canadian enterprise, and that, along with Hydro-Québec, it had played a major role in the development and promotion of francophone executives. Now, according to the committee, the SGF had to go, too. They could not look upon it as something normal and ongoing. Simply because the company was publicly owned, they marked it for elimination.

For believers in privatization, companies like SOQUEM and the SGF must not be allowed to stay around. Privatization advocates are a bit like Lady Macbeth, inflamed in their case by the ambition of their doctrine, wiping their hands and muttering, "Out, damned spot." Out, out, damned public-enterprise example.

"It takes all sorts to make a world," concluded oil-industry specialist Paul Frankel in his biography of Enrico Mattei. He was referring not to Mattei but to public enterprises and the role they played in economies "as a complement of and an antidote to" privately owned corporations. Other, similar reflections come to mind: "The more the merrier," for example, or "Variety is the spice of life." The desperate absolutism of privatization doctrine doesn't like to think about it.

12.
Air Canada:
Kindly Shoot Public Ownership

When it comes to public enterprises competing in market situations, nothing has made privatization advocates quite so apoplectic as the public ownership of Air Canada. Here is the *Globe and Mail*, in the late spring of 1987, more and more exasperated, nay reaching the end of its tether, about the Conservative government's shilly-shallying over the affair. "It's time to sell Air Canada," read the headline of an angry editorial. "Will the Conservatives mark out their own territory or be content with carrying out the old Liberal game plan?" the editorial shouted. "... Air Canada is the immediate issue [in the matter of privatization] and the case is overwhelming for its sale." The "overwhelming case," boiled down, was that a Crown corporation should not be involved in straight commercial competition. The editorial picked on "sentimental" defenders of Air Canada's public ownership, and lashed them for an outdated mentality that wants to keep "a national airline at whatever cost."[1]

Who would have ever thought the restrained *Globe and Mail* would show such emotion? Something had gotten under its skin, and under the skin of academic apologists for privatization who proclaimed again and again that there was simply no excuse to keep Air Canada as a Crown corporation, as if its public ownership were positively sinful.

THE PRIVATIZATION PUTSCH

Why this desperate urge to get rid of the public ownership of Air Canada, particularly when it has been such a successful and well-run enterprise? There is the answer: it has been such a successful, efficient and well-run enterprise. Privatizers declaim about how public enterprise is so inefficient, but it is really the success of public enterprise which they cannot tolerate. They privatize the winners with a vengeance. Ultimately, if allowed to go on, they would leave public enterprise with just the lame ducks of private-enterprise failure and with the orphans, which they can then point to, like stigmata, as proof of public enterprise's degraded economic character. Instead of Nathaniel Hawthorne's scarlet letter "A" for adultery, it would be scarlet letter "P" for publicly owned.

Air Canada's particular problem, for privatization ideologues, was not just that the company has been such a fine example of the success of the Canadian public-enterprise tradition. It was also an airline. Hence it carried with it all the imagery of the romance of air travel. The romance of railways has long since gone. Rail transport in Canada has declined drastically as a carrier of passengers. Even as a carrier of freight it has been pushed into the background by trucking. There is not much romance to a CN unit train carrying coal to Prince Rupert. Air transport, on the other hand, is people going places fast, business, holidays, excitement, family, meeting old friends or making new deals, destinations, foreign countries, flight attendants in designer uniforms, courtesy and service, speed, pilots sitting in front of all those dials, expertise and modernity, technology that one can almost touch, great silver birds floating through the sky and, most of all, crossing Canada. This is not the imagery that a privatizer likes to see associated with public enterprise. It is no accident that the Thatcher government had scheduled British Airways as its first major privatization, only pushing it down the list when the airline ran into financial turbulence.

If there were any practical rationale to privatization, Air Canada would be the last Crown corporation one would think of privatizing. By the animus of privatization ideology, on the other hand, it was the first one that had to go.

Most Canadians probably aren't aware of how great an entrepreneurial story publicly owned Air Canada has been. In its origins (it was then called Trans-Canada Air Lines), Air Canada brought to sparsely populated Canada a service and technological expertise which compared with, and often ranked ahead of, that of the Americans despite the advantages the latter airlines had in size and traffic densities. This was at a time when in most other sectors it was simply accepted that Americans did things better than us and that we could only follow their lead or sell out our companies and let them do it for us. At a time, too, when Canadians were used to paying more for everything than the Americans, air fares in Canada (Air Canada was the sole trunk-route carrier) were cheaper than fares for comparable flights in the U.S. Because of its policy of cross-subsidization and its public-service mandate, Air Canada also offered smaller cities in the country, like Saskatoon, Regina and cities in the Maritimes, a level of service which was the envy of similar-sized cities in the U.S. Air Canada managed all this in the face of constant hostility from a small but vocal minority of travellers who disliked the very idea of a publicly owned airline and who took it as ordained that only American private enterprise could do things rights.

This early Air Canada efficiency and tradition, in fares, service and technology, has continued to this day.

Air Canada was the first airline in North America to introduce turboprops (the famous Vickers Viscount) for commercial service, in 1955 – an innovation only surpassed later in the industry with the introduction of full jets. Air Canada was actually involved in the functional specifications of the Viscount. It subsequently became the first major airline to have an all-turbine fleet. The Viscount in particular, with Air Canada in the lead, revolutionized air travel in North America, bringing to it speed, comfort, high productivity and lower maintenance costs and making air transport a widespread and popular means of travel for the first time.

Air Canada has also been a technical innovator of its own. Some of the innovations will come as a surprise. Air Canada, in 1958, played an active role in the development of the multi-channel flight recorder, working on airworthiness and maintenance aspects (later, multi-channel versions of the recorder, known as the "black box," were widely adopted by the industry). Its RESERVEC system (automation of reservations inventory), implemented in 1961, was a world first as well as a Canadian original, and fostered extensive growth in computer-communications processes in the industry. Other developmental work, while less striking, had its own importance. Publicly owned Air Canada over the years has pioneered a whole range of de-icing technology for everything from windscreens and aerodynamic surfaces to engine chambers and jet fuel. It developed principles and methods of detecting early engine-failure warnings. In that and other ways, it has kept the airline in the forefront of technology. It has one of the largest and most efficient maintenance bases in the world, and is known in the industry for its high standards of safety and maintenance.

Air Canada, as it got older, only got better. In 1982, it won the Technical Management Award given by *Air Transport World*, a leading international aviation magazine published in Washington.[2] Air Canada was cited for "its consistent record of excellence over the years in achieving maximum productivity in the technical aspects of airline operations." Air Canada's "maintenance, fleet management and operations management," the citation continued, "are continually judged by other airlines to be among the best in the world." Air Canada was also commended, in the announcement, for "having one of the finest fuel conservation programs in the world." In the seven years leading up to 1982, the airline had produced 28 per cent more air transportation per unit of fuel through modifications to aircraft, new operating procedures and new equipment. "Perhaps the best testimony to the excellence of Air Canada's technology management," the citation concluded, "is the airline's on-time performance which continually ranks among the highest of all airlines in North America despite often severe weather conditions."

A few years later, for 1985, the airline won *Air Transport World*'s coveted Passenger Service Award from among 700-odd airlines around the world.[3] "What we look for in airline service," stated the magazine, "is the best combination of investment in the product coupled with the airline staff's ability and willingness to carry it off . . . Air Canada has over the years produced an excellent balance of these two main ingredients." Several aspects of the airline's service were singled out in the citation, among them its physical plant (aircraft), the ReserVec II computerized reservation system, the special services for handicapped passengers, the success of its "En Route" credit card system. Particularly noted was the in-flight service, especially on the North Atlantic routes where it was described as "one of the better kept secrets in the industry." Perhaps most important, in the magazine's view, was the well-trained and courteous staff itself.

Air Canada continued to innovate. In early 1986, it introduced non-smoking flights, a North American first. Beginning in 1984, following a tragic lavatory fire, it initiated a development program to improve aircraft safety measures for fire and smoke, resulting in a whole series of innovations. Even in what has become a progressively more cutthroat competitive environment, with airlines in the U.S. in particular paring safety procedures to the regulatory minimum (and sometimes below the regulatory minimum), Air Canada's public-service character remained very much alive.

If Air Canada had been just half the airline it was, it would still have been not too bad, but the performance of a public enterprise has to be superb to avoid the slings and arrows of privatization doctrine's wrath. Air Canada happened to be such a case. It was useless for privatization apologists to resort to ideological denunciation of the airline and impossible for them to attack Air Canada head-on. Air Canada, from its past, also still elicits in many Canadians an identification with its role as a national airline binding the country together and with its success as a national enterprise. When it came to Air Canada, privatization advocates found themselves halfway up an ideological precipice, with their thumb joint squeezed tight in the last hand-hold but without the usual ropes of ideological slanging and exhortation to lift them any higher.

Privatization apologists tried the most desperate and daredevil intellectual manoeuvre of all. They argued that Air Canada needed to be privatized if the full benefits of deregulation were to be realized. If Air Canada remained publicly owned, they explained, it could become a high-price leader, and its newly merged national competitor (Canadian Airlines International) would simply shelter under that umbrella, leaving consumers with a high-price, high-cost duopoly.

The manoeuvre was most breathtaking for being executed upside down. No mention was made of the likelihood, or even the possibility, of a price-leadership arrangement or of collusion between two privately-owned operators in a duopoly, or among several such operators in an oligopoly for that matter. There is no shortage of examples of such cases. If only the schoolroom proponents of privatization had reread Adam Smith's cautionary aside about private-enterprise collusion, this time with their eyes open, or reread some of their own lectures on competition.

No mention was made, either, of public enterprise's role in checking price-gouging in a duopoly or oligopoly. The checking or preventing of such abuse is one of public enterprise's time-honoured purposes, unlike private corporate enterprise whose very goal is to collect the highest possible profits for its shareholders. It is worth repeating that in the past Air Canada kept profit margins in the industry so tight that CP Investments – the kind of pick-and-choose holding company always looking for higher-than-average returns – eventually gave up on the industry.

In a book on public-enterprise management which appeared in 1982, the co-editors explained in their introduction how this competitive dynamic worked in railways. "Were the two railroads in Canada private enterprises," they explained, "we strongly suspect that they might collude or at least 'closely coordinate' their behavior . . . . In this case [with one of the railroads a public enterprise], they engage in active rivalry."4 One of those co-editors was privatization partisan William Stanbury who now, in his eagerness to have Air Canada privatized, has conveniently misplaced the argument.

The omissions in argument, by these privatization advocates, is both startling and revealing. But how else were they to get out from under where they were and to find that Air Canada had to be privatized regardless? Duopoly or oligopoly only adds to the case for a publicly owned participant.

Any old argument or excuse for privatization is grabbed at by its apologists. Earlier, they argued that Air Canada had to be broken up before deregulation because otherwise the airline, being so much larger, might overwhelm its competitors. Deregulation, of which these same people were also doctrinaire advocates, would, according to their scenario, bring in a utopia of multiple competing airlines – that is, if only Air Canada were cut into pieces. With all that wonderful untrammelled competition, we wouldn't need a publicly owned airline to keep prices down anyway. Similarly, when Air Canada acquired regional carrier Nordair, there were screams and howls about this cross-ownership of trunk and regional carriers. The government, in the name of all that was holy, refused to allow Air Canada to consummate the takeover.

Later, Canadian Pacific Airlines, subsequently taken over in turn by Pacific Western Airlines, acquired Nordair. There were no screams and howls from the usual quarters now. Instead, as takeover followed takeover, an effective duopoly developed, with a third carrier, Wardair, on the side. At the same time, it was becoming clear in the United States — the fount of private-enterprise doctrine — that a multiplicity of competing carriers, with easy entry in and out of the market, was just a foolish pipe dream. Airlines went belly up or were taken over. As the smoke began to clear, there were fewer major carriers than before, and regional and commuter airlines had become tied to the majors through working relationships or takeovers. It gradually began to dawn on people that integration was the sensible way for air transport to go, and that air transport would inevitably evolve in that direction unless there were rules to prevent it. Advocates of the privatization of Air Canada had to find a new set of arguments.

In fact, the best option for a market the size of Canada is *no* market competition, with public ownership of the carrier to prevent fare-gouging. The most important economic variable in air transport is the passenger load factor — how full airplanes are. Competition American-style, as airlines chase for business with more flights, reduces the load factor. A monopoly, on the other hand, can not only achieve higher load factors, it can also do so with the best spread of flight frequencies (a plus in service), the most equitable route pattern (a social and economic plus), the use of the largest airplanes (a financial saving), and the subsequent lessening of airport congestion and requirements (another financial saving). The publicly owned Air Canada would still be just a fraction of the size of the large U.S. airlines.

Nor would competition be missing. Domestic fares and service would be under the greatest pressure to match or better American fares and service. International competition (something in the order of 40 per cent of kilometers flown by the airline) would also keep the carrier on its toes. At the same time, the strengthened Canadian carrier would be able to compete more effectively against the much larger major U.S. airlines and similar international competitors like

British Airways. This is where the most important competition is taking place, with airlines building secure fortress-like hubs which they dominate and from which they can take on outsiders. Instead, in Canada, we weaken our home base with unnecessary internecine competition. We also end up with with our airlines directly helping foreign competition to eat into our own business. Interlining by Canadian Airlines International with American Airlines, for example, competing against Air Canada's trans-border traffic, simply takes trans-border traffic away from Canadian air transport and gives it to the Americans.

The very idea of a public monopoly would make a deregulator's hair stand on end. Canada, however, once did have such an efficient air travel system, with Trans-Canada Air Lines (Air Canada) in the 1950s. It was an industry leader. Load factors were high, efficiency was good, flight frequencies were balanced, the most applicable and economic aircraft could be used given the route patterns, and comparison with U.S. carriers and international competition helped push the airline to excel. The Trans-Canada Air Lines monopoly was broken up for ideological reasons — doctrinal assumptions about competition borrowed from the United States — not too much different from the doctrinal kowtowing to American fashions now.

The only argument left to privatization advocates was that Air Canada needed more equity capital to update its fleet. Estimates for the update (bringing in newer and more efficient aircraft) ranged from $2 to $3 billion. The announcement of the order for Airbus A320s put the total price tag at $1.8 billion. Of course, the need for aircraft purchases was not an argument for privatization, only an argument for aircraft purchases. If more equity capital was required to finance the update, then the government, acting for the shareholders (all of us), should simply have put the financing in place.

The airline's domestic competitors, Canadian Airlines International and Wardair, had raised large sums of capital through new equity issues. These airlines objected vociferously to new public equity for Air Canada, as if public money for underwriting a public enterprise should be taboo, although private money underwriting a private enterprise was perfectly all right. In ideologically rigged times, anything can be argued.

The equity requirement, in any case, was always exaggerated because the cost would be broken down over a long period, and would be largely covered by depreciation, retained earnings, and the sale of older aircraft. Air Canada, before the recent privatization measure by the government, requested only $300 million in additional equity in the context of aircraft expenditures of $2 billion plus.

Nor was there a short-term financial problem with providing any necessary equity. There was plenty of money. The government gives away an estimated $11 billion annually in tax concessions to private corporations, not to mention direct grants.[5] This is money, moreover, that the public never sees again. On the other hand, any new equity requirement for Air Canada would have been relatively small and would have been a business investment, the value of which, in assets and future dividends, would remain with the Crown, that is, with all of us. For that matter, the cost of a few by-election gifts would have covered the equity requirement. Most relevant, the Crown, for business investment, simply does not have a capital problem. It can raise the money at any time if it wants to.

So the problem isn't, and never has been, public ownership or public financing which are, indeed, advantageous ways of under-writing enterprise. The problem is the current government's privatization ideology. Trying to pass off the financing argument was much like choking a person while at the same time complaining that the person doesn't know how to breathe.

Air Canada, still majority-publicly-owned, is, in one sense, just an airline. It is a large and significant company, with $3 billion annually in sales, but there are many hundreds of other companies in the world that are larger. The largest, General Motors, has annual sales of $135 billion. Yet privatization advocates, given their ideological obsession, have been right to target Air Canada. They know that the privatization of Air Canada will weaken the Canadian public enterprise tradition itself by taking away one of its most interesting examples, and one in a competitive market situation at that.

Supporters of the public ownership of Air Canada also appear to sense what is involved — over and above the obvious, common-sense reasons for the airline's public ownership — although they haven't always been able to put their finger on this underlying feeling. The

Globe and Mail, intent on the airline's privatization, has characterized any such feelings as outdated sentimentality, and then mocked them: "the mentality of a newly-minted nation state that feels the immediate need for two proofs of its existence — epaulets on the president's shoulder and a national airline." The core of the feeling behind Air Canada's public ownership is something else, though: the sense of Air Canada as an expression of an ongoing entrepreneurial culture so indigenous to the country, and so important and creative a part of it, that to privatize Air Canada is a form of sadism.

An entrepreneurial culture, after all, is not a collection of graphs and charts in old textbooks. Entrepreneurial cultures are organic and continuous. They are experience, history, precedent, a presence in society, a legitimacy accepted, the building of entrepreneurial community and commitment, shared struggle and achievement, lessons learned and applied, existing organizational examples to draw on and to stimulate interest, a body of enterprises through which evolution occurs and from whose existence ideas for new enterprises arise, and finally an awareness and sensitivity among the people of a country, not least its young people as they enter the working world, as to what the entrepreneurial culture is and what it can accomplish. Anything that seriously wounds that culture, like the gratuitous amputation of one of its major enterprises, damages the culture and the community's economy well beyond the fate of the particular enterprise. Similarly, the enterprise's history, kept alive in the culture, is as important for the future as it was for the past.

Air Canada has been a vivid expression of such an entrepreneurial culture — a culture, moreover, that is bound up with the way we are, and one which privatization advocates most ardently want to suppress.

"Kindly shoot public ownership," they are shouting.

13.
Public-Enterprise Decentralization of Power Versus Private-Enterprise Concentration of Power

The easy capture of a dominant one-third interest of privatized Teleglobe Canada by BCE (Bell Canada Enterprises), the huge Montreal-based conglomerate, not too long after Teleglobe was sold by the federal government, was decentralization of economic power privatization style – in other words, more concentration of economic power. Hardly anybody commented. It happened under the umbrella of privatization mythology.

According to the mythology, a Crown corporation, although it is owned by the whole population, is supposed to be centralized economic power because decision-making is in the hands of the government of the day which has so much other power as well. Scary phrases like "big government" and "the heavy hand of the state" are used in the telling and retelling of the myth. One privatization advocate, in a compilation of enterprises owned wholly or partly by the public, referred to the state, the abstract under which this ownership was categorized, as "The Leviathan" – a terrible monster indeed, for the leviathan is the biblical whale that swallowed Jonah. Private enterprise, by contrast, in the mythology, decentralizes economic power by its very nature. Individuals, with no other leverage in society than their separate votes at election time, hence no leverage at all, struggle against each other in the marketplace.

Meanwhile, in the real world, concentration of ownership in the private sector, and political leverage with it, is as startling as ever. Public enterprise, on the other hand, with legislatures acting for the public, decentralizes the power of ownership, exactly what one would expect it to do. Even more at odds with the privatization mythology: much of public enterprise in Canada has been established to decentralize entrepreneurial decision-making power and activity geographically, towards Canada and its regions, against the flow of private-enterprise centralizing forces.

The story of heightened corporate concentration in Canada is well-known. There are the family dynasties of the Reichmanns, Irvings, the two branches of the Bronfman family, Paul Desmarais, the Westons, Ken Thomson and others, and the huge holding companies like BCE (Bell Canada Enterprises) and Canadian Pacific Investments. The "Five Families" leading the list control or possess a significant minority interest in nearly 500 companies in the country. The large chartered banks have grown more powerful, with mushrooming financial assets, and are now taking over investment-dealer companies. There is growing cross-ownership between non-financial and financial companies (in the form of trust companies) on top of the old interlocking boards which tie the banks to their major conglomerate customers. The tax dodges which have helped build up these empires at public expense have become notorious.

With that economic power, too, indirectly comes political muscle. Criticism and alarm are coming from unlikely quarters. The chairman of the Ontario Securities Commission, Stanley Beck, has argued that big corporate conglomerates "exercise power that extends far beyond their obvious function as efficient producers of goods and services...the large corporation yields power that controls, directs and influences large segments of society."[1] This includes the crucial power over capital and reinvestment. Bernie Ghert, the former head of Cadillac-Fairview, has referred to "the ability to redirect corporate locational decisions."[2] This ability also carries with it leverage over the terms of the investment: the level of pay and benefits; the kinds of jobs; how the work is organized; what subsidies will be required; where research and development functions will or will not be located; who gets the supply and service contracts; even safety and environmental factors.

DECENTRALIZATION VERSUS CONCENTRATION

More and more, people are talking about the power of corporate and family groupings over the political process. "Their opinions and preferences must necessarily carry great weight in government councils," says Beck. Ghert talks about "expenditures on lobbying, advocacy advertising, public relations [and] campaign contributions," as well as the power over who gets new investment. David Crane, economics editor of the *Toronto Star*, writes about how "big businesses, and the people who control them, have considerable access to the media and to government officials and politicians. They finance political leadership races and election campaigns, sponsor various lobby groups, and support public-policy think tanks."[3]

The main ideas that emerge for public debate today come from bodies financed mainly by these centres of power — such as the Conference Board, the Fraser Institute, and the Business Council on National Issues (BCNI, representing 155 of Canada's biggest privately owned companies). What this means, Beck notes, is that "increasingly, the public is subjected to, and government responds to, a narrow range of ideas." A former "associate" of the BCNI itself, Deborah Coyne, in a long article in 1986 entitled "Corporate Over-Concentration," also raises concern over the "extremely high concentration of corporate control of our newspapers and electronic media" and the "unseemly reverence of corporate power" to which these media have contributed.[4] Diane Francis, herself an apologist for the ideology of private corporations, says point-blank, "our private sector is already an economic oligarchy and may be hurtling towards a form of economic feudalism."[5] Not that there is anything particularly new here. Ever since the early American railroad syndicates began corrupting legislatures in the U.S., there has been bitter criticism of the dangers of concentrated corporate wealth and power.

Large multi-national companies, a good part headquartered in the United States, have a parallel concentrated power in the Canadian economy. They can allocate reinvestment for manufacturing and exploration, or import products for use or resale, where they will. If they don't like a particular tax policy or royalty, they can deny reinvestment to Canada, even of profits earned here. These are "capital strikes," the most lethal of industrial actions. As of the end of 1987, General Motors had $116 billion in assets, Exxon $98 billion, General Electric $52 billion, IBM $84 billion. Add to this the centralization of Canadian business power in Central Canada — concentration within concentration.

Every once in a while, an advocate of privatization will express chagrin about this corporate concentration. UBC professor William Stanbury declares that the corporate mergers "are putting too much power in the hands of too few people."[6] Tom Kierans, who served as an adviser on privatization to the British government, writes that "major new power concentrations have been formed...the spectre of conglomerates utilizing complex financing mechanisms to leverage an expanding asset base...raises troublesome issues."[7] (Kierans' own firm, investment dealer McLeod Young Weir, was subsequently taken over by the Bank of Nova Scotia, in the concentration march.)

The declarations against concentration by one or two of the more religiously pure of privatization proponents don't mention the tough measures needed to break up the wealth and power, and there is no call to take on the fierce political fight which it would involve. One is reminded of members of esoteric sects, muttering old prayers in the cellars of closed communal houses.

Privatization, as with the BCE acquisition of its Teleglobe share, or British Petroleum's acquisition of Britoil, throws more assets into the pot for concentration to feed on. Sometimes management personnel are significant buyers of shares in a privatization scheme but this is no safeguard against concentration. Management can be just as eager as ordinary shareholders to sell out in a takeover offer; where they don't have majority ownership, a hostile takeover is possible in any case. In some instances, privatization legislation will limit individual shareholdings to a small percentage — and much political play will be made of that — but, as with the BCRIC case, that limitation probably won't last long. It also flies in the face of privatization doctrine itself, for a main tenet of the doctrine is that takeovers will discipline management for poor performance, by booting them out. If a takeover is impossible because of the limitation on share ownership, there goes the discipline. Shareholders, the revered divine instruments of privatization, meanwhile, will begin to holler not so divinely that the value of their shares is being held down by the ownership limitation, and will demand, in the name of private enterprise itself, that it be lifted.

In Italy, even the supporters of privatization are wary that privatization may lead to further concentration of economic power. There, a handful of groups – the Agnellis and De Benedettis of the country – sit astride private corporate empires much like the family dynasties and huge holding companies in Canada in their relative size. This accelerated concentration is already happening in New Zealand, where Petrocorp, the state-owned oil and gas producer, went to Fletcher Challenge, the country's biggest company (an earlier deal, withdrawn because of the local outcry, would have had Petrocorp going to the even bigger, privatized British Gas).

Public enterprise, owned by all the people of a region or country, democratizes ownership instead. Crown corporations in Canada are not allowed to make contributions to favoured political parties, to avoid their skewing the political system. At least at the federal level, where the issue arose, they are not allowed to retain "public affairs consulting groups" – those public relations and lobbying groups with often special access to the powers-that-be. They cannot get together and launch, with corporate money, well-heeled think tanks with self-serving ideological and political objectives (even if, at the same time, the generous private corporate funding of the BCNIs and the Fraser Institutes puts the idea of public enterprise at a political disadvantage). Nor do Crown corporations indulge in blatant advocacy advertising with ideological or political overtones (save for loaded institutional advertising – a copy of private corporate practice which should be checked across the board).

Such limitations are part of the corporate culture of public enterprise and of what the diverse public expects from its ownership of Crown corporations. Governments, which make the rules for public enterprises, moreover, need to be re-elected periodically. Their decisions about publicly owned enterprises are made under the glaring scrutiny of all elected representatives (and often require legislation). Acting as shareholders' agents are elected representatives of different parties, covering the geographic, demographic and political landscape.

Most important, Crown corporations cannot lever public policy with the threat, explicit or implicit, of a capital strike – the crucial power over capital and reinvestment that comes with ownership. Nor, unlike the cross-ownership of the Thomson and Irving conglomerates, can a Crown company also operate and control newspapers or radio and television stations while also operating in non-media sectors (although CN, in the 1920s, did begin network radio). The publicly owned broadcasting companies themselves are carefully distanced both from the government of the day and other Crown companies.

Only with the very largest Crown corporations, like Ontario Hydro and Hydro Québec, might the publicly owned company unduly influence public policy because of size, and there the problem would stem largely from an information gap between the management of those companies, on the one hand, and legislature and government on the other. This is a gap which the latter should close, as part of its administrative responsibility. The same administrative check would have to be established if the utilities were privately owned.

This decentralization of the power of ownership is aside from the sheer asset-ownership of public enterprises and the wealth they generate, belonging equally to everybody in the community.

Public enterprise also decentralizes economic power in another, quite different way — by decentralizing entrepreneurship and owner-ship in North America towards Canada or towards regions within Canada, or by simply keeping a company out of the hands of a private empire. This decentralizing function goes back to the earliest days of public enterprise in the country. The Welland Canal and the publicly conceived, benefited and protected CPR were aimed at keeping economic and territorial power from falling into the hands of an immensely more powerful U.S. nation and economy. The CNR was pulled together, and kept going in the disastrous depression of the 1930s, to make sure the mighty CPR did not end up with everything. Ontario Hydro was created in good part to protect small western Ontario manufacturing, as well as ordinary ratepayers, from rate-gouging by powerful Toronto financial interests.

Similarly, Hydro-Québec shifted power from English-Canadian interests to French-Canadians on their own home territory where otherwise a leading role in corporate enterprise had been denied them. Petro-Canada repatriated part of our oil industry from multinational, largely American, domination and expertise, headquartered far from the western Canadian oilfields. The Canadian Wheat Board, and before it the co-operative wheat pools, freed the well-being of millions of people in prairie farm families from exploitive elevator companies and from the manipulations of a small clique of operators of the old Winnipeg Grain Exchange. The publicly owned automobile insurance companies put the investment capital from insurance premiums, and with it the revenue generated from that capital, under home control instead of under the control of insurance companies largely run elsewhere.

One of the greatest decentralization initiatives in Canadian history was the establishment of the Canadian Radio-Broadcasting Commission, later to become the CBC, without which network radio here would have fallen into the hands of American companies. "The state or the United States," was how Graham Spry, a leader in the public radio movement, put it. This decentralization of power was doubly significant because it involved culture and information as well as the sheer economic activity of program production. The same applies to television and film-making today. Private enterprise puts the leading production power in Los Angeles and New York. Private television stations in Canada are adjuncts of the American television and film industries. Public enterprise decentralizes some of that power towards Canada.

(The CBC, because it was publicly owned, also established rigorous democratic rules which, among other things, denied special access to the network for wealthy individuals and corporations who wanted to buy time to propagate their views on matters of public controversy. It was also the first mass medium in North America, and today remains the only mainstream mass medium on the continent, not owned and controlled by private business groups – in Canada, now, by an increasingly concentrated group of corporate owners.)

The whole series of post-war provincial Crown corporations, from the Société générale de financement (SGF) in manufacturing in Quebec to the resource companies in oil, mining and potash in Saskatchewan, were attempts to build regional entrepreneurship independent of the whims and the demands of large, outside-owned corporations and holding companies – companies whose head offices were usually elsewhere as well.

In some cases, decentralization has been maintained at an even more local level, with municipal ownership. Prince Rupert has its own telephone system. So does Edmonton ('edmonton telephones'), which an AT&T consultant recently described, with some envy, as a "model telephone organization," with indices as good as, and in most cases better, than any telephone company in the United States.[8] Thunder Bay, Kenora, Dryden and some other, smaller communities in Ontario have their own telephone systems. Winnipeg Hydro produces half its own power, from long-existing dams. Edmonton Power, which also generates some of its own supply, is Alberta's second-largest electrical utility. Medicine Hat has an electrical utility and supplies its own power. Medicine Hat also has its own gas utility, established in 1902 when the city had only two thousand residents. The gas comes from the utility's own wells. The Medicine Hat Gas Utility is now an oil producer, from a small field discovered while drilling for gas. Ontario cities and many other cities across the country — among them Calgary, Red Deer, Lethbridge, Saskatoon, Swift Current, and Saint John — have their own electricity distribution utilities, and a few smaller centres also have generating stations. (Even in the ideologically constricted U.S., municipally-owned enterprise is not unknown. There were 1900 municipal electrical systems scattered across the U.S. in 1981, about a quarter of which generated power for their systems. There are also district and co-operative electrical utilities in the U.S.)

With exceptions like the above cases, most of which were established in the early years of the century, the idea of municipal public ownership as an instrument of decentralized ownership and control has gone begging in Canada. It remains of great potential. The sale of West Kootenay Power and Light in British Columbia by Cominco in 1987 provided a singular opportunity for local public ownership. The provincial government, privatization-mad, went along with its sale to an American holding company instead.

Public enterprises owned by different-sized communities (people coming together in different ways) can participate in the same sector and compete or form joint ventures. Alberta Government Telephones and 'edmonton telephones' interlock. SaskOil (now effectively privatized) and Petro-Canada operated side by side in the oil industry. The CBC and provincial broadcasting networks (most importantly TV Ontario and Radio-Québec) are another example of different public enterprises in the same sector.

Now, according to the privatization doctrine, this decentralization of economic power, through public enterprise, is not to be allowed. The takeover of Block Brothers in British Columbia by a few brothers in Toronto, the Reichmann organization – controlling, through Olympia & York, non-financial assets now variously estimated at $20 to $30 billion – is perfectly all right. So is the takeover of Daon Development by BCE (Bell Canada Enterprises, $26 billion in assets) and so is the real-estate power of the CPR, latterly through Marathon Realty. But for the people of British Columbia to own one small land development company in their own province (Dunhill Development Corporation, later the Housing Corporation of British Columbia, privatized in 1978 and 1979) is, according to the doctrine, a terrible evil to be suppressed as quickly as possible.

Similarly, the control of MacMillan-Bloedel by Edper (just two people in effect, again in Toronto), not to mention the rest of Edper's enormous non-financial and financial empire, is perfectly all right according to the doctrine. But a provincially owned Cancel (privatized in 1979), with a tenth the sales of MacMillan-Bloedel, is taboo.

The control of a major chain of important mass media, including the *Globe and Mail,* by just one man, Ken Thomson, not to mention the other Thomson holdings and the conflict of interest from the cross-ownership, is similarly legitimate and desirable, according to the doctrine. So are the sweeping media holdings of the Irving family in New Brunswick with, at the same time, a feudal-like economic empire in other sectors in the province. But the public ownership of the CBC or of a full-fledged provincial public broadcaster is taboo.

Or take banking. The Royal Bank of Canada has over $100 billion in financial assets. Its interlocking board connects it to a seemingly endless list of powerful corporate organizations – almost, it seems, the whole private corporate community. The bank is run by a management autocracy and a board to suit; not that they control the bank directly but the shareholdings are widely dispersed by law, which gives management and its board control. The bank refuses to disclose the remuneration of the chairman or president, but a calculated guess would put it, in each case, at the $700,000 level, excluding stock options, and perhaps higher. These and other top executives eat in the executive dining room and get haircuts for a nominal price ("below market" is the official euphemism) from the full-time barber who serves senior executives and directors. Such perks are among the psychological tokens of power.

THE PRIVATIZATION PUTSCH

When the bank's chairman speaks — and he may speak on everything from inflation to public expenditures — governments listen. The bank makes substantial donations to the political parties of its choice. It belongs, of course, to the Business Council on National Issues with its high-level lobbyist's access to government circles. It naturally also supports organizations like the Conference Board which produce literature and hold conferences reflecting the bank's ideological and political leanings. It contributes generously to single-issue political campaigns of its liking; it gave $150,000 to a corporate business coalition pushing for free trade. Many of these political and lobbying expenditures are tallied as expenses against net income, hence are paid in part by the public in foregone taxes inasmuch as the banks do pay taxes (the chartered banks have not been backward in taking advantage of loose government tax rules).

The publicly owned Alberta Treasury Branch, by comparison, has just $6 billion in financial assets, one-eighteenth of the Royal Bank figure. Its depositors are ordinary Albertans. All its deposits are re-invested in Alberta. The Treasury Branch does not make donations to political parties, much less to single-issue political causes; that would be an abuse of its mandate and its public ownership. It has branches throughout the cities and towns of Alberta, maintaining agents in some of the smallest of villages. In 72 locations it is the only financial institution represented. These are places to where the Royal Bank and the other large banks can't bother going because the volume of business or the rate of return isn't great enough to satisfy them. The superintendent (the chief executive officer) of the Treasury Branch is paid from $67,000 to $99,000 a year. If the Treasury Branch ever abused its powers or noticeably failed to be sensitive to the needs of the local Alberta population and economy, it would ultimately have to answer to the legislature, where elected representatives — shareholders' delegates, in effect — chosen regularly in highly publicized and contested campaigns, speak for the citizenry. The presence of a vocal and highly visible opposition reinforces the accountability.

Which bank is the Leviathan and which is the Jonah?

According to the privatization doctrine, the Royal Bank is a creation of divine private-enterprise will while the Alberta Treasury Branch has no right in practice or theology even to exist.

DECENTRALIZATION VERSUS CONCENTRATION

In one panegyric to privatization, Trevor Lautens, a *Vancouver Sun* newspaper columnist, describes Canadians as "a herd people, God's natural collectivists," because they won't reject the idea of public enterprise. He sees them as "sheep."[9] It's a pastoral-ideological picture, like an old religious oil painting, with the sheep waiting to be turned into gazelles if only some miraculous privatization event would occur. But, in fact, the creation of public enterprise in Canada has been one case after another of bold defiance of the powers that be, animated by that least sheep-like of qualities, the spirit of self-reliance.

Think of the individual cases. Ontario Hydro was a movement for people's power; the citizenry organized meetings and knocked on doors, fighting not just against Toronto financial interests but also against the American electricity trust. The rural frontier governments of the prairies were not impressed by the American Bell company and took over and built their provinces' telephone systems themselves quicker, cheaper and better. The campaigners for public radio told the American networks and their moneyed station-owner friends in this country to go fly a kite. The war-time companies refused to be cowed by the technological demands of radar, optics, aircraft and other advanced manufacturing, or by the pompous and condescending view of others, and did things Canadians weren't supposed to be capable of doing. Atomic Energy of Canada took on what, for its time, was the most futuristic and unbelievable venture of all: nuclear power. And so on, case after case, to modern times where Petro-Canada was created in the face of opposition from powerful global corporate giants, or where the Allen Blakeney government in Saskatchewan defied at one and the same time the American government, the Canadian federal government and a phalanx of mining companies with potash interests to establish the Potash Corporation of Saskatchewan. The automobile insurance cases and the introduction of medicare in Saskatchewan (in contrast to private corporate insurance operations) were also acts of defiance. In each instance there were gutsy individuals, sometimes larger than life and sometimes unassuming, making bold decisions which flew in the face of the clubbish and conservative circles opposing them.

The newspaper columnist got his zoological classification of Canadians exactly backwards. The Canadian sheep are the ones who

14.
Holding One's Own in the West

As 1986 wound down, Jim Pattison from Vancouver was named Canada's businessman of the year by the editorial board of the *Financial Post*. He was chosen for his role as chairman of Expo 86 but, were it not for his reputation as a businessman proper, it's not likely the *Financial Post* would have thought of him. Pattison was well known as head of the Jim Pattison Group with annual sales in 1985 of $1.2 billion. Just a month earlier Pattison had told the Sales and Marketing Executives of Toronto, who had also given him an award for his Expo work, that most of his future business initiatives would be in the U.S. "because the return on your efforts is so much higher there."[1] The British Columbia economy at the time was struggling.

When the going gets tough, the not-so-tough go to the United States. The decision to reinvest capital elsewhere is a decision that has been made again and again, decade after decade, by others taking profits out of the West's resource economy and by corporations whose activities span the country and often the world, including western Canada. The West gets left in the lurch, gasping for diversification like a fish out of water gasping for oxygen.

Public enterprise, by contrast, is an instrument for westerners' control over their own economy. Provincial Crown corporations are entrepreneurially rooted in their regions. Their very purpose is to build and strengthen their regions' economies. They don't run off to

Toronto or Los Angeles or New York when there are tough times at home. Inasmuch as they are strong enough, they make sure that the West gets its fair share of investment capital from profits made in the West.

The sheer existence of Crown corporations, particularly in the natural resource sector, fends off economic blackmail: the threat by private corporations, more often than not owned outside the region, to pull out or to cut back on development and capital investment if they don't like royalty or tax rates. The publicly owned company is around to move into the vacuum. Its existence undercuts the threat and helps to ensure that the West gets the maximum "rent" for its resources.

The Potash Corporation of Saskatchewan (PCS) was formed by the provincial government after a bitter fight with private potash producers, largely foreign-owned, over the level of royalties. The world price for potash had more than doubled and the companies were making large windfall profits. At stake was a reserve tax to recover some of that windfall for the public, the owner of the resource. The companies protested but refused to provide the production and financial data necessary for the government to assess their position — necessary in fact for the government to administer a "rent" system that wouldn't end up with the public being shortchanged by intracorporate accounting manoeuvres. The companies also shelved an expansion plan as part of their battle against the government, this at a time when the market was growing. It was a "capital strike." They launched a series of court actions and deliberately fell behind in the payment of taxes.

The establishment of the PCS and its takeover of 40 per cent of potash production recovered regional Saskatchewan control over its own potash resource. The location of the company's head office in Saskatoon at the same time made Saskatchewan the centre of potash expertise in the western world.

The creation of SaskOil and of the Saskatchewan Mining and Development Corporation recovered for Saskatchewan some of the same control in the oil and gas and uranium sectors. This established a significant public enterprise in each of the region's mining resource sectors. Saskatchewan was the only province which followed through on the realization — or was independent enough to realize — that public enterprise was the most effective decentralizing force of all. The result was that Saskatchewan was getting a higher rent in percentage terms from its natural resources than was Alberta, although Alberta otherwise, by the sheer size of its oil and gas industry, was in a stronger position.

Saskatchewan had historically been in the position of having to accept the industry's terms for resource development or not getting development at all. It was a weak sister—virtuous, hard-working, intelligent and inventive, true, but always vulnerable to being roughed up if it complained about its allowance. Its public enterprises changed that.

Alberta was in a similar position, although its later oil wealth tended to hide the fact. When, in 1974, a federal tax combined with provincial royalties was deemed too onerous by the oil companies, they threatened to cut back exploration and development and move activity across the border to the U.S., although profit levels and cash flow, and hence the capital for reinvestment, were soaring. Alberta backed down. Ottawa was labelled the devil in the affair, but what if Alberta by itself had raised "rents" to the same aggregate level? Presumably, the oil companies would have made the same veiled threats, and Alberta would have had to take the punishment again.

How much more solid Alberta would be today if it had had a major publicly owned oil company of its own all those years and was able to build on the spin-offs both industrially and in entrepreneurial culture that would have come with it. Imagine if this company had been established in 1906 along with Alberta Government Telephones, or in 1938 along with the Treasury Branches. Remember that the existence of the Devonian formation running through Alberta was established by the Canadian Geological Survey in the nineteenth century. It was known that oil and gas was in the ground under Alberta. It only required the enterprise to develop it. The Canadian company which eventually discovered the Turner Valley field in 1914 lacked the capital for the long run and sold out to Imperial Oil (Standard Oil of New Jersey). Other foreign, largely U.S., companies moved in. Later, when Leduc No. 1 and other big wells were discovered, the American companies took out most of the exploration reservations for promising territory. Appeals for financing by Canadian operators to eastern chartered banks and Bay Street met with indifference, a source of bitter animus against the East to this day. It virtually forced the industry into American hands, went the refrain.

But this wasn't the case at all. If Alberta had put a Crown corporation into the field the way Saskatchewan eventually did, it would at the least have occupied some of the entrepreneurial territory itself, and it would have been in a position to buy all those Canadian companies which sold out over the years, instead of seeing them go to the big outsiders. The multi-national oil companies, meanwhile, were favourite customers of the eastern chartered banks and came to have friendly interlocking board relationships with them. It was both safer and more lucrative for the banks to deal with these companies, with their huge world-wide assets as collateral, and to finance their takeovers, and to cater to the psychology of dependence, rather than to underwrite mere Albertans. And many of the Canadian companies were only too happy to let the Americans take them over, for a price. With all these sell-outs went Canadian control over the downstream cash flow and hence investment capacity generated by the operations.

Without public enterprise in the West, the centralization of business and financial power accelerated.

A Crown corporation, where it exists in any given sector, can also capture the spin-off activities, technology, employment and new ideas generated by its base operation. This is a crucial factor, because new work is usually created out of old work. Regional public enterprises can keep processing, engineering, technology, and the maximum of supply functions at home. Instead, they may be lost to a foreign-controlled head office or automatically assigned outside the region to companies in larger centres which happen, for the moment, to have a bit more expertise or maybe, even, just status, or, more often, have an existing relationship with the parent company. This is what happened, with a vengeance, in the oil industry (the whole story is told by writer David Crane in his 1982 book *Controlling Interest*).[2]

One of the limitations of western Canadian economies is that, outside of utilities and sometimes resources, public enterprise has been largely limited to assistance programs and to hospitalization cases with marginal viability. The so-called "development" corporations are really just lenders of last resort. This is not a sufficient base for entrepreneurial subdivision and proliferation.

To make matters worse, when a public enterprise of real strength does appear outside of certain limited sectors, it is more than likely privatized by ideologically perverse governments. Cancel (the forest company) and Dunhill Corporation (the land developer) in British Columbia are examples. The B.C. Petroleum Corporation, whose charter allowed it to become actively involved in exploration and development but which was then emasculated, is another. Ideological charges ring through the air that companies in these sectors shouldn't be publicly owned, that they are invading private enterprise territory. Why such territory must necessarily be reserved to private corporate forms, including huge conglomerates controlled by some character or other half way around the world, is never satisfactorily explained, because it cannot be.

The same prejudice limits what public enterprises in place might do. The prejudice dictates that a public-enterprise entry into this "private-enterprise territory" is taboo. Sometimes, where the linkage is very close, the taboo is broken. AGT (Alberta Government Telephones) has two wholly owned subsidiaries providing consulting, technical assistance, software and customized systems, and high technology training. Consulting subsidiaries are an area where public enterprises generally in Canada have been allowed to venture. The company also is involved in the manufacturing and marketing of cellular mobile radio telephones and systems, but in a joint venture with Nova Corporation of Alberta although the technological expertise comes from the AGT side.

Another partial contra-example is IPSCO (formerly the Interprovincial Steel and Pipe Company). IPSCO was established in 1959 by a merger of a pipe company and a small steel manufacturer making primary steel out of scrap. Its real creator, though, was the Tommy Douglas CCF government which offered loans and loan guarantees and promised to purchase the output. The government was intent on diversifying Saskatchewan's economy and not afraid of public investment to do it. In exchange for interest on loan guarantees, used when the company ran into early financial difficulties, the government acquired equity.

IPSCO's presence is taken for granted now but its creation was a bold venture in regional enterprise: a steel company in the middle of the prairies of all places, without even the blessing and expertise of a

Stelco or Dofasco. IPSCO has been under mixed ownership since the 1960s. As of early 1987, its control rested with Saskatchewan (16 per cent), Alberta Energy Company (10 per cent) and Nova Corporation of Alberta (10 per cent). Alberta Energy, in turn, is owned 36 per cent by the province of Alberta. This mixed ownership makes IPSCO a poor target for ideological woolheads. They don't quite know where to direct their thunder. If, on the other hand, IPSCO were publicly owned by one province, they would be clamouring for its privatization until the sun stopped rising. If that meant a sellout to, say, pipeline maker Algoma Steel (recently taken over by Dofasco from Canadian Pacific Limited) and the possibility later of "rationalization" moving certain functions to Sault-Ste-Marie, no matter, because the privatization ideology says it must be so.

As long as there is an ideological barrier artificially protecting economic territory for exclusive private-enterprise operation, the spin-off of new work from old is inhibited. The very first step of that entrepreneurial process, which is thinking in terms of linkages, is going to be inhibited.

Regional Crown corporations, because they are rooted both physically and psychologically in their own regions and have their head offices in their respective regions, also benefit by all the advantages that local ownership provides: pools of indigenous expertise at the highest levels, strategic decision-making experience and self-confidence, a keener awareness of new economic possibilities arising at home that might be overlooked, ignored or co-opted by absentee ownership, and a vital people knowledge about the region.

The very public ownership of a regional Crown corporation can give it a special entrepreneurial energy and commitment — the energy that comes from regional patriotism, a powerful motivating factor in economic history. A regional public enterprise which is allowed to grow and explore both expresses this patriotism and puts it to work. The greater the commitment to the region by the people in the entrepreneurial culture, the more intense the entrepreneurship. The characteristic that privatizers attack and inveigh against — public ownership — is actually the characteristic that makes public enterprises so entrepreneurially valuable given half a chance. This is especially so for the West.

At the bottom of this regional patriotism is the profound desire to control one's own fate. This is fundamental to the vigour of a region socially and economically, especially regions like western Canada at the edges of other peoples' worlds. For controlling one's own fate, there is no substitute for the spirit of self-reliance and for keeping hold of one's resources, including profits and savings for re-investment. Privately owned corporations don't accept this regional, decentralist way of thinking. Expecting large private corporations or banks to think Saskatchewan and Alberta first is to expect the Second Coming. Even a head office in the West doesn't necessarily mean much. Think only of the Jim Pattison case. The Jim Pattison Groups and the Exxons of the world, as business enterprises, don't ultimately give a hoot about western Canada. When resource prices are down or when for other reasons a western Canadian economy is declining, their attention and capital inevitably drift away.

Indeed, if you tried to argue against such a development, pointing to the capital in their coffers which was generated in the West, they would be outraged. "It's our capital," they would say, "and we can do anything we want with it." Interference with this right would be tantamount to expropriation, they would say. Not to move capital to where it can get a higher return would be to shortchange their shareholders to whom they owe primary allegiance (at least in theory, which allows them to bring up the argument). For them, and for privately held companies like The Pattison Group, such a constraint would simply betray the laws of capital, would be a sin against nature. If the western Canadian economies don't grow fast enough, people should leave, as many people have done in the last few years, and should stop whimpering.

In a few words: Them's the breaks. One is reminded of how British capital drifted away to the United States and other frontier countries, for such as railway-building projects, because the return was higher there, and how, although these investments established a rentier class in Britain, they marked the beginning of a long economic decline at home.

This mechanical and bureaucratic corporate world simply does not have room for the idea that the communities of western Canada — the four provinces — should come first or even have any relevance other than to be referred to sentimentally as great places to

THE PRIVATIZATION PUTSCH

live. Privatization doctrine is a branch of the same bureaucratic and other-worldly thinking—the same shiny and thin tinfoil doctrine. If control over a privatized company falls into outsiders' hands, or if the reinvestment capital generated by the enterprise is then allocated outside the West, all the better that privatization took place, for such loss of power and of economic activity from the West to other areas was in the stars—was in the pre-ordained orbiting of market forces. (One need only ask where a remote and backward region like Japan might have been today if it had so feebly submitted to the doctrine.)

Forget, too, that the orbiting is actually manoeuvred by corporate bureaucracies who are prisoners of their own business circles, prejudices, locales, reading habits, routines and comforts. According to the doctrine, they are not so much human beings as atoms in the market universe, hence functioning perfectly ("rationally" is the doctrine's code word) even when, as individuals, they appear to make mistakes.

Eric Kierans, in his Massey lectures *Globalism and the Nation-State*, points out the irony in how the idea of community has been discarded.[3] The new doctrine purports to harken back to the "classical" economists of the nineteenth century and their free market thinking. In actuality it betrays those early thinkers' philosophy. Kierans writes of "the profound respect that classical economists held for people and for community." He continues that those nineteenth century thinkers "were not merely economists but were possessed of a political philosophy as well. Men and women were citizens, the foundation and source of national strength, custodians of the traditions, beliefs, language, laws and customs of the nation. They were the substance of the state, not mere instruments and factors of production to be transferred to foreign lands at the dictate of capital flows and feedback systems."

He cites David Ricardo, one of those thinkers, as writing approvingly of the "natural disinclination which every man has to quit the country of his birth and connexions." Economic theory was designed to build financial power, employment and industrial strength at home. Ricardo would have understood western Canada and the Atlantic provinces. More than that, though, the key to developing economic strength at home, and contributing productively to both one's own region and one's trading partners, was sovereignty and economic independence. "Sovereignty," as understood in nineteenth century thought, Kierans adds, "not only depended on a strong citizenry proud of their rights, it also depended on the control of one's resources."

Control of one's resources, in today's economy, means holding on to the expertise, market share, spin-off work, financial capacity, and re-investment capital generated in a region, not just keeping ownership of raw natural resources which, by themselves, are a declining force. Regional or, as appropriate, local public enterprise — because of its roots in the community and how it is owned, which is to say because of its nature — is such a decentralizing economic vehicle.

This brings us to the ultimate irony for western Canadians: the rhetoric of politicians full of a superficial western patriotism but who aid and abet the centralization of economic power in Canada by denigrating and suppressing public enterprise in their regions.

In British Columbia, premier Bill Bennett's privatizations of Cancel and Dunhill Development through BCRIC were extremely important — as his coterie knew — although the companies themselves were quite small. Limited as they were in size and diversity, they had nevertheless established a public-enterprise presence in commercial sectors. The BCRIC privatization scheme was created to eliminate that presence. At the same time, Bennett pretended to be a western patriot. "B.C. is not for sale," he said, when a takeover of control of MacMillan-Bloedel by CP Investments was in the offing and he moved to block it.

The Bennett mentality in fact ushered in a period of spectacular sellout which is continuing to this day. MacMillan-Bloedel went. B.C. Forest Products was traded from outsider to outsider. Premier Cablesystems went. Daon Development went. Block Brothers went. West Kootenay Power and Light went. Woodward's real estate and supermarket holdings went. CP Air head office was lost to PWA just as PWA head office was lost earlier, to Alberta, through government purchase. The Bank of British Columbia went. (A revealing side-light: Daon, Woodward's, and the Bank of B.C. were the businesses of three of the five original privatized BCRIC directors. Control of a fourth, Okanagan Helicopters, was also lost to outside the province.) The B.C. economy began to look like a regional clearance sale.

The regionally rooted entrepreneurial power of these corporations, including control over the re-investment capital that goes with them, was lost. The operation of the existing businesses might be given the necessary capital to exploit the resources in place (forests, hydro-electricity) or to hang on to subscribers or depositors whose money is essential to the companies (cable, banking), but what of the development of new possibilities in the region? The ownership roots are no longer there. They were weak in the first place, with many of the previous owners being either non-British-Columbians or having only a financial interest in the enterprises. Without the rootedness of regionally based public enterprise, what could one expect?

The result was that the Bennett government became an investment beggar and a sitting duck for cockeyed, desperate schemes like northeast coal. The Vander Zalm government is another investment beggar. The option it leaves itself is to bend the knee to outside entrepreneurship: to weaken labour unions; lower labour costs (although labour costs are not high in Canadian terms); and otherwise make B.C. attractive to outside investment. However, there is no substitute for vital indigenous entrepreneurship. Beggars of investment ultimately beggar their own societies. They represent a surrender to outside economic power, a bitingly negative declaration that British Columbians don't have what it takes, that they are second class and have to depend on others . . . a western capitulation.

The privatization of SaskOil is a western surrender in another way, with a majority of its privately owned shares already held outside the province. Publicly owned SaskOil gave to Saskatchewan an ownership and entrepreneurial role which private enterprise had failed to do. Its public ownership was also a good idea in itself. SaskOil had established itself in an inhospitable environment of multinational giants and had become consistently profitable. The impressive accomplishment of public ownership did nothing, of course, to deter the Devine government from privatization, just the opposite. Public ownership success is bad karma for transcendental privatization devotees.

The meaning of the SaskOil privatization is found in the 1985 annual report, the year of the changeover. On the cover is an artistic mockup of men and women watching the stock exchange electronic ticker. The ticker is showing the SaskOil symbol and price. Three of the people are raising an arm in a hosanna of praise and gratitude. Some of the men are wearing hardhats, no doubt to protect them from falling paper. The original of this work has been placed in the main reception area in the SaskOil Tower in Regina – Regina, Saskatchewan, the annual report notes, just in case some farflung shareholder doesn't know where Regina is.

In the inside of the report is a glossy full-page picture of a luminescent-glass high-rise office building projecting into the sky. It isn't, though, the SaskOil Tower in Regina, Saskatchewan. It's the Toronto Stock Exchange building in Toronto, Ontario, where the electronic ticker portrayed on the cover is located.

This Bay Street stock-exchange culture and the banking and corporate world surrounding it are the same world that wouldn't give Saskatchewan the time of day while its people were struggling to create a place in the sun for themselves. It's a world that noticed Saskatchewan only when it could take something out of it. Now the people of Saskatchewan are supposed to humble themselves in front of its totems – Saskatchewan fellaheen prostrating themselves towards the East – as if those totems were the gods of a superior universe. John Diefenbaker, who fought that smug and self-centred Bay Street crowd all his life, for good reason, must be turning in his grave.

The Toronto Stock Exchange is part of a mechanistic bureaucracy whose electronic ticker is incapable of registering a region's will to be itself and to run its own affairs.

The Crown can nominate a number of directors to the Saskoil board, corresponding to its percentage of share ownership. This number will henceforth be a minority, but the government has declared it will not vote its shares anyway. On the other hand, it has limited individual shareholdings to 4 per cent of the company so that, ideally, nobody else can take SaskOil over either, particularly not some predatory oil company or holding company. It's a case of *privatus interruptus*. If the Devine government believes in privatization, then why doesn't it believe in privatization?

Pressure is already starting to remove the 4 per cent limit. As of the end of the 1986 financial year – within one year of the original privatization share issue – the largest ownership of privately traded shares was in Ontario. Outsiders held 75 per cent of both common and convertible preferred non-Crown shares. If the 4 per cent individual shareholding limit is eliminated, it is likely effective control will soon exit the province. The parties arguing for removal have a solid case in privatization doctrine. They point out that the limitation hurts shareholders because it rules out any takeover interest. A takeover interest would, naturally, boost the share price. One of the cardinal rules of privatization doctrine is that takeovers by anybody and everybody should be allowed, whatever the citizenship or character of the bidder. The privatization of Saskatchewan Mining and Development Corporation (with Eldorado) allows for an individual or institutional shareholding of up to 25 per cent. Two out-of-province shareholders means absolute control. Out-of-province SaskOil shareholders can be expected to demand the same liberal arrangement.

One Saskatchewan cabinet minister, mimicking the jargon, talks about how privatization will create "giant, world-class corporations" with "head offices in Saskatchewan," but, as the SaskOil share issue has already shown, privatization ships out control more likely than not. If and when, down the line, the Saskatchewan economy is in the doldrums, SaskOil then may still be making money, but that money won't be ploughed back into the province. It will be allocated elsewhere or drained off by the outside shareholders. Investors won't be interested in taking up the slack. Without the interest of outside investors, the people of Saskatchewan, co-operatively, will have to get together all over again. Anybody in Saskatchewan easily impressed with the machinery of corporate transactions and of distant investment dealers and pension-fund managers is more of a petty provincial, and less of a worldly realist, than he imagines. That's the illusion.

It's part of the whole psychology of privatization in the West. Here is the Edmonton Chamber of Commerce, recommending the privatization of "edmonton telephones," and also the merging of "edmonton telephones" and AGT, but only if the resultant creature is sold. Among the proposed ways of disposing of these two systems is to sell them to Bell Canada or GTE. Another possibility is to sell to a non-phone company interested in diversification.

This putting out for sale, to takeover machinery, of a region's economic life fits the psychology of privatization where huge, outside-controlled bureaucratic corporations are considered the cat's pajamas but, most of all, it also fits the doctrine of privatization – a doctrine which boasts as a virtue that it is community-blind.

Alberta Report, the doctrinaire Alberta news magazine – published in other western provinces as *Western Report* – gives us another glimpse of privatization's superficial westernism, where ideological self-indulgence comes before the West. One of Alberta's historical *bêtes noires* has been the eastern banks. One by one, the new western financial institutions have gone under or sold out: Northlands Bank (bankrupt), Canadian Commercial Bank (bankrupt), the Principal Group (bankrupt; pieces picked up by a New York insurance company), the Bank of British Columbia (sell-out to a Hong Kong bank). What about a publicly owned bank, or banks, for the West? All kinds of countries have them: Australia, Italy, Austria, France, Sweden, West Germany. Even Alberta has a small but creditable one (the Treasury Branches). *Alberta Report* prefers to continue railing against the East, in heated ideological onanism. Not surprisingly, *Alberta Report*, on privatization, ran an adulatory feature on British lecturer Madsen Pirie and on the Fraser Institute, militant advocates of privatization, without allowing even a hint of possible negative implications for the West.

One of the stock eastern-Canadian villains for the magazine and many other Albertans is Petro-Canada. "It's the feds," goes the argument, which is as good as saying, "It's those easterners, who have always controlled the federal parliament." There is something to the argument. How much of the animus, though, is because of Petro-Canada's public ownership in itself, for which the anti-Ottawa animus is just a cover of convenience? Petro-Canada at least decentralizes power one level, from autocratic global corporations with a powerful lobby down to the Canadian community of which we are all a part. If those discontented Albertans were serious about regional economic power, they would be militating for a major provincial Crown corporation in the field. There haven't been complaints about eastern or foreign control of telephones in Alberta since 1906, when the problem was taken care of properly.

There is something at once painful and humorous in the way that Alberta avoids publicly owned enterprise – avoids it especially in name. Alberta, with its nationalism, realized that, left to the community-blind decisions of private corporate bureaucracies, it would forever be an exploited hinterland and lose the development possibilities that its temporary oil wealth might bring. It also realized the need for an active public entrepreneurial role. But full-frontal public enterprise? No, no, anything but that!

Alberta Gas Trunk Lines (AGTL) — what is now Nova Corporation of Alberta — was a public-enterprise creation. The original impetus came from within government circles, in the days of E.C. Manning. The company itself was put in place by the government. In its original incorporation, two of the seven-person board of directors were appointed by the provincial government (now, with the board expanded to a maximum 20 members, four seats are reserved for government nominations). All directors were to be Canadians living in Alberta (this requirement has since been changed to a "majority" of the board). Shareholder voting rights for operational issues and for most board positions were limited to companies in the natural gas industry; ordinary shareholders' rights were severely restricted. The company was given a quasi-monopoly to gather and carry the province's natural gas for export. This guaranteed it a lucrative revenue. AGTL was, in other words, publicly gifted in order to build up Alberta ownership and control where private enterprise proper had so patently failed. Some critics of AGTL claimed that regulation of its rates was deliberately kept loose, to the cost of consumers and producers, so that AGTL could build up its capital quickly and leverage its assets to increase its size.

As it happens, a good part of Nova's subsequent growth also has its origins in public enterprise. Polysar was acquired in 1988. Its central property, the petrochemical operations, came from the original and highly successful entrepreneurial pioneer, Polymer, the federal Crown corporation. Polymer was arbitrarily privatized with its sale, at a bargain price, to the hapless Canada Development Corporation (which later adopted the Polysar name). Nova's 50 per cent participation in NovaTel, producer of cellular telephones, came through an offer from AGT, the publicly owned telephone company. Much of the entrepreneurial drive behind Nova's own entry into petrochemicals came from the Alberta government which, having made up its mind, conferred the mandate on Nova and amended the company's original charter so it could take the necessary steps.

Robert Blair, the c.e.o, who joined the company in 1969, is, or at least was, both an Alberta and Canadian nationalist. Like a good public enterpriser, he does not think that making money should be the sole determinant of a company's direction. Nova has been both a vehicle of public policy and has expanded by riding on the back of public policy. "Blair walks around the legislative building as if it's Alberta Gas [Trunk Line]," an Alberta oil journalist once remarked.[4]

To actually make a public enterprise out of all this public enterprise, however, was taboo. People kept thinking that Nova was a Crown corporation anyway. So Nova spent $1 million on advertising, in an attempt to erase forever any such mischievous notion. According to one report several years later, most Albertans still believed Nova was a Crown corporation.

The Alberta Energy Company (AEC) is a similar case, and a bit of an energy giant in its own right. It ranks ninth in proven reserves among Canadian oil and gas companies. In addition to its oil and gas properties, it wholly owns the pipeline to the Syncrude project in Fort McMurray and has a two-thirds interest in the project's utility as well as a small direct interest and royalty rights on production. AEC also owns and operates a forest products company (Blue Ridge Lumber) and a technical services group, and has substantial interests in a nitrogen fertilizer company, a coal mine, a natural gas liquids extraction plant and IPSCO.

AEC is 36 per cent publicly owned. It operated for two years under complete public ownership, but the intention was always to sell half the shares to private investors, which the government did. Just to make sure the private-sector powers-that-be did not mistake it for a publicly owned company, the government later sold back another chunk of shares to the company, reducing the public's interest to well below half. Privatizers offered congratulations. AEC also holds a 49.995 per cent interest (and a 40 per cent voting interest) in gas marketer Pan-Alberta Gas Ltd., with Nova holding the rest; because of the .005 per cent extra that AEC doesn't own, which would bring it to 50 per cent, nobody can accuse Pan-Alberta of being a Crown corporation, even twice removed.

The private-enterprise facade of AEC is ideological smoke and mirrors, to soothe both the private sector and ideology while public-enterprise initiative can do what has to be done. According to the articles of incorporation, the government can appoint four of the ten-member board. Or it can waive that right and vote in general meeting for all the directors. Since the Crown holds 36 per cent of the shares and no other shareholder is allowed to hold more than 1 per cent (and most of those holdings are spread out in tiny fragments), there is little doubt who would prevail. Over and above that is the government's legislative authority.

The result has been quasi-public enterprises held in private hands, with intimate connections between parts of the private business community (whose members sit on the boards of these new private corporate bureaucracies) and the government. (Don Getty, who as a cabinet minister put forward the idea of AEC, later sat on the board of Nova before returning to politics and the premiership of the province. Mervin Leitch, the energy minister who followed Getty in that portfolio, is now on the board of AEC.) This is as far removed from the "free-enterprise system" as one could imagine, except on one point – who gets what is to be gotten.

AEC's 46,500 private shareholders, while a large number by themselves, are just a fraction of the Alberta population, and even that small total is slowly shrinking. The government, meanwhile, as quasi-public entrepreneur, has been turning over rights and properties to the company – "[feeding AEC] provincial energy delicacies with a silver spoon," as the *Financial Post* reported with admiration.[5] The big gifts were the energy resources hidden below the Primrose and Suffield military ranges – heavy oil and natural gas respectively. The rich and enormous Suffield range in particular was a prize. The original sweetheart deal for the Suffield range, to the benefit of AEC's private investors, was $54 million (only $24 million down) plus up to 50 per cent net production revenue to the Crown after development costs had been recovered. A decade later, when the revenue-sharing part of the agreement loomed on the horizon, it was scrapped for only $51 million in payments by AEC to the Crown. "Generous pal," said the *Globe and Mail*'s Report on Business, of the government.[6] One analyst put the true value of the surrender at several times the settlement price. Public enterprise initiatives become private property of a relatively few behind the rhetoric of private-sector doctrine and "people's capitalism."

The final irony is that the more the two companies become private enterprises, which is what ideologically they are supposed to be, the less their public-enterprise entrepreneurial spirit, committed to the development of Alberta, which is what, in reality, they were created for. Genuine private enterprise left to itself would never have created a petrochemical industry in the province. The changes have already begun. Ordinary shareholders in Nova have been given full voting rights and any one shareholder may own up to 15 per cent of outstanding common shares. This was to help Nova raise more money through the Toronto Stock Exchange and other outside financial markets. Outside institutional investors have now become major Nova shareholders (two-thirds of Nova shares are held by institutional investors — not the local Alberta storekeeper, cowhand, teacher and farmer for whose ownership the company was created).

Nova has recently been listed on the New York Stock Exchange where, because of the takeover of Polysar, it became a hot item, with the arbitrageurs having "a real ball," according to one analyst. The "new toy on Wall Street," said another.[7] In the churning, Canadians became net sellers and Americans net buyers. One of the attractions to the Americans of Nova shares, as compared to the shares of U.S. petrochemical companies, was its pipeline operation which guarantees growth in earnings and offsets the notoriously volatile chemical industry cycle. The pipeline was the original legacy of E.C. Manning used to create and build up AGTL (Nova) in the first place, for the purpose of injecting a degree of Alberta ownership into an industry dominated by foreign money. Into Wall Street games and outside ownership do Alberta legacies go, as if by private-enterprise pre-determination.

Pressure is growing on AEC to follow the same route. The law limiting individual shareholders to 1 per cent was "antediluvian," a financial analyst recently fumed. It "keeps the company from using modern corporate financing techniques. You can't do bought deals if you have to offer shares first to Joe in Red Deer. And the 1 per cent rule kills the ability of institutions to continue to buy the stock — it cuts away all the people who lead the stock market."[8] The analyst is altogether right, in privatization terms. Joe in Red Deer can take a walk.

THE PRIVATIZATION PUTSCH

The same dogma stifles public-enterprise possibilities elsewhere in Alberta, although public initiatives and public money are involved. AGT has a venture-capital subsidiary, Alta-Can Telecom Inc., for telecommunications high-technology industry, but once any investment succeeds it is supposed to get rid of it ("full-cycle investment" is the euphemism for this self-inflicted entrepreneurial masochism). Alberta in 1987 took over two failed trust companies (North West Trust and Heritage Savings and Trust), merged them into a 99 per cent Crown-owned company and quickly returned the operation to profitability; private investors had refused to step in without guarantees against losses well into the future. Instead of amplifying this initiative into a new publicly-owned financial institution, however, the Alberta government is obliged by its own dogma to sell the rehabilitated trust company to the same kind of people who had refused to take it in the first place.

Similarly, as of the spring of 1987 the Alberta government had invested $35 million in shares of small technological, export-oriented companies, in an attempt to promote diversification. It had already tried other similar programs. Its Alberta Opportunity Co. is a much-subsidized lender of last resort. Through the Heritage Savings Trust Fund it lent $200 million to help establish Vencap Equities Alberta Ltd., a venture capital firm. The new policy of purchasing equity, often in the form of preferred shares, really constitutes just another policy of making loans. It is ideologically safe commercial intercourse, thanks to the use of a preferred-share condom. But as for doing it the natural, public-enterprise, way . . . better to forego that than to risk picking up some dreadful ideological infection.

15.
Scapegoating and the
Canadair Case

In the name of private-enterprise ideology and all that it stands for, people will attack public enterprise no matter what it does or what its particular advantages. They will scapegoat it in the darndest ways. They will even vilify public enterprise for the sinful ways of private enterprise itself.

One old favourite was the case of Churchill Forest Industries (CFI) in the 1960s. It was condemned as a "government corporation" horror story that cost the Manitoba taxpayer huge wads of money. The truth is that the Churchill Forest Products fiasco was a private enterprise, yet funded by public money in one of the screwiest deals private-enterprise proponents have ever perpetrated on an innocent public. The responsible party was a pro-private-enterprise Conservative government (the New Democratic Party in opposition attacked the giveaway). The government was so anxious to make a deal that it even went along with the refusal, by the company in question, to reveal the names of its principals. The government's own Treasury Department had recommended that, given the economic disadvantages of the location, a small pilot project be built instead and the government maintain as full control as possible. The recommendation was rejected. (The story has been told in all its ludicrous and incredible detail, first by Philip Mathias in *The Financial Post* and *Forced Growth,* and then by Sandford Borins in *Investments In Failure.*[1])

Or take the Bricklin case, New Brunswick's exercise in Edselism. It was another instance of a provincial government desperate for development and being taken in by a foreign promoter of dubious reputation. Although the government insisted on a 51 per cent ownership share because it was putting up most of the money, Bricklin was no more a public enterprise, least of all a Canadian public enterprise, than a crater on the moon. Malcolm Bricklin was American. The Bricklin executive offices were in Scottsdale, Arizona, and the design shop was in Livonia, Michigan. Bricklin was a technical incompetent and an even worse administrator. He appointed his parents, sister, brother-in-law, uncle and girlfriend to managerial positions. It was a private-enterprise parody of entrepreneurship which denigrators of public enterprise were only too glad to cite as a government corporation, and no wonder!

A variation of this scapegoating is to pick out individual difficulties or disasters, even when hospitalization cases are involved (and, in enterprise of any kind, there are going to be difficulties and disasters, particularly where new technology is part of it). The trick is not to look too closely for explanations and, at the same time, to avoid talking about private-enterprise weaknesses, failures, losses, scandals and debacles. For example, in 1987 journalist Walter Stewart brought out a book entitled *Uneasy Lies the Head: The Truth About Canada's Crown Corporations.*[2] It was meant to be a scathing and muckraking expose. To make the case, though, so much had to be left out that what was left behind was not much of the truth at all. The omissions included most of Canada's public enterprises themselves. Even the reviewer of the private-enterprise *Financial Post* took after Stewart.

Or public enterprise will get blamed for not being allowed to do what it should have done simply because it was a public enterprise and wasn't supposed to invade private enterprise's sacrosanct territory. Stewart, for example, excoriated Ontario Hydro for having signed uranium contracts with two private companies that would cost between $6 and $7 billion and would guarantee the two firms $1 billion in profits. To make matters worse, by the mid-1980s the price of uranium had tumbled and Ontario Hydro, because it was locked into an agreed price, was paying an enormous premium.

The unmentioned question: If Ontario Hydro was going to guarantee an enormous profit of $1 billion, why did it not do the mining itself? It looked all too much like another case of private-enterprise ideology getting in the way of public-enterprise common sense. That, indeed, was what happened. It was recommended to Ontario Hydro's board that it would be possible and profitable to acquire Denison Mines, the major uranium producer. This vertical integration would both guarantee uranium supplies and do so at reasonable cost. However, the government of William Davis rejected that alternative because, as *Maclean's* delicately put it, "it was not in line with Conservative philosophy on public ownership."[3]

People shouted "rip-off" over the deal that was pushed through instead, when it was made public. The opposition pointed out that the contracts involved huge windfall profits for the two companies. The NDP was particularly critical and called for the government to acquire either Denison Mines or Denison's uranium assets. To rub salt in the wound, Denison and Preston (the other company involved) both got $340 million in interest-free loans to expand the operations of the mines. The Ontario government of Bill Davis sloughed off all the criticism. "I want to emphasize to you that Ontario Hydro has a good deal," declared Stephen Roman, the head of Denison Mines and, incidentally, a good friend of the premier.[4]

Another favourite case where public enterprise gets blamed for private-enterprise ways is Petro-Canada's 1981 acquisition of Petrofina — an old item whose usefulness for scapegoating nevertheless appears to be ageless. Stewart got excited about that one, too.

Petrofina's stock price at the time was $90. Petro-Canada ended up paying $120. Stewart quoted Petrofina's founder as saying that the price paid was "so far beyond what any company would pay for it, or what the market was indicating, that I wonder how it makes any sense." And Petrofina's Canadian president: "As a Canadian taxpayer, I am convinced the government acted irrationally." Given all the tumult, the government asked accounting firm Ernst & Whinney to do a study on the takeover. Stewart's dismay was only redoubled when he discovered that Ernst & Whinney considered the money paid to be "within the range . . . of a fair price." He didn't want to believe it. The Ernst & Whinney study was, in fact, a step by step analysis of the procedures and consultations undertaken by Petro-

Canada in the matter of the sale. It shows that Petro-Canada acted in a responsible and professional way, arriving at its price in time-honoured, private enterprise, stock-market fashion.[5] Stewart should have been criticizing private-enterprise procedures instead.

One way to bring a large company like Petrofina into public ownership is to nationalize it, with a fair price to be decided by assessment. The Liberal government of the day, though, wanted to avoid that at all costs. Nationalization and an assessed price involve legislation and debate, in which the government would be accused of being socialist and would otherwise be vilified by opponents. The Liberal Party by its nature would not want to face the ideological prejudice a debate would unleash, even if it were so inclined, which it wasn't. A takeover in the stock market, within Petro-Canada's originally legislated mandate, bypasses all that. When, earlier, Petro-Canada acquired Phillips Petroleum, the cabinet virtually crowed that the takeover wasn't nationalization at all, but a straight commercial deal.

Takeovers in the stock market, on the other hand, involve hefty premiums. The lust of corporate empire-builders inflates the premiums paid when control is involved. Shareholders have come to expect it. The non-lustful must bid against the lustful or against what the lustful could be expected to pay. Also involved are tax-avoidance possibilities that come from combining two companies with different financial situations and tax accounts. Sure enough, in the Petro-Canada calculations for the takeover of Petrofina there was a tax-avoidance factor, a factor which Ernst & Whinney took as not only acceptable but also as essential in assessing the purchase price – the way these things are done.

At that, the Petrofina premium of 7-15 per cent over assessed "fair market" value (33 per cent over the prior stock price) was minor compared to what goes on in the trade. Takeover premiums go much higher, to as much as 125-150 per cent. One of the most notable: a premium of 127 per cent over trading price paid in 1974 by Inco for battery company ESB; the captured company then began to deteriorate and, before too long, disappeared.

The case with the greatest scapegoating capacity, though, was Canadair. Stewart called it "the Champ" of screwups. Canadair's adventures with the Challenger executive jet, its main product, seemed to have no end of horror stories and bizarre incidents, starting with a crash of one of the prototypes during flight testing in early 1980. There were questionable buybacks to maintain prices. Management was invariably over-optimistic about its market. Modifications added considerably to costs. Delays on engine deliveries created enormous sales and financial problems, and when the engines were delivered, many of them were faulty, in a couple of cases forcing emergency landings. Orders were cancelled because of the recession. The government was obliged to keep providing Canadair with additional funds. In 1982, $1 billion was written off, and by the time it was all over, the government was out approximately $2 billion.

It's a great story and, in the telling, all public enterprise was found guilty by association. On the other hand, according to the private-enterprise doctrinal assumption, private enterprise by its nature is immune from such inept and profligate behaviour...is, in fact, our veritable salvation.

Or is it? Because airframe manufacturing requires so much capital up front and a long period of sales before costs are recovered, and because new technology may be involved, it is enormously risky. So screw-ups are not unknown.

Probably the company most deserving of the tin medal in this arena was Lockheed Aircraft. Part of the Lockheed tale is told in a book by British journalist David Boulton, *The Grease Machine: The Inside Story of Lockheed's Dollar Diplomacy.*[6] In the story, huge development sums are scrubbed, one technical debacle follows another, planes fall out of the sky killing people (one of the planes, the military F-104, was known as the "widow maker"), governments are corrupted, bribes and other cumshaw are distributed Pink Panther style, cost overruns skyrocket, records are falsified, whistle-blowers are intimidated, there are enough retired military officers on the payroll (rank of colonel and above) to fill a barracks...it's an investigative journalist's orgy. The technical and costing fiascos occurred despite Lockheed's advantage of size and its having been long established in the business.

Next to Lockheed's adventures and manoeuvres, the Canadair story appears altogether ordinary. Lockheed, of course, is a private-enterprise company. Ironically, the company owes its survival to a public enterprise happening — the takeover in 1971 of bankrupt Rolls

Royce by the Heath Conservative government in Britain, which allowed for completion of development of the RB211, the engine to be used on the Tristar. This, plus a U.S. government loan guarantee for Lockheed itself (a bit of public enterprise of another sort), saved Lockheed's bacon.

Nor, as a commercial failure in general, was Canadair exceptional in this period. There were the Dome Petroleums, the Massey Fergusons and the pathetic privatized BCRIC and, growing out of this period, the western Canadian banks falling out of the sky and the $3.4 billion in write-offs of third-world loans by the big Canadian chartered banks. The U.S. was no different. The American industrial heartland was slathered in red ink. Steel, automobiles, heavy machinery and agricultural equipment were running up huge losses. In banking, Citicorp by itself was ultimately to write off $4 billion in third-world loans, and the losses and failures of small and not-so-small banks were to reach startling proportions (by 1987, the losses of insolvent or near-insolvent savings banks, known as "thrifts," would hit $18 billion for the year and the ultimate cost of bailing them out would be estimated at anywhere from $60 to $120 billion). Losses, bungling and gross inefficiencies were also hidden inside large corporate or conglomerate operations (one software analyst calculated, in the mid-1980s, that General Motors was losing up to $775 million a year because of redundant and incompatible computer systems; the leakage alone from GM's huge medical benefit costs would have paid for an entire airframe development program in Canada).

Even measured in terms of a sheer handout—to keep alive an integrated aircraft industry in Canada and maintain employment in Montreal in a down time—the Canadair expenditures were not exceptional. A good deal of Canadair's accumulated cost was due to interest; the company had been financed almost entirely with debt. The government could as easily have carried the debt on its own books as it does with the cost of subsidies and grants to private corporations. On that annual cash-flow basis, comparable to other subsidies and grants, Canadair's net cost to the government was $1.36 billion. Spread over the eight development years of the project (1976-1983 inclusive), before Canadair was stabilized and turning a profit, that comes to $170 million a year. If a lawsuit for $480 million against an engine-maker is successful, the net subsidy cost will work out to roughly $110 million a year.

Compare that to the subsidies, grants and "tax expenditures" to corporations of about $18 *billion* a year as of 1984, as noted by Linda McQuaig in her book on the tax system, *Behind Closed Doors*.[7] The notorious Scientific Research Tax Credit (SRTC) alone, much heralded by the private business community, went through $2.8 billion in the short ten months it was in existence in 1984 (including follow-up allocations), virtually all to private corporations and businesses. Agricultural subsidies and price supports reached a reported $8 billion per year in 1988. The restraints on Japanese automobile imports – a subsidy to the automobile industry, in effect – cost Canadians up to $900 million a year calculated as a percentage of U.S. figures, as the restraints took hold in the early 1980s.

Nor, as an example of inadequate monitoring of government expenditure, was the Canadair case unique. It is impossible to say what the cost of government monitoring weakness was, but it would be a fraction of the $110-$170 million annual pay-out. For a real monitoring nightmare, one needs to look at something like U.S. defence procurement. According to some critics, wastage, duplication and just plain cheating by defence contractors could be costing the American taxpayer $31 billion *each and every year*. Bribery, padded labour costs, inferior materials, shoddy work, improper inspection, and in some cases falsified lab reports and forged correspondence have been involved. Add to that the cost of non-cheating "contract nourishment," overruns and technical futility (of which there are many colourful and extremely expensive cases). These are deeds of private corporations all.

That puts the Canadair losses in perspective. Nevertheless, there was inadequate government monitoring in the Canadair case. And the Challenger was an expensive commercial failure. It was supposed to cover its own costs, including the cost of its capital. The details are instructive.

The Challenger began as a self-financing commercial project. It was pushed by the private-enterprise management group from the old company – people who were supposed to know about these things. Canadair was also meant to be under public ownership only temporarily; the scenario was a private-enterprise one. The government's original loan guarantee was small ($70 million). The prospects for the Challenger, based on the order book, were exceptional. In part because of such factors, no commitment was made to build up shareholder (government) technical expertise in a major way.

Then the Challenger's prospects changed very quickly from great to dismal, as we'll see. Because of the inadequate monitoring expertise, however, the implications were hidden from the government. To make matters worse, the government's representative on the board of directors was a project booster (and would soon join Canadair in an executive capacity); he put Canadair in the best possible light. He was also *de facto* head of the government's interdepartmental review committee (he attended most of its meetings and the committee was chaired by a subordinate)! Management, for its part, was not altogether frank with the board. It also used aggressive accounting practices which made Canadair appear in a better financial position than it was. Moreover, the firm's prestigious private-sector auditors, who were supposed to catch unrealistic projections and call for write-offs, accepted the forecasts instead.

There was also controversy about the role of the board of directors. Charges flew through the air about its passivity. The board, in private-enterprise theory, is supposed to represent the shareholders. On the board were such private-enterprise notables as the chairman of Comstock Construction, the chief executive officer of the Provincial Bank of Canada, the chairman of the Aluminum Company of Canada and the chief executive officer of Canadian General Electric. A lot of excuses were made for the board, but in the crunch these private-enterprise luminaries flunked the test. One board member did raise the alarm — a former Liberal cabinet minister.

When the seriousness of the troubles finally surfaced, the monitoring was beefed up with a task force, then with tight supervision and an independent outside analysis of prospects. Then the Canada Development Investment Corporation (CDIC) was formed to take charge directly. A financial restructuring and management shake-up followed. This was a normal business progression, exactly what should be done in these situations. Commercial viability was eventually achieved.

The government was lambasted for its lack of sufficient monitoring, in some quarters as if the very idea of public enterprise were somehow to blame. But adequate monitoring of a costly development project is exactly what the public-enterprise model calls for. Part of the problem, again, was that Canadair, and also publicly owned De Havilland, were meant to be returned to the private sector. No systematic, step-by-step strategic approach to building up an aircraft industry, under public ownership, was taken. Whenever a government provides loan guarantees, however, whether for a publicly owned company or for a privately owned one, it should have sufficient monitoring expertise in place to assure the money is well spent and the project is on target.

That's the monitoring side. The enterprise side is the more interesting and revealing part of the Canadair case. It shows that Canadair was far removed from mainstream public enterprises in the aerospace sector, like Aérospatiale in France, Aeritalia in Italy and the former British Aerospace (nicely profitable and hence quickly privatized by Margaret Thatcher). The Canadair story was more a case of private enterprise in public-enterprise drag.

The private-enterprise press lauded Canadair. *The Financial Post*, in a glowing "special report" in 1980, called it "the poor-boy-makes-good of Canadian business" and a "rags-to-riches story." It had "all the elements of a first-class corporate melodrama," the paper reported. The "bad guys" were the indifferent former U.S. owner, General Dynamics. The "good guys" were the Canadian government for providing the backing. The leading management figures were "heroes...who had faith through all the lean years" and had triumphed. And there was an exciting plot, "a race against time to justify the green light for a brand new type of aircraft the company had never built before, the business jet now known as the Challenger."[8]

Canadian Business called the Challenger project "the making of a miracle" and "the most important single project in Canadian aviation history."[9] It noted with approval the government's intention to put Canadair back into private hands. *Maclean's* called the Challenger "a glittering success story in an otherwise gloomy Canadian manufacturing scene."[10] A book on government in business, published by the right-wing C.D. Howe Institute in 1981, saluted Challenger's success and approvingly cited Crown ownership for having "created an environment in which managerial ingenuity was allowed to flourish." The "costly gambles...are now beginning to pay off," the book reported.[11]

After the roof fell in, in 1982, the same management that had been so ecstatically praised in the business press was all of a sudden abandoned. Over-indulgent sales contracts, underestimating technical and production difficulties, errors of judgement in key decisions and over-optimism came to light. Management's inexperience in producing civil aircraft was brought up. Forgotten in the shouting was that these men and their management and marketing style were the product of private-enterprise branch-plant manufacturing in Canada; they were the best that the private-enterprise stream in Canada had produced in the sector, where only private enterprise had been permitted. Unfortunately, nobody knew their level of incompetence until they were allowed to reach it.

What altogether kayoed Canadair, though, was the disastrous effect on its market of private-enterprise weakness in the United States. The Challenger business-jet project wasn't just something cooked up on the back of an envelope. Canadair had got hold of a fine design, by Bill Lear of Learjet fame. The plane was a generational advance on existing executive jets. The company began development and production with a bulging order book and amid considerable excitement. The slump in the early 1980s, culminating in the deep recession of 1982, changed all that. Private-enterprise corporate America was being buffeted. Some of the losses in the early 1980s were staggering. Corporate America was cutting costs and battening down the hatches.

But this was the Challenger's major market. Before, speculators had been buying up Challenger order positions and selling them at a profit to bidders who did not wish to wait the regular time for delivery. Now, with the economic downturn, order positions could not even be sold at a loss. Canadair's order book began to crumble just at the most vulnerable moment, with almost all its development costs up front. Also, a key order of 25 planes effectively collapsed when deregulation in the U.S. allowed a freight carrier (Federal Express) to use larger planes. Resale value went down and, with that, so did the potential margin for new units where a high margin was expected and required to amortize the development costs. Prior market analysis had shown that the market for executive jets was "recession-proof." What this market analysis had not shown was deep-rooted decay in private-enterprise industrial America. In the ideological conventional wisdom of the U.S. (and Canada), such an idea was both unthinkable and unimaginable. With Canadair's dependence by and large on a single product—without defence contracts and Pentagon "contract nourishment" to help out—the little Canadian company was a sitting duck.

Canadair also took it on the chin from skyrocketing interest rates, the product of U.S. monetarist policy favoured at the time by private-enterprise ideologues. These extraordinarily high interest rates, too, were completely unforeseen. The effect was a double whammy. The high rates were a primary cause of the recession, which in turn undermined the Challenger's market, leaving Canadair helplessly holding the debt on its development costs. Then Canadair, to service this debt, also had to pay the extraordinarily high interest rates themselves, charges, moreover, which kept compounding. The way Canadair's financing had been structured by the government—entirely through debt, until the crisis hit—heightened the effect.

There was an added irony here. Any company starting out in such a risky business should have been financed with a good deal of equity. Indeed, given that aircraft development work, in case of commercial failure, can be sold only at a heavy discount, the best part of Canadair's financing should have been provided by equity. But neither the Canadair principals nor the government wanted to do it that way. They wanted to pretend that the venture wasn't a public enterprise in the ordinary sense, with the government actually providing equity—"Look, see, all the money is coming from private markets"—and the announced intention was that, as soon as Canadair was on its feet, it would be turned over to the private sector. A private enterprise by blood, as they saw it, would be returning to its family after being in a foster home with sufficient groceries in the fridge to build up its health. So, for that private-enterprise wishfulness, the Canadair corporate books had debt instead of equity, and ended up showing an extra $600 million in losses from interest and exchange.

Private-enterprise engine-maker Avco-Lycoming also hurt Canadair badly. Nothing is more devastating to the manufacturer of a new aircraft, with its large costs up front, than delays. That's what happened with the engines. Avco-Lycoming eventually delivered only 45 of the 114 engines which it had agreed to supply, many of them defective. General Electric supplied the others. Those engines which conked out and burned out, and created many embarrassing incidents, were private-enterprise engines. Canadair eventually sued Avco-Lycoming for $480 million for lost sales and for added costs due to delays; the case is still before the courts.

How had the aerospace industry gotten into such a sorry state in the first place? It was private enterprise again: two branch-plant operations. Canadair had been owned by General Dynamics in the U.S. De Havilland was owned by British-based Hawker Siddeley. When the slump hit the world market for aircraft in the 1970s, General Dynamics' limited orders went to its U.S. plants. Hawker Siddeley turned thumbs down on financing the Dash 7 for somewhat the same reason; they preferred to develop such an aircraft at home. Hawker Siddeley kept its major civilian aircraft work, and the expertise and experience that went with it, back in Britain.

General Dynamics, in its Canadair subsidiary, had waxed profitable as a manufacturer of military aircraft with federal money. It had also received over the years large sums of grant money which were meant to develop technical competence and productivity so the aerospace industry would have some continuity. Public money had always been flowing into the aircraft industry, in grants and military contracts. The one significant attempt at a new passenger aircraft — development of the Jetliner by Hawker Siddeley subsidiary A. E. Avro — was largely financed by government, too. Now, with no lucrative military contracts from the public purse in the offing, General Dynamics and Hawker Siddeley were abandoning the Canadian aerospace industry to the industrial desert, which is where the government-owned Canadair began. Canadair, itself, got left with limited engineering capability. Moreover, because of General Dynamics' focus on military aircraft, Canadair management had no significant experience in marketing civilian aircraft (they hired an American hotshot to build up the primary order book).

The negative effects of foreign ownership were at their clearest here. Even those who habitually cried Hosanna at the mention of foreign ownership saw it differently this time. At the same time, no

Canadian company in the private sector was prepared to get involved, and particularly not to expend the massive sums of money required for research, development and equipment modernization.

The one thing in particular that General Dynamics and Hawker Siddeley hadn't done, and wouldn't do, was to build up their subsidiaries' mercantile power through alliances and project-sharing with companies in other countries or through diversification. In civilian aircraft manufacturing, against giants like Boeing — giants also in marketing — co-operative arrangements for large projects were a virtual necessity, and could make sense even for lesser projects. However, the corporate strategies of General Dynamics and of Hawker Siddeley were oriented to their home countries.

Exclusive dependence on a project like the Challenger — and, in the desert, any oasis is welcome — left the new Canadair highly exposed.

So that's the story of the Canadair financial loss: private-enterprise branch-plant legacy, private-enterprise business reporting, private-enterprise scenario, private-enterprise management, private-enterprise corporate downturn and disarray (the market for the Challenger), private-enterprise suppliers, public money, public-enterprise scapegoat.

Imagine, instead, if public enterprise had not been banished from aircraft manufacturing, by tribal taboos, before the industry was allowed to run down. Canada once did have a publicly owned manufacturer, when the National Steel Car Company in Malton, a privately owned and inefficient aircraft manufacturer, was nationalized during World War II. The crown company's name was Victory Aircraft. It raised efficiency and became an impressive operation. Also during the war, the government built an aircraft plant in Montreal which was operated at first by a British subsidiary and then, in 1944, was taken over by a newly formed crown corporation. The name of the new company was Canadair. This new crown company engaged in conversion and development work, including development of the North Star.

Victory Aircraft was sold to none other than Hawker Siddeley and run under a newly formed subsidiary, A.V. Roe Canada (Avro), later to become part of de Havilland. Canadair was sold, of course, to General Dynamics. A crown company, on the other hand, would have been free to use the momentum and experience of the decades of government contracts after the war to evolve new structures and strong mercantile links, as the publicly owned aircraft manufacturers in western Europe had done.

The same blindness, fed now by privatization doctrine, turned over de Havilland and the Dash 7 to Boeing, after Canada had created the technologically new and successful aircraft with its own money, and suffered the vicissitudes of the process. It's back to branch-plantism, and its limited possibilities, again. This was done despite an independent study which concluded that a publicly owned de Havilland would sell 457 Dash 8s worth US$3 billion over the next decade, about the same market share that Boeing was projecting. Similarly, the official reason for the sale of Canadair, which had begun to make a modest profit, was the "belief that [crown] ownership limited the further development of Canadair and of the Challenger aircraft which was considered to be a leader in its market segment." This "belief" was simply forced ideological doctrine.

For the story of full-fledged public enterprises in aerospace one needs to look at companies like Aérospatiale and Aeritalia in Europe. They are involved in a multiplicity of projects – civilian aircraft, helicopters and missiles in Aérospatiale's case; civilian and military aircraft and satellites for Aeritalia. Aérospatiale is one of the leading Airbus Industrie partners (38 per cent). The other, Messerschmitt-Bolkow-Blohm (MBB), with an equal share, is 45 per cent owned by the state governments of Bavaria, Hamburg and Bremen taken together. In addition, almost all the underwriting of the German Airbus share has been public, in the way of loans and guarantees. Airbus has now reached the point where it is taking on American giants Boeing and McDonnell-Douglas. France also has a major engine maker, SNECMA, which is publicly owned.

One might also look retrospectively at British Aerospace (profitable, and privatized in 1981) and Rolls Royce (profitable, and privatized in 1987). Without the 1977 public takeover of the major British aircraft companies and their reorganization in British Aerospace, the British industry would have faltered badly. And without the public acquisition of Rolls Royce in 1971, as it plunged towards receivership, the famed engine maker might now be just a shadow of itself.

SCAPEGOATING AND THE CANADAIR CASE

Aérospatiale is the 13th-largest industrial company in France, with sales in 1986 of $6.8 billion and 43,000 employees. SNECMA, the engine maker, is the the country's 24th-largest industrial company, with sales in 1986 of $3.1 billion and 26,000 employees. Aeritalia is a subsidiary of IRI, the third-largest industrial company in the world outside the United States, as measured by sales, and the largest as measured by number of employees.

The problem in the aerospace industry in Canada was not too much public enterprise but not enough public enterprise — not any public enterprise in the mainstream sense of the tradition.

16.
The Abject Media:
Houses of Dogma

Public enterprise is also downgraded by a structural bias in the media, as dogmatic as it is extraordinary.

Mention bias and people immediately think of slanted news and one-sided columnists and editorial writers. In Britain the overwhelming majority of newspapers are pro-Conservative. This didn't hurt Mrs. Thatcher's privatization march at all. A lot of people have worried about this and its effects on public debate and public opinion. They point out that it is fundamentally wrong in a democracy to have such an unrepresentative press. All that objectors can usually do, though, is grit their teeth. Things have gotten so bad in the 1980s — coincident with the privatization putsch — that, when a group of investors and journalists established a new paper, they expressly called it *The Independent* and marketed it as a paper which readers could depend on to be free of the Conservative warp of the British press scene.

Privatization advocates can ride the back of a similar kind of media bias in Canada. In a study almost a decade ago, two journalism researchers compared coverage of both privately owned and publicly owned corporations in nine newspapers across Canada.[1] Note that this was even before privatization was hyped as it is now. The researchers, classifying items as favourable, neutral and unfavourable, and comparing ratios, found a heavy bias against public ownership.

Reports of negative news – decline in profits, losses or even bankruptcy – were not counted as unfavourable treatment. An item was classified as "unfavourable" for reasons over and above that. The bias against public enterprise was especially strong in the editorial and opinion-piece category.

The survey dealt with slanted news and one-sided commentary, real and alleged. "Structural bias," on the other hand, has to do with what subjects are chosen for coverage in the first place. The effect of this bias goes much deeper than slanted coverage or opinion. It influences readers' very perceptions of what the world consists of. It also influences not just what editorial writers and columnists can get away with, but also how they themselves perceive, think, and relay the scene to us.

Pick up your newspaper and look for news and information about the practical life of making things and providing services. You will find what most newspapers call a "business" section. In that "business" section will be detailed, often colourful, reports of corporate takeovers and takeover attempts – with often a cornucopia of minutiae about the manoeuvres. Some of these stories, like the disposition of ownership of Canadian Tire or Dome Petroleum, take on a soap-opera quality because they appear to go on forever. The movers behind these takeovers are treated as business prototypes and described accordingly.

The daily papers are not the only media that carry these stories in detail. In the specialized "business" press, like the *Financial Post*, we are told not only about the transactions but also, by columnists, about some of the play-by-play action and the colour and anecdotes of the personalities. *Maclean's* is almost like a magazine version of the *Financial Post*, its sister-publication. It carries endless stories in the same vein in its own "business" section. For Canadian Tire, it even did a cover story. Peter Newman, in his weekly column for the magazine – its "business" column – writes assiduously and admiringly of the same scene. Often the front-section columnist in *Maclean's* also deals with that "business" scene. The endless deals and takeovers are also discussed breathlessly on the regular "business" report of CBC radio's *Morningside*. *Venture* on CBC television does the same thing (as did *Business World* on CBC radio, recently cancelled). The business reports on private radio and television also follow the pattern.

THE ABJECT MEDIA: HOUSES OF DOGMA

The ins and outs of small privately owned businesses are also widely portrayed. Questions about incorporating, financing, debt-equity ratios, hiring employees, delegation of work, pitfalls to watch out for, and where to get advice are dealt with in how-to fashion. Stories about small-business successes are offered to provide role models for readers.

Most pervasive is coverage of stock markets and related bureaucratic areas. "Business" sections of newspapers have pages of stock market listings every day, plus articles explaining what is happening in the stock market. Newspapers now carry extensive financial advice columns dealing with, among other things, putting money in the stock market or in mutual funds which, in turn, put money in the stock market. A newspaper financial section may even play the stock market itself for a feature series, sharing the results with its readers. It may also have columns written by representatives of brokerage houses, offering their advice. The *Financial Post* weekly has a thick section every issue on the subject: "The Investor's Guide." Sometimes it expands to two sections.

In addition, every morning, mid-day and afternoon we get a stock market report on the radio. Television goes so far as to flash the DOW, TSE and (at least in Vancouver) the VSE averages on its early evening news program, plus gold, Canadian dollar, and sometimes silver values, presumably for speculators in those commodities. *The National*, on the CBC — the leading mass-media codifier and legitimizer in the country — flashes the DOW and TSE averages, plus gold and Canadian dollar values. These numbers and symbols are the artifacts and icons of the private sector. Most people, if not all, probably don't pay any attention to the actual reading on any given day. The flashing at us of these icons, however, does tell us that this is what is important, this is what "business" consists of and how it measures itself. The ultimately destructive world of paper entre-preneurship and the making of paper profits is glorified.

The presentation of the artifacts and icons of corporate takeovers and of the stock market overflow from "business" coverage into the news. When the television news wants to highlight business reaction to something — even something quite prosaic — we often get shots of the stock market floor and comments about the stock market, as if they meant something. This is really a ceremonial presentation of symbols:

these symbols, the imagery says again, represent business. We get feature items about children playing the stock market. Takeover power games, holding company structures, and playing the paper market (stock markets) are heralded as higher forms of life, getting reverence from the mass media that would embarrass the saints — this, notwithstanding the occasional jibe over particulars.

Where are the symbols and imagery of public enterprise? We never see them. Nor are its icons and models passed on to us any other way by the mass media save incidentally and weakly in newspaper reports about Crown corporation results or controversies. Public enterprises are treated like entrepreneurial exiles in their own land.

Venture, on CBC television, is a good example. In the program's prospectus, for internal use, Crown corporations were simply omitted. At first glance, this was astonishing — leaving out public enterprise in a program about business in Canada! But a closer look at the program's prospectus shows how it happened. "The motivation in business is making money," the outline said.[2] This was how business was defined and also how the imagery of the program was conceived. The title sequence of the eventual program, appropriately, was made up of piles of money.

This definition of business was as astonishing as the omission of Crown corporations in the projected subject matter. Many public enterprises, like public utilities, exist to provide the best possible service at cost. Making money is not the motivation at all. Even a more "commercial" publicly owned company, like Air Canada or CN, does not exist solely to make money, if at all. The company needs to make a profit in order to provide additional capital for necessary re-investment. It may want to make more profit in order to reduce debt and put itself in a stronger financial position. It may also be be required to pay its shareholders (the public, through the Crown) dividends reflecting the public's investment in the enterprise. But, even then, making a profit is instrumental. The motivation is to successfully create and manage a national, regional or municipal enterprise, to be competitive, to excel as an enterprise, to innovate, to grow, to thrive and contend, to keep Canada (or Saskatchewan, or Quebec, or Manitoba . . .) in the economic stakes, to build up the community and make it economically strong (economic nationalism), to be part of economic development generally, to contribute to progress, perhaps also to provide well-paid, safe and interesting work.

Even where a public enterprise is pushed to maximize profits, or is making large profits because of commodity prices or transactional arrangements (like the B.C. Petroleum Corporation in the early 1970s), the motivation is to garner the highest possible return for the community. The enterprise is community-centred.

Venture's definition of business misses the best part of private enterprise as well. It misses the entrepreneurial spirit of creation, innovation (including organizational innovation) and competitiveness which has moved entrepreneurs to far greater heights than the greed of simply making money. It would exclude a good part of the private-enterprise side of economic development of many western European countries – Germany, France, Italy, for example – where economic nationalism has played a considerable role. It would exclude Japanese economic development, where a deliberate effort was made to eliminate short-term profit-making as a business motive and to replace it with more economically creative and constructive objectives: increasing productivity, technological innovation, capital formation, the ability to compete against other countries.

The bizarreness of *Venture*'s definition of business becomes silly in its specific applications. It means, for example, that public automobile insurance companies like the Insurance Corporation of British Columbia are disqualified although public automobile insurance is one of the smartest consumer-service innovations in Canadian business history. The operations of a company like ICBC, too, are sophisticated and instructive. On the other hand, privately run automobile insurance companies, which are conceptually retrograde, costly to consumers and as bureaucratically self-interested as they come, qualify for *Venture*. They can be portrayed – to borrow from the prospectus – as "images of the business ideal."

Similarly, *Venture* can offer for viewers' delectation the operators of private television and cable in Canada. These operators may be simply bureaucratic paper builders of holding companies, manipulating a captive regulatory agency and making their money by distributing American programs – as parasitic and derivative a bunch of paper shufflers as ever existed. They, however, qualify, as "images of the business ideal." Several such items have been carried. The

CBC, on the other hand, the product of one of the greatest, boldest and most defiant entrepreneurial innovations in North American business history—and a real creator, not to mention the proprietor of *Venture* itself—does not qualify.

By the same token, Ontario Hydro and Hydro-Québec, with their large investment programs (not to mention huge sales and plant) and annual research and development budgets of $100 million and $60 million respectively, don't qualify. Nor does Manitoba Hydro with its Limestone project. Nor did industry leader and award-winner Air Canada qualify (although Canadian Airlines—ex-Pacific Western—and Wardair do, and have had items on *Venture*). Air Canada qualified only inasmuch as it was being considered for privatization. Municipal public ownership, like Edmonton Power or 'edmonton telephones'—preserving local ownership despite large capital requirements—doesn't fit. And so on, through the whole panoply of commercial Crown corporations. The business report on *Morningside* recreates this same strangely altered world (as did, also, *Business World* on CBC radio).

Where does this extraordinary structural bias come from? In its prospectus, *Venture* envisages itself as "the visual equivalent of the front page of the *Wall Street Journal.*" *Venture* was a derivative, American-inspired, ideologically exclusionary and dogmatic mistake to begin with. But how was the mistake made?

Cynics would say it was to protect the CBC's flank from criticism from private corporate business, and also from the Conservative Party (and, beginning in 1984, the Conservative government) which reflect the same interests. In the 1970s a special corporate business lobby had been formed to pummel the CBC for some investigative items on "*the fifth estate,*" *Marketplace* and *Ombudsman*, and did succeed in applying a few bruises. In 1984, as *Venture* was being put together, CBC president Pierre Juneau delivered a speech to a gathering of corporate people arranged with the co-operation of the Association of Canadian Advertisers and co-chaired by the president and c.e.o. of Imperial Oil. Juneau mentioned *Venture* to show that the CBC wasn't being hostile or indifferent.

However, even if corporate pressure was a factor, it did not occur in a vacuum. The structural bias built into *Venture* was a product of the structural bias of the media all around it. First were the print media. Second were the electronic media precedents: programs like *Wall Street Week* on PBS and others in Canada. The title of a program carried for several years by City-TV in Toronto provides a clue: *The Money Game*. *Everybody's Business*, produced for many years by Global and syndicated to other stations, was captive to private corporate business, which underwrote it.

The New Bureaucracy — the bureaucracy of private corporate transactions and stock exchanges — has gained overweening power in the U.S. and now in Canada, at the cost of real entrepreneurship. The media help this bureaucratic power along.

In fact, the media have become more and more part of this New Bureaucracy. The rapid rise in what is called "business journalism" is in good part a rapid rise in catering to the New Bureaucracy and promoting participation in its stock exchange branch. At the same time, a growing amount of media revenue comes from this New Bureaucracy. Investment-dealer, mutual-fund and other investment-fund advertising, including advertising connected to the business of corporate acquisitions and mergers, is expanding quickly.

The result of this structural media bias is that the culture of public enterprise is downgraded or, in cases, suppressed. So is co-operative enterprise to a significant extent. This is how dogma works. It excludes things from the picture or pushes them to the margins. It's like a photograph of an extended-family gathering where, for some reason, several of the families, including many of the most venerable and important ones, are left out. We know they exist and are somewhere around, but we don't see them.

This simultaneously pushes into the margin the different aspects and workings of public enterprise. The exclusion weakens public enterprise politically. It also holds it back as an evolving entrepreneurial form and even hinders its performance. It culturally pushes public enterprise to imitate private enterprise — no other model is shown — instead of elaborating and strengthening its community-centred character and showing the way.

Our economic imagery has this gaping hole in it. Privatization advocates try quickly to dash through the door which the structural bias of the media has opened for them.

17.
Moving Public Enterprise Forward

In an illuminating talk in 1985, John Langford, a University of Victoria professor of public administration, speculated on the "heavy hitters" in the pro-privatization camp.[1]

At the top of the list were investment groups and individual corporations, looking to pick up a good business – preferably a monopoly – at a good price. Then came some senior executives of Crown corporations which might be privatized. They want the freedom from shareholders that a diffuse equity ownership might bring and also salaries and benefit packages more in line with their private-sector counterparts. Next were the "abominable no-men," "drys" or "razor gangs" within the cabinets and caucuses of those governments pre-occupied with the privatization issue. They want ideological satisfaction. Business-oriented interest groups came next. They want smaller government, less competition from Crown corporations, and a "U.S.-friendly" economy relatively untainted by public enterprise. Finally, on the short-list, are the investment dealers, consulting companies and law firms vying for a piece of the privatization action – members of the New Bureaucracy, in short. They want to make money.

"This helps to explain," Langford commented, "why privati-zation – despite its lack of mass public support – has made it onto the political agenda at all. Privatization has the backing of groups or constituencies which generally have more resources and far better access to the policy making process than the average citizen or those groups and constituencies opposed to privatization."

For many of these special interests pushing for privatization, "it is accepted dogma that most [Crown corporations] should be sold to the private sector," Langford noted. It is "a matter of faith, not reason." To which one might add that, if their particular interests may be served by privatization, all the more ardent their faith.

If that weren't enough, private-enterprise ideology falls on us day and night, often unnoticed, like acid rain. A lot of it, too, like acid rain, floats across the border from the U.S., the world's largest producer of the ideology. Privatization advocates in Canada, ideologically opposed to public enterprise, get this helping environmental boost. The New Democratic Party, the most active exponent of public enterprise, treads warily for fear of being tarred as doctrinaire socialists out to nationalize everything that moves, so the entrepreneurial culture does not get the defence and exposition it should have. Many people, particularly younger people, aren't aware of where public enterprises come from historically and how much they have made Canada what it is with just a fraction of the country's corporate assets. Others take their Crown corporations for granted in another way. They cannot imagine that anybody would seriously want to wipe them off the map. It would be a kind of lunatic genocide. So, when an attack is suddenly launched, as it is now most clearly in Saskatchewan, for example, they are caught unawares.

The impressive thing about public enterprise in Canada, given all this, is not that some privatization has occurred but that public enterprise continues to exist with such strength and vigour. It demonstrates how deeply rooted in Canadian life public enterprise is—how much a part of us it is—and most of all how successful an entrepreneurial stream it has been.

One shouldn't after all be surprised, despite the ideological rainfall. Public enterprise goes back to the time of the pyramids and to the construction of control dams on the Yellow River in the earliest days of the Han empire. Private corporate enterprise as we know it today is only about 100 years old and control of such enterprises is growing increasingly bureaucratized and removed from communities. The historic accomplishment of Crown enterprise in Canada and of other publicly owned enterprises in western democracies is that they have combined the age-old natural characteristic of public enterprise – a relationship to community – with an entrepreneurially creative and a democratically owned form. They did so in the face of vested interests and often despite hostile ideology – a testimony to how natural and appropriate the form is.

Putsches take advantage of very particular and awkward circumstances – moments of weakness. The privatization putsch in Great Britain was no different. The 1970s were a difficult and depressing decade economically for Britain and the Thatcher government was able to make the nationalized industries the scapegoat. A look at the particulars in Britain and in other western European countries gives us a different picture from the one presented by doctrinaire privatization advocates. Even a brief glance at the historical development of public enterprise in western Europe is an eye-opener.

Another of the curiosities of privatization Margaret-Thatcher style is that it derives from American ideology and ideas exactly at a time when the American system is sputtering and those ideas are coming under question. It's an expression of British provincialism: antipathetic to the French, condescending to the Canadians (all the more desperately condescending as Britain's power declined and its inferiority complex grew), but enviously gawking at the Americans. Canadians, next door to the U.S., know Americans' strengths and weaknesses better, particularly the weaknesses and blindspots of their absolutist ideology.

And here is an unexpected result from the privatization campaign: the challenge will do public enterprise good, wherever, that is, unlike Britain, the privatization drumbeating has failed to stampede people and governments. Privatization in Britain and sell-offs elsewhere have forced people to look around and to ask themselves questions about their economies. It also has forced them to look again at their public enterprises. They will rediscover public enterprise's entrepreneurial role in the past, in western industrial society.

They will also discover added potential in public enterprise for the future, such as new ways of decentralization and of anchoring indigenous entrepreneurship – providing alternatives to private corporate dynasties.

They will discover, too, earlier than they might otherwise, the rise of a new and disturbing bureaucracy – a bureaucracy of private corporations, financial managements, stock exchanges, and related branches (media, law, accountancy), of which paper entrepreneurship is just one part. This is perhaps the most important, and hidden, aspect of privatization and of the push behind it. A revolution is indeed underway, largely going unchallenged – the expansion of this new, increasingly globalized and mechanical, bureaucratic order.

Finally, people will rediscover the inherent advantages of public enterprise in their own communities: its democratic ownership; its decentralization of economic power; its enhancement of competition in market situations; its regional or national spirit and the entrepreneurial impulse which comes with it; its indigenous control of reinvestment capital; its role in helping to gather maximum resource "rents"; its structural efficiencies; its freedom from the debilitating paper entrepreneurship of the private corporate sector; its putting long-term development, productivity, technology, and reinvestment ahead of short-term profit.

Now is the occasion to defend the entrepreneurial stream against its predators and to move it forward as an entrepreneurial form.

Notes

Chapter 1
The Rigged Debate

1. Philippe Simonnot, "Les nationalisées saisies par le capitalisme," *L'Express*, 13 December 1985, p. 48.

2. Trevor Lautens, "On exposing private parts: the Thatcher phenomenon," *Vancouver Sun*, 16 May 1987.

Chapter 2
Britain: Ideological Tag Teams and Roman Circuses

1. George Yarrow, "Privatization in theory and practice," *Economic Policy*, April 1986, p. 360.

2. Samuel Brittan, "The Politics and Economics of Privatisation," *Political Quarterly*, April-June 1984, p. 113.

3. Heidrun Abromeit, "Privatisation in Great Britain," *Annals of Public and Co-operative Economy*, 57:2 (June 1986), p. 155.)

4. Anita van de Vliet, "Mrs. Thatcher's Private Prospects," *Management Today*, March 1987, p. 64.

5. John Moore, *Privatization Achievements*, speech 18 July 1984, ms. p. 2.

6. J. D. Kay and D. J. Thompson, "Privatisation: A Policy in Search of a Rationale," *The Economic Journal* 96 (March 1986), pp. 29 and 25.

7. "Vote-buying starts early," *The Economist*, 16 November, 1985, p. 57.

8. "Don't just sell, compete," *The Economist*, 27 August, 1983, p. 35.

9. Douglas W. Caves and Laurits R. Christensen, "The Relative Efficiency of Public and Private Firms in a Competitive Environment: The Case of Canadian Railroads," *Journal of Political Economy* 88:5 (October 1980), pp. 958-976.

10. D. R. Pescatrice and J. M. Trapani, "The performance and objectives of public and private utilities operating in the United States," *Journal of Public Economics* 13 (1980), pp. 259-76.

11. J. Finsinger and M.V. Pauly, eds., *The Economics of Insurance Regulation: A Cross-National Study*, London: Macmillan, 1985; J. Finsinger, E. H. Hammond and J. Tapp, *Insurance – Competition or Regulation?* IFS Report Series, London: IFS 1985.

12. Richard Pryke, *The Nationalised Industries: Policies and Performance Since 1968*, Oxford: Martin Robertson, 1981, p. 174.

13. Ibid., p. 265.

14. Abromeit, "Privatisation," p. 154.

15. Pryke, *The Nationalised Industries*, p. 253.

16. Charles Collyns and Steven Dunaway, "The Cost of Trade Restraints: The Case of Japanese Automobile Exports to the United States," *International Monetary Fund Staff Papers*, March 1987, pp. 150-75.

17. Yarrow, "Privatization in theory," pp. 337-338.

18. Ibid., p. 341.

19. Van de Vliet, "Mrs. Thatcher's."

20. "Can you hear us?" *The Economist*, 5 September 1987, p. 51.

21. "Survey puts the heat on British Gas," *Sunday Times*, 27 October 1987.

22. "Privatisation: A Powerful Worldwide Trend," *The Amex Bank Review*, 13:10 (1 December 1986), p. 8.

23. Paulette Roberge, "Britain shifts foundation of privatization model," *Financial Post*, 6 July 1987.

24. Brian Milner, "A better life is objective of worldwide privatization push," *Globe and Mail*, 3 March 1987.

25. Brittan, "The Politics and Economics," p. 110.

26. Yarrow, "Privatization in theory," p. 359.

27. "The State in the Market," *The Economist*, 30 December 1978, p. 41.

28. J. A. Kay, *The State and the Market: The UK Experience of Privatisation*, Occasional Papers No. 23, London and New York: Group of Thirty, 1987, p. 26.

29. "Who needs privatisation now?" *The Economist*, 19 December 1987, pp. 49-50.

Chapter 3
The Historic Failure of British Private Enterprise

1. Van de Vliet, "Mrs. Thatcher's," p. 63.

2. Michael Edelstein, *Overseas Investment in the Age of High Imperialism: the U.K., 1850-1914*, New York: The University Press, 1982.

3. E. J. Hobsbawm, *Industry and Empire*, London: Penguin Books, 1969.

4. Ibid., p. 178.

5. David Thoms and Tom Donnelly, *The Motor Car Industry in Coventry Since the 1890's*, London: Croom Helm, 1985, pp. 197-200.

6. Van de Vliet, "Mrs. Thatcher's," p. 63.

7. "Rover Group: co-driver wanted," *The Economist*, 16 January 1988, p. 67.

8. Ian Williams and Philip Beresford, "Rover Hitches A Ride," *Sunday Times*, 6 March 1988.

9. Edward Townsend, "British Steel 'is ready for privatization,'" *The Times*, 8 July 1987.

10. Geoffrey Foster, "National Freight's Private Road," *Management Today*, April 1983, pp. 40-41.

11. Pryke, "The Nationalised Industries," p. 12.

12. Ibid., p. 31.

13. Richard Pryke, *Public Enterprise in Practice*, London: MacGibbon & Kee, 1971, p. 59.

14. W.W. Daniel, *Workplace Industrial Relations and Technical Change*, London: Frances Pinter 1987.

15. Theo Nichols, *The British Worker Question*, London: Routledge & Kegan Paul, 1986; see also Robert Heller, *The State of Industry*, London: BBC Publications, 1987)

16. "Not wholly guilty," *The Economist*, 11 June 1988, pp. 91-92.

17. "The State in the Market," *The Economist*, p. 57.

18. Ibid., p. 54.

19. Ibid., p. 45.

Chapter 4
The European Dossier

1. "The State in the Market," *The Economist*, p. 40.

2. Ibid., p. 39.

3. Ibid., p. 50.

4. Ibid., p. 49.

5. Ibid., p. 53.

6. "Mitterand makes French state bosses earn their keep," *The Economist*, 13 October 1984, p. 77.

7. Simonnot, "Les nationalisées," p. 48.

8. "Socialism à la française," *International Management*, May 1984, p. 20.

9. Roger Ricklefs, "Concerns Nationalized by France Put Profits Ahead of Social Goals," *Wall Street Journal*, 18 April 1985.

10. Simonnot, "Les nationalisées," p. 49.

11. Ibid., p. 52.

Chapter 5
Shareholders' Democracy: The Counterfeit and the Real Article

1. Yarrow, "Privatization in theory," p. 359.

2. Ibid., p. 357.

3. Abromeit, "Privatisation," pp. 160-61.

4. Karin Newman, *The Selling of British Telecom*, London: Holt, Rinehart and Winston, 1986, pp. 167-68.

5. "Pile 'em high and sell 'em cheap," *The Economist*, 30 June 1984, p. 47.

6. Yarrow, "Privatization in theory," p. 357.

7. "How Maggie sold us £2 billion short," *The Guardian*, 4 December 1984.

8. United Kingdom, Public Accounts Committee, Seventeenth Report, 16 May 1984.

9. *The Economist*, 30 June 1984, p. 19.

10. "Britain's new capitalists," *Maclean's*, 1 December 1986, p.42.

11. "The Big Year of the Small Shareholder," *Sunday Times*, 21 December 1986.

12. Pearson Phillips, "Taking stocks to stores," *The Times*, 28 April 1987.

13. "The Big Year of the Small Shareholder," *Sunday Times*, 21 December 1986.

14. Adolf A. Berle and Gardiner C. Means, *The Modern Corporation and Private Property*, New York: Harcourt, Brace and World Inc., 1932; see especially pp. 65, 78 and 116.

15. Foster, "National Freight's," pp. 39-45, 120.

16. Christopher Hird, "Sell-out of the People's Bank," *New Statesman*, 18 January 1985, pp. 8-10.

Chapter 6
Propaganda Inc. (in Britain, Propaganda PLC; in France, Propagande SA)

1. Philip Norman, "Telecom Britain," *Sunday Times*, 13 July 1986.

2. Christopher Hird, "The Hyping of British Telecom," *New Statesman*, 23 November 1984, pp. 8-9.

3. Richard A. Melcher and Sarah Bartlett, "The Hard Sell That's Turning British Telecom into a Hot Stock," *Business Week*, 3 December 1984, p. 42.

4. "Can you hear us?" *The Economist*, 5 September 1987, p. 51.

5. Kenneth Fleet, "The TSB a hard act for British Gas to follow," *The Times*, 2 October 1986.

6. In the *Sunday Times*; cited in Stephen Handelman, "Everyone wins in $10 billion British Gas stock lottery," *Toronto Star*, 2 December 1986.

7. Philip Revzin, "France Urges Citizenry To Break With Habit, Become Stockholders," *Wall Street Journal*, 5 November 1986.

8. Ibid.

210

9. Sabine Delanglade, "Saint-Gobain part en campagne," *L'Express*, 31 October 1986, p. 35.

10. Shawn Tully, "Europe Goes Wild Over Privatization," *Fortune*, 2 March 1987, p. 69.

11. Philippe Gavi, "Privatisation: les premiers gagnants," *Le Nouvel Observateur*, 10 October 1986, pp. 20-21.

12. Ibid., p. 21.

13. Sabine Delanglade, "Un journée de Jacques-Henri David," *L'Express*, 21 November 1986.

Chapter 7
The New Bureaucracy

1. Cento Veljanovski, cited in "Share and share alike," *The Economist*, 10 October 1987, p. 89.

2. Quek Peck Lim, "The Perils of Privatization," *Euromoney*, February 1986, p. 65.

3. Ibid., p. 67.

4. John Rossant, "Come One, Come All, To The Great French Sell-Off," *Business Week*, 22 September 1986, p. 46.

5. Ibid.

6. "Merrill Lynch: Paris nous intéresse," *L'Express*, 16 January 1987, p. 25.

7. Abromeit, "Privatization," p. 159.

8. Eric Dadier, "Bourse: faut-il vendre?" *L'Express*, 3 April 1987, pp. 26-30.

9. Peck Lim, "The Perils," p. 62.

10. Cited in Hugh Thompson, "All aboard the shares train," *Sunday Times*, 31 August 1986.

11. Cited in Revzin, "France Urges Citizenry."

12. Dadier, "Bourse," p. 27.

13. Tully, "Europe Goes Wild," p. 68.

14. Phillips, "Taking Stocks."

15. Cited in Peck Lim, "The Perils," p. 62.

16. Seymour Melman, *Profits Without Production*, New York: Alfred A. Knopf, 1983.

17. Georges Valance, "Privatisations: les hommes de l'ombre attendront," *Le Nouvel Observateur*," 12 September 1986, pp. 11-13.

18. Rossant, "Come One, Come All," p. 46.

19. "Digging into coal's accounts," *The Economist*, 1 August 1987, p. 49.

Chapter 8
Back In Canada: BCRIC and Other Privatizations

1. Patrick Durrant, "A Sickly Discard Learns to Stand," *Executive*, June 1976.

2. *B.C. Hansard*, August 31, 1977.

3. Zane A. Spindler, " 'Bricking up' Government Bureaus and Crown Corporations," in T. M. Ohashi and T.P. Roth, *Privatization: Theory & Practice*, Vancouver: Fraser Institute, 1980.

4. Cited in Rick Ouston, "One BCRIC director stands to make $2.49 million profit," *Vancouver Sun*, 13 September 1980.

5. Cited in Patrick Durrant, "BCRIC stock price slump a puzzle," *Vancouver Province*, 22 March 1981.

6. Der Hoi-Yin, "Shareholders' anger buried under proxies," *Vancouver Sun*, 15 May 1982.

7. Marjorie Nichols, "A toast to the good fortune of BCRIC shareholders," *Vancouver Sun*, 22 July 1982.

8. Cited in Der Hoi-Yin, "No Kaiser valuation stuns BCRIC-watchers," *Vancouver Sun*, 6 September 1981.

9. Dale Eisler, "Economic gurus spread the word," *Leader-Post*, 26 January 1988.

Chapter 9
Canadian Public Enterprise in Economic History

1. David U. Himmelstein and Steffie Woolhandler, "Cost Without Benefit: Administrative Waste in U.S. Health Care," *The New England Journal of Medicine* 314:7 (February 13, 1986), pp. 441-445.

2. Tom Kierans, "Commercial Crown," *Policy Options*, November 1984.

3. Cited in Cathryn Motherwell, "Privatization trend faces test over Big 3," *Globe and Mail*, 28 February 1987.

4. Herschel Hardin, *A Nation Unware: The Canadian Economic Culture*, Vancouver: J.J. Douglas, 1974.

Chapter 10
Community-Centred Enterprise

1. Herman E. Krooss and Charles Gilbert, *American Business History*, Englewood Cliffs: Prentice-Hall, 1972, p. 273.

2. Gustav Ranis, "The Community-Centred Entrepreneur in Japanese Development," *Explorations in Entrepreneurial History*, December 1955, pp. 80-98.

3. P.H. Frankel, *Mattei: Oil and Power Politics*, London: Faber and Faber, 1966, p. 157.

4. Ibid., p. 157.

5. Robert B. Reich, *The Next American Frontier*, New York: Times Books, 1983. See especially Chapter 12, "Political Choice."

6. Andrew Pollack, "U.S. Chip Makers Plan Consortium," *New York Times*, 6 January 1987.

Chapter 11
Public Enterprise in the Competitive Marketplace

1. "Selling points," *Globe and Mail*, 7 April 1987.

2. R.F. Cranston, "Regulation and Deregulation: General Issues," *UNSW Law Journal*, 5 (1982), p. 20; cited in Kevin La Roche and Kernaghan Webb, "Bureaucrats Among the Businessmen: Influencing the Private Sector Through Crown Corporations," in *Government Enterprise: Roles and Rationales*, Ottawa: Economic Council of Canada, 1984.

Chapter 12
Air Canada: Kindly Shoot Public Ownership

1. "It's time to sell Air Canada," *Globe and Mail*, 10 July 1987.

2. *Air Transport World*, January 1982, p. 74.

3. *Air Transport World*, January 1986, p. 76.

4. W. T. Stanbury and Fred Thompson, eds., *Managing Public Enterprise*, Montreal: The Institute for Research on Public Policy, 1982, p. 5.

5. Linda McQuaig, *Behind Closed Doors*, Toronto: Viking, 1987, p. 85.

Chapter 13
Public-Enterprise Decentralization of Power Versus Private-Enterprise Concentration of Power

1. Cited in David Crane, "Takeovers give Big Business economic *and* political clout," *Toronto Star*, 5 April 1986.

2. Cited in Diane Francis, *Controlling Interest*, Toronto: Macmillan, 1986, p. 239.

3. Crane, "Takeovers give Big Business."

4. Deborah Coyne, "Corporate Over-Concentration," *Policy Options*, April 1986, pp. 14-17.

5. Francis, *Controlling Interest*, p. 230.

6. Cited in "The new takeover frenzy," *Maclean's*, 7 April 1986, p. 28.

7. Kierans, "Commercial Crowns," p. 29.

8. *'et' cetera*, January 1985.

9. Lautens, "On exposing."

Chapter 14
Holding One's Own in the West

1. Cited in Pat Brennan, "Ottawa 'spending money we don't have' says millionaire salesman Jim Pattison," *Toronto Star*, 21 November 1984.

2. David Crane, *Controlling Interest: The Canadian Gas and Oil Stakes,* Toronto: McClelland & Stewart, 1982.

3. Eric Kierans, *Globalism and the Nation-State*, Toronto: CBC Enterprises, 1984.

4. Cited in Paul Grescoe, "Bob Blair and his All-Canadian Pipeline," *Weekend*, 1 March 1975.

5. "Alberta Energy Co. has come a long way in very short time," *Financial Post*, 22 September 1984.

6. Dennis Slocum, "Province proves a generous pal during Alberta Energy's travails," *Globe and Mail*, 8 December 1986.

7. Deirdre McMurdy, "Nova newest rising star on Canadian, U.S. markets," *Financial Post*, July 2, 1988.

8. Cited in Barry Nelson, "Alberta Energy floats an $80-million issue," *Financial Times*, 4 April 1988.

Chapter 15
Scapegoating and the Canadair Case

1. Philip Mathias, *Forced Growth*, Toronto: James Lewis & Samuel, 1971; Sandford Borins, *Investments in Failure*, Toronto: Methuen, 1986.

2. Walter Stewart, *Uneasy Lies The Head: The Truth About Canada's Crown Corporations*, Don Mills: Collins, 1987.

3. Angela Ferrante, "I, Stephen," *Maclean's*, 26 June 1978, p. 27.

4. Ibid., 28.

5. Ernst & Whinney, "A Review and Assessment of the Acquisition of Petrofina Canada Inc. by Petro-Canada," Final Report, 11 pp., Canada: Energy, Mines and Resources, 1985.

6. David Boulton, *The Grease Machine*, New York: Harper and Row, 1978.

7. McQuaig, *Behind Closed Doors*, p. 85.

8. Anderson Charters, "Canadair's Challenger: Rags-to-riches story," *Financial Post*, 31 May 1980.

9. Stephen Dewar, "Canadair: into the wild blue yonder," *Canadian Business*, December 1978, p. 80.

10. Ian Urquhart, "New bird in town," *Maclean's*, 10 July 1978.

11. Marsha Gordon, *Government in Business*, Montreal: C. D. Howe Institute, 1981.

NOTES

Chapter 16
The Abject Media: Houses of Dogma

1. James P. Winter and Alan Frizzell, "The Treatment of State-Owned vs. Private Corporations in English Canadian Dailies," *Canadian Journal of Communications*, Winter 1979-80, pp. 1-11.

2. "Venture: The Business Show," ms. 6 pp., undated.

Chapter 17
Moving Public Enterprise Forward

1. John Langford, "Privatization: A Political Analysis," in *Papers on Privatization*, eds. W. T. Stanbury & Thomas Kierans, Montreal: The Institute for Research on Public Policy, 1985.

Members of the Institute

Board of Directors

The Honourable Robert L. Stanfield, P.C., Q.C. (Honorary Chairman)
Ottawa

Roger Charbonneau, O.C. (Chairman)
Président du conseil, NOVERCO, Montréal

Rosalie S. Abella
Chair, Ontario Labour Relations Board, Toronto

Robert Bandeen
President and Chief Executive Officer, Cluny Corporation, Toronto

Nan-Bowles de Gaspé Beaubien
Vice-présidente du conseil d'administration, La Corporation Télémédia, Montréal

Larry I. Bell
Chairman and Chief Executive Officer, B.C. Hydro & Power Authority, Vancouver

Allan F. (Chip) Collins
Special Advisor, Provincial Treasurer of Alberta, Edmonton

Peter C. Dobell
Vice-President & Secretary Treasurer, Institute for Research on Public Policy, Ottawa

Rod Dobell
President, Institute for Research on Public Policy, Victoria

David Hennigar
Atlantic Regional Director, Burns Fry Limited, Halifax

Susan McCorquodale
Department of Political Science, Memorial University of Newfoundland, St. John's

Jean Monty
Executive Vice-President, BCE Inc., Montreal

Robert Normand
Président et éditeur, *Le Soleil*, Québec

217

219

David Leighton
Director, National Centre for Management Research and Development
University of Western Ontario, London

Terrence Mactaggart
Toronto

Judith Maxwell
Chairman, Economic Council of Canada, Ottawa

Milan Nastich
Canadian General Investments Ltd., Toronto

Roderick C. Nolan, P.Eng.
President, Neill & Gunter Limited, Fredericton

Robert J. Olivero
United Nations Secretariat, New York

Gordon F. Osbaldeston, O.C.
Senior Fellow, School of Business Administration, University of Western Ontario,
London

Garnet T. Page, O.C.
Calgary

Jean-Guy Paquet, O.C.
Québec

Leonard Russell
Summerside, Prince Edward Island

Eldon D. Thompson
President and Chief Executive Officer, Telesat Canada, Gloucester

Israel Unger
Dean of Science, University of New Brunswick, Fredericton

Louise B. Vaillancourt
Outremont

Ida Wasacase, C.M.
Winnipeg

R. Sherman Weaver
Executive Director, Alberta Environmental Centre, Vegreville

Blossom Wigdor
Director, Program in Gerontology, University of Toronto

Government Representatives

Roger Burke, Prince Edward Island
David R. Cameron, Ontario
Joseph H. Clarke, Nova Scotia
Ron Hewitt, Saskatchewan
Lynn Langford, British Columbia
Donald Leitch, Manitoba
Francis McGuire, New Brunswick
Barry Mellon, Alberta
Norman Riddell, Quebec
H.H. Stanley, Newfoundland
Gérard Veilleux, Canada
Louise Vertes, Northwest Territories

Institute Management

Rod Dobell	President
Peter Dobell	Vice-President and Secretary-Treasurer
Yvon Gasse	Director, Small & Medium-Sized Business Program
Jim MacNeill	Director, Environment & Sustainable Development Program
Steven Rosell	Director, Governability Research Program
Shirley Seward	Director, Studies in Social Policy
Murray Smith	Director, International Economics Program
Jeffrey Holmes	Director, Communications
Parker Staples	Director, Financial Services
Walter Stewart	Editor, *Policy Options Politiques*

Fellows- and Scholars-in-Residence:

Tom Kent	Fellow-in-Residence
Eric Kierans	Fellow-in-Residence
Jean-Luc Pepin	Fellow-in-Residence
Gordon Robertson	Fellow-in-Residence
Gilles Paquet	Scholar-in-Residence
David Cameron	Scholar-in-Residence
Klaus Stegeman	Scholar-in-Residence
Eugene M. Nesmith	Executive-in-Residence

Related Publications Available
– December 1988

Order Address

The Institute for Research on Public Policy
P.O. Box 3670 South
Halifax, Nova Scotia
B3J 3K6
Phone: (toll free) 1-800-565-0659

James Gillies	*Where Business Fails.* 1981 $9.95
Allan Tupper & G. Bruce Doern (eds.)	*Public Corporations and Public Policy in Canada.* 1981 $16.95
Irving Brecher	*Canada's Competition Policy Revisited: Some New Thoughts on an Old Story.* 1982 $3.00
W.T. Stanbury & Fred Thompson	*Regulatory Reform in Canada.* 1982 $7.95

Robert J. Buchan, C. Christopher Johnston, T. Gregory Kane, Barry Lesser, Richard J. Schultz & W.T. Stanbury	*Telecommunications Regulation and the Constitution.* 1982 $18.95
R. Brian Woodrow & Kenneth B. Woodside (eds.)	*The Introduction of Pay-TV in Canada: Issues and Implications.* 1983 $14.95
Mark Thompson & Gene Swimmer	*Conflict or Compromise: The Future of Public Sector Industrial Relations.* 1984 $15.00
Samuel Wex	*Instead of FIRA: Autonomy for Canadian Subsidiaries?* 1984 $8.00
Paul K. Gorecki & W.T. Stanbury	*The Objectives of Canadian Competition Policy, 1888-1983.* 1984 $15.00
W.T. Stanbury (ed.)	*Telecommunications Policy and Regulation: The Impact of Competition and Technological Change.* 1986 $22.00
Stephen Brooks	*Who's in Charge? The Mixed Ownership Corporation in Canada.* 1987 $20.00
Louis Raymond	*Validité des systèmes d'information dans les PME: analyse et perspectives.* 1987 20,00 $
Jacques Saint-Pierre & Jean-Marc Suret	*Endettement de la PME : état de la situation et rôle de la fiscalité.* 1987 $15.00
R.S. Khemani, D.M. Shapiro & W.T. Stanbury (eds.)	*Mergers, Corporate Concentration and Power in Canada.* 1988 $29.95
Allan Tupper & G. Bruce Doern (eds.)	*Privatization, Public Policy and Public Corporations in Canada.* 1988 $34.95